STORIES OF FREEDOM
IN BLACK NEW YORK

James Hewlett imitating Edmund Kean in the title role of Shakespeare's *Richard III*, as shown in an engraving distributed to the audience in New York in 1827. Courtesy of The Harvard Theater Collection, The Houghton Library, Harvard University.

STORIES OF FREEDOM IN BLACK NEW YORK

SHANE WHITE

HARVARD UNIVERSITY PRESS

Cambridge, Massachusetts
London, England
2002

Copyright © 2002 by the President and Fellows of Harvard College
All rights reserved
Printed in the United States of America

Library of Congress Cataloging-in-Publication Data

White, Shane.
   Stories of freedom in Black New York / Shane White.
      p. cm.
   Includes bibliographical references and index.
   ISBN 978-0-674-02578-3
   1. African Americans—New York (State)—New York—History—19th century.
   2. African Americans—New York (State)—New York—Intellectual life—
   19th century.   3. African Americans—New York (State)—New York—Social
   conditions—19th century.   4. New York (N.Y.)—History—1775–1865.
   5. New York (N.Y.)—Race relations.   6. New York (N.Y.)—Intellectual life—
   19th century.   7. African American theater—New York (State)—New York—
   History—19th century.   8. African Company (New York)—History.
   9. African American actors—New York (State)—New York—Biography.
   10. Slavery—Social aspects—New York (State)—New York—History—
   19th century.   I. Title.

   F128.9.N4 W48 2002
   978.7′100496073—dc21   2002068540

FOR

GRAHAM WHITE

AND

RICHARD WATERHOUSE

CONTENTS

STORIES OF FREEDOM
IN BLACK NEW YORK

INTRODUCTION

On a muggy fall day in 1939, a black youth in his mid-twenties trudged from tenement to tenement in New York City's San Juan Hill, home to a small pocket of blacks who would be displaced by the Lincoln Center. He was employed by the Federal Writers' Project, but on this afternoon the time was his own, and he was spending it by collecting signatures in support of a petition for some worthy cause or other. As he quietly walked down the dimly lit hallway in the basement of one of these buildings, he heard—it would have been impossible not to hear—loud voices booming out from behind a door. Years later he would write that "they were male Afro-American voices, raised in violent argument," and that "the language was profane, the style of speech a Southern idiomatic vernacular such as was spoken by formally uneducated Afro-American workingmen." What he overheard was disturbing; indeed, it was "a mystery so incongruous, outrageous, and surreal that it struck me as a threat to my sense of rational order." The unseen African Americans were exhibiting "an intimate familiarity with a subject of which, by all the logic of their linguistically projected social status, they should have been oblivious," confounding all the well-schooled young man's assumptions about "the correlation between educational levels, class, race and the possession of conscious culture." "Impossible as it seemed," he explained, "these foul-mouthed black workingmen were locked in verbal combat over which of two celebrated Metropolitan Opera divas was the superior soprano!"

Screwing up his courage, the petitioner knocked on the door, and was welcomed by an irritated shout of "Come in!" On entering, he found himself "in a small, rank-smelling, lamplit room," where "four huge black men sat sprawled around a circular dining-room table, looking toward me with undisguised hostility." Apprehensive, the young black man explained his mission to the hulking fellows—coalheavers by their appearance—who were still obviously unamused by the interruption. Nevertheless, once the interloper got talking, they were impressed to learn that he worked with the Writers' Project and that he had studied music at Tuskegee—one of the men allowed that "They got a damned good choir down there. . . . They had that fellow William L. Dawson for a director"—and told him to pass his piece of paper across. Although the leader of the black workers thought the petition worthless, he observed to his friends that "Home here's a musician, it won't do us no harm to help him out. Let's go along with him." Each man then painstakingly added his signature with a blunt pencil, a process that took some time. When they had finished, the young man blurted out that he would like to ask one question: "where on earth," he wanted to find out, "did you gentlemen learn so much about Grand Opera?" The four men convulsed in laughter, "erupt[ing] like a string of giant firecrackers." Eventually one of them curbed his merriment, "wip[ed] the coal-dust stained tears from his cheeks," and said "we learn it down at the Met. Strip us fellows down and give us some costumes and we make about the finest damn bunch of Egyptians you ever seen. Hell, we been down there wearing leopard skins and carrying spears or waving things like palm leafs and ostrich-tail fans for *years!*"[1]

This book is about something just as challenging to our usual understanding of the way things worked as the puzzle that confronted Ralph Ellison—the young man of our story. The book is set in New York City in the early decades of the nineteenth century, a time when restive blacks were becoming rather more than extras able to dissect the performances of the whites on center stage. In the early 1820s, even as the institution of slavery still lingered on in New York, a group of African New Yorkers, many of them ex-slaves, formed a black theater company. They put on various of Shakespeare's works and at least one drama created by one of their number, before mixed audiences of whites and blacks. The black company was only tolerated by white New Yorkers for a couple of years, but James Hewlett, its principal actor, would make a living for almost another decade performing his one-man shows before a mostly white public.

If the very idea of blacks acting on stage was improbable to contemporaries, just as important was what they had in mind as they were doing it. Even well into the twentieth century there was something unusual and daring about so-called "colorblind" casting, that is, having African American actors performing roles usually assumed to be for whites only. In 1967, a sixteen-year-old Ricardo Khan, later to be a Tony Award winner, purchased a ticket for a matinee performance of *Hello Dolly* at the St. James Theater. Thirty years later, he remembered vividly the "awe" he had felt when the raising of the curtain revealed Cab Calloway and Pearl Bailey in the lead roles. "I wasn't inspired because it was on Broadway, but because it was an all-black cast." "It was a cast," Khan told a *New York Times* writer, "that looked like me." There is no surviving direct testimony from 1821, but the spectacle of a former slave performing as Richard III must have thrilled black members of the audience in much the same way.[2]

For this remarkable story of pioneering black effort it is easy enough to come up with a list of "firsts." By decades, the black theater company was the first venture of its type; its members built the first black theater; they performed the first play written by an African American; and gave the first stage representation of slavery by black people. Ralph Ellison, patrician and opera lover, would probably have been surprised to discover that the debut performance by an American-born singer of Italian Opera in front of a paying American audience was given by James Hewlett, a black man. Hewlett was also, if not the first, one of the very earliest American one-man performers, the progenitor of an enormous range of American entertainers, from vaudeville performers through to the likes of Richard Pryor and Robin Williams. All of this is true enough, but a mere trapping of lives on the pages of some sort of *Guinness Book of Records* is about as lifeless a form of memorialization as can be imagined. Hewlett and his fellow black actors deserve far better. What I have sought to do in this book, therefore, is to locate the theatrical endeavors of this group of African American performers within the rambunctious and unsettling response of slaves, ex-slaves, and free blacks to slavery's protracted demise in New York. I wish to show how the audacity and brashness of their attempt to open up the stage to black people reflected something of the exhilaration and exuberance that characterized African New Yorkers' life in those years.

My subject has suffered a double erasure. Historians have known about the African Company for decades, but that pioneering institution has mostly been treated as an oddity, hardly to be taken seriously. James Weldon Johnson, the African American poet and writer, set the tone in *Black Manhattan*, when he concluded that, except for nurturing the great black actor Ira Aldridge, the black company's "early high-brow theatrical effort" was "pathetically ridiculous."[3] For the most part, the early theatrical efforts of these black performers are simply absent from the history of the theater. In the last decade or so, fleeting mentions of the first black theater by historians of African Americans in the North, or in New York, or of the city itself, manage to cram an impressive number of factual errors into very few sentences. To be sure, in the past year or two, some scholars have made determined and resourceful attempts to research the history of the African Theater, but most historians of America—let alone those members of the public interested in things historical—are completely unaware of its existence.[4]

The second erasure concerns the larger developments in African American history that were associated with the ending of slavery in New York, developments of which the theater was a notable part. On the one hand, during the last decade or so scholars have rewritten the history of slavery in New York—and indeed in the North—to the point where bromides about the "mildness" of the northern slave system are now seldom heard. On the other hand, however, the logical corollary of this discovery or rediscovery (northern slaves themselves were hardly under any illusions about the nature of the regime that kept them enslaved), namely, that freedom mattered a great deal to African New Yorkers, has barely been examined.

Under the impetus of slavery's demise, black life in New York displayed a kind of edgy vitality in these transitional years, a mood expressed not only in dance, music, and street parades, but also, more surprisingly, in theatrical endeavor. In the performance spaces available in the city, ordinary African Americans created a vibrant culture, one that not only reflected their new and exhilarating status as free people, but that also fascinated and not infrequently horrified white onlookers. The resulting conjunction between black creative activity and white voyeurism was unprecedented, and would not recur until the Harlem Renaissance of the 1920s.

Nothing illustrates the new assertiveness of the city's blacks better than the audacious decision to create the black theater company, the very existence of which gives some sort of indication of the strength of the cultural convulsion that accompanied slavery's demise. The African Company's first public performance in 1821—the staging of Shakespeare's *Richard III* by black actors before an audience whose members had either been slaves or were, at least, the children of slaves—was certainly seen as a bold intrusion onto what had been considered exclusively white cultural terrain. During the conflicted course of this African New Yorker theatrical venture, the myriad private and individual dramas through which the city's blacks tested the limits of their freedom would be played out in more public and spectacular form. The vitality of black life in the early decades of the nineteenth century also prompted an unprecedented interaction between black and white. Whites mimicked black behavior, particularly black speech. Conversely, on the other side of the color line, the black actor James Hewlett was able to make a living for nearly ten years by imitating white actors in their most famous roles. As well, contemporary newspapers were full of stories of "passing," and of whites being mistaken for blacks and vice versa.

This is a book about slavery and its lingering death in New York. It is also an examination of the struggle over the meaning of freedom in one of the first societies voluntarily to abolish the institution. As well, the book is about theater, and the pioneering attempt of a group of black men and women to break down whites' unthinking assumption that members of the theatrical world must necessarily be white. Most of all, however, it is a book about the city of New York in a time of unsettling transition. In the early decades of the nineteenth century, the metropolis was becoming a recognizable version of its modern self—at once dynamic and cruel, invigorating and infuriating—and, although this fact has often been ignored or forgotten, the ending of slavery and the troubling (for most whites at least) presence of liberated African New Yorkers were a vital part of this story.

1 | THE END OF SLAVERY

It was the smallest of stories, worth only a few lines in the *New York Sun*, not even mentioned in other city newspapers. In August 1834 two unnamed African New Yorkers had come across Edmond Willis, "an aged black man," in the middle of a street. Willis was clearly distressed; he was making strange sounds "and exhibiting all the frantic movements that reason dethroned seldom failed to produce." The concerned passersby managed to carry Willis to the Police Office, where he presented a frightening spectacle; "his eyeballs appeared to be starting from their sockets," the *Sun* reported, "and rolled with a phrenzied motion that denoted horror of mind." As the police fought to restrain Willis, he suddenly "screamed out in a frightful tone of voice" that reverberated to every corner of the building "O, my master! my master! O, my dear master!" Having unburdened himself of these words, he went limp and thereafter remained calm until removed to the lunatic asylum, "a melancholy monument," the *Sun* observed alliteratively, "of madness complete."[1]

Edmond Willis may have been born free or may have come from another state; it is much more likely, however, that he had been subjected to the rigors of the New York slave system. His terrible and at the same time puzzling cry, with its evocation not only of past horrors but of ambivalent loyalties, marks a useful point of entry, an appropriate place to begin to tell the story of what freedom meant for African New Yorkers. Sufficient attention has not been paid to the damage that northern whites did to their slaves, nor to the intensity or the importance of the sense of relief, even exultation, at slavery's demise on the part of those who, unlike Edmond Willis, negotiated the process with some measure of success. The early decades of the nineteenth century were the liminal years of slavery's gradual withering and final freedom. These were years of struggle, frustration, and often cruel disappointment, but that is only part of the story, for black life in these awkward transitional decades possessed a distinct edge, a particular kind of restless vitality. Not only did recently liberated slaves incorporate exuberant signs of their freedom into the performances of everyday life, but, prompted by their memories of slavery and of those, like Edmond Willis, left broken by the wayside, they also brought with them an impatient aggressiveness that decisively influenced the black culture forged in these years on the streets of the metropolis.

The best way to understand the transformation freedom wrought is to listen to the stories of individual African Americans, stories that reveal the gritty details of New York life. And such material begins to abound in contemporary newspapers and archives, much more than it had done before the slave system came under serious challenge. The increased notice, if not scrutiny, of black lives was a product of slavery's demise. In part, this interest, ranging from mild curiosity to something verging on voyeurism, was prompted by distance, as the lives of New York blacks were increasingly separated off from those of most whites, but it was also induced by the free blacks' new ways of behaving. Whites told all sorts of stories about blacks, many of which, like that of Edmond Willis, ended up being recorded in one form or another;

moreover, blacks told stories about themselves. "Tell us your history," intoned the magistrate in a Police Office in late 1827, addressing "a tall, well looking mulatto man" arrested as a possible runaway from New Orleans.[2] This sort of interrogatory was also put to any number of other black residents of New York, and not only to those who appeared in court. In a variety of situations blacks were forced to recount their stories in order to prove that they were free and to justify their presence in the city. This requirement was a condition of their freedom, a sign that even though blacks had become free, they were hardly to be treated in the same way as white citizens.

Poor and powerless blacks were not the only ones required to tell their free stories. In the early decades of the century only a few hundred of the better-off black New Yorkers met the property requirements needed to vote, but under the provisions of an act passed in 1815, a black person who wished to vote also had to prove "his freedom, the place of his birth, his age, the time when he became free, as nearly as can be ascertained the length of time he has resided in said city, the street and number of the house . . . in which he resides, whether he is a freeholder." As an angry editorial in the *New York Herald* pointed out, blacks were being "required to give a history of their lives and circumstances, and to state and prove a number of facts," conditions that were neither prescribed in the constitution nor required of whites.[3]

African New Yorkers needed to be able to tell a story and to tell it well. In February 1826, a black man named William Johnson was accused of stealing a cloak that he claimed had been given him in payment of a debt. Arraigned before the courts, Johnson, according to the *New York American*, "made an ingenious and able defence," giving "a history of his life which amused the court not a little." Several years earlier, the accused testified, he had left New York for New Orleans in the brig *Flood*, and had subsequently enlisted in General Jackson's army and fought in the battle of New Orleans, "in token of which he said he had lost one hand and his left eye." Johnson conceded that "he had no one to speak for his character, and knew that without friends and without counsel, he was as much exposed to punishment as though he had committed the crime." Yet his performance was certainly a winning one. A prominent attorney, who was waiting for another case to be called, was "induced" by that performance to say a few words on Johnson's behalf. The accused's "conduct and appearance [speak] volumes in his favour," the attorney declared, and, although the man was unable to adduce favorable evidence as to his character, "he had told here a very straightforward story," one, moreover, that was the same as the story he had earlier recounted at the police office. After deliberating for all of a couple of minutes, the jury acquitted the prisoner.[4] Perhaps William Johnson was telling the truth, or perhaps he was just very good—at this distance who can tell?

For all of Johnson's evident storytelling prowess, we are left with only secondhand accounts of his performance, one from the reporter, the other from the attorney who became his *pro bono* mouthpiece. The fact that Johnson's and similar stories come to us in the form of paraphrases and summaries, larded with the occasional direct quotes, underscores the extent to which blacks were second-class citizens, compelled to speak but having no control over what was done to their words. The clearest example of this heavy editing is contained in the most plentiful source of material on the lives of African New Yorkers in the early decades of the nineteenth century—the thousands of depositions from blacks taken by the district attorney, depositions that are housed today in the city's Municipal Archives. These statements, varying in length from a few lines to ten or more pages, were taken from a surprisingly broad range of blacks. To be sure, many were "criminals," but it is important to remember that the number of blacks hauled into court was way out of proportion to their percentage of the city's population. Sooner or later, it seems, even the most prominent African New Yorker citizens ended up telling some sort of story, as witness, victim, or accused, to the district attorney's clerk. Occasionally in these transcriptions the dynamics of the interview bubble to the surface. Irritated by questions about stints he had served in the state prison, Edward Latham, a "no nosed black man" accused of burglary in 1816, retorted "The writer knows as well when he was Discharged from the State prison as this examinant and therefore it aint worth while to say any thing about."[5] Or this, at least, was how the clerk rendered Latham's speech, that is to say, in the third person, which was characteristic of these documents. As well, there are the usual problems, encountered the world over, with material taken by judicial authorities: the sheer number of confessions without which the blacks who had been charged could never have been found guilty; confessions which specifically mention that those who made them had not been treated violently (a notation which looks decidedly suspect when put in the third person); cases in which prisoners who resolutely refuse to speak on one day, give the next day a full and helpful catalogue of their various sins.

These difficulties notwithstanding, the plethora of storytelling by and about African New Yorkers—in newspapers, in the records of the district attorney, and elsewhere—has created an immensely rich record of black life. By collecting these stories from an avalanche of paper and by trying to read them imaginatively and often against their own grain, I have been able to fashion my own story of the ending of slavery in New York. It is a story of the way in which, through thousands upon thousands of individual encounters with other African New Yorkers and with whites, the city's blacks shucked off the hated legacy of slavery and discovered for themselves what their newly won freedom meant.

The myriad small dramas of these black New Yorkers were

played out against a backdrop of rapid economic expansion in a city which, by early in the nineteenth century, had become the most dynamic in the New World. Recovering quickly from the destructive effects of British occupation during the Revolution, the city's total population had increased in almost exponential fashion, from 33,131 in 1790, to 60,489 in 1800, to 96,373 in 1810, to 123,706 in 1820.[6] Already the premier economic and financial center in America, New York had received an enormous stimulus from the opening of the Erie Canal in 1825; as the London *Times* confidently predicted, this event would make the city "the London of the New World."[7] By 1830 the population of the metropolis stood at more than 200,000, having increased by over sixty percent in the previous decade.[8] Yet for all its burgeoning signs of modernity, New York in the 1820s still struggled to escape the long shadow of slavery. Begun in the previous century, the long and tortuous process of emancipation still had some years to run (at the start of the decade, there were more than 500 slaves in the city); the troubled legacy of a grudgingly conceded freedom would last much longer.

Abolition was always going to be more disruptive and difficult in New York and its surrounds than anywhere else in the North. For most of the eighteenth century, the city had ranked second only to Charleston, in British Mainland North America, in the number of slaves held by its inhabitants. In 1790 one in every five white households contained a slave, and in the immediate hinterland, within ten to fifteen miles of the metropolis, the figure was four in every ten households, a rate of slave ownership higher than that existing in the states of Virginia or South Carolina. Holdings were generally small, with very few whites owning more than one or two slaves, but slave ownership was widespread and was not confined to the elite. Numerous small farmers, artisans, shopkeepers, widows, and sea captains, as well as lawyers, merchants, and members of the gentry relied to some extent on slave labor. Not only was slavery firmly entrenched in and around New York City, but in the 1790s the institution had actually expanded. That decade saw a 22 percent increase in the city's slave population and a massive 33 percent increase in its slaveholders.[9]

In 1799 the New York State legislature had passed a bill ending slavery, but the measure was a compromise that clearly demonstrated both the power of the slaveholding interests and the respect accorded property rights, even if the property was other human beings. On the one hand, it was now clear that slavery was going to end and that New York would align itself with the other northern nonslave states. On the other hand, however, and particularly as far as African Americans in New York City were concerned, the legislature had ensured that abolition would occur at a pace that could only be described as glacial. Under the terms of the act, all children born to slave women after July 4, 1799, were to be free, but males were to remain in a form of indentured servitude until they reached the age of twenty-eight, and females were to be so bound until they were twenty-five. Those who were still slaves on July 4, 1799, were abandoned to their fate; not until 1817 would the legislature finally agree to free such persons and even then that was not to occur for another decade, until July 4, 1827.

In the event, many slaves took things into their own hands and negotiated individually with their masters. Most of the advantages in such transactions still lay with the owners, but for once the deck was not stacked entirely against the slaves, and many played their cards very skillfully indeed. Not only was slavery in New York legislatively doomed, but the city's free black population was rapidly increasing, making the successful pursuit of runaway slaves much more difficult. Moreover, implicit in every negotiation was the threat that if some arrangement were not agreed upon, the owner would be left with either a sullen, refractory slave, or, if the slave decamped, nothing at all. In these circumstances, many owners took the path of least resistance, settling for whatever they could get from their human property. Some accepted money. Ann Grasey was able to buy her freedom in 1806 from Richard Dean, a fruit merchant, for $125. Three years later, Harry, a thirty-year-old slave, paid the executors of his master's estate $150 and walked free. Other owners used the promise of future liberty to extract pledges of good behavior. Elizabeth Fine agreed, in January 1805, that if her slave Margaret behaved "in an orderly manner as a servant ought to do," she would free her eight years hence. Similarly, in 1807, Edward Griffin undertook to manumit his slave Samuel if he behaved well for a decade.[10]

As such stories suggest, to a large extent the details of slavery's demise in and around New York City were worked out on an individual basis. Often, however, the term "self-purchase" was a misnomer. The raising of the substantial sums needed to buy one's freedom could require the combined efforts of one's family and in many cases those of other members of the black community and even of benevolent whites as well. Negotiations were often highly complex. In 1814, the slave Titus wished to buy out of slavery the members of his family—his wife Betsey, a sixteen-year-old son, a daughter aged five, and another daughter not yet one year old. These slaves were the property not of Titus's owner but of the estate of one Walter Berg, whose executors were proposing to sell Titus's family at auction. Although Titus managed to scrape together enough money to free his kin, he could not do so in his own name, for if he, a slave, bought them, they would become the property of Titus's owner. With the help of the Manumission Society, Titus arranged for his family to be bought and for the bill of sale to be endorsed to the Reverend James Thomson, a black living in Brooklyn, who subsequently freed them.[11]

Titus's caution was understandable: a slave had little or no legal recourse if his or her owner decided to renege on any agreement. The minutes of the Standing Committee of the New York Manumission Society are littered with cases in which owners, ignoring previously agreed to terms, cruelly squeezed the last drop of profit out of their unfortunate human chattels. Adam Mitchel, originally from Hackensack, was owned by the four Miss Nicols. For nearly fifteen months Mitchel had been "working for his freedom," his wages being put by his owners toward his purchase price. In the event, however, the avaricious sisters not only shortchanged Mitchel by failing to credit him with the money he earned for them, but had him committed to prison for six days "because he does not bring them Money as fast as they Wish." In another case, in February 1813, Robert and Mary Rhea entered into a written contract with their slave Violet Waters, agreeing to free her in consideration of payment of $150. Within two years Waters had paid off $100 and had saved up a further $50, but her mistress refused to accept the remaining money or to give her a discharge, declaring that she would "have her again as her slave." Other owners were even more unscrupulous. Samuel Williams arranged to have his wages put toward buying his freedom from Nathaniel Prime, but after taking Williams's money, Prime sold him to a buyer from Georgia, and then went with the new owner and a constable to the slave's residence in Beekman Street, seized him, and confined him on a Savannah-bound ship in the harbor. Somehow Samuel managed to make his way back to New York, where in February 1812, as the records of the Manumission Society show, he appealed to that organization for help.[12]

In large part it was New York slaves who bore the costs of the tangled and often capricious process of emancipation, and for many, stuck in poorly paying jobs, those costs must have been huge. There were emotional costs, too, in this frequently demeaning process; having to behave like the perfect slave for a specified number of years must have been galling. To gain one's freedom depended, of course, on the slave's ability to bargain and earn money, but also to a large extent on just plain luck. Because of the small size of holdings in the city, slave families were usually dispersed among several owners, and while one member might secure freedom, his or her spouse or children, the property of more obdurate owners, might have to wait years longer. The frustration and anguish involved in such situations must have been immense.

Worst of all, the gaining of freedom was an agonizingly protracted process. Unlike Lincoln's Proclamation in 1863, which freed southern slaves at a stroke, emancipation in New York took decades. To be sure, by the time the legislature's deadline of July 4, 1827, came around, there were virtually no slaves left in the city; by then, and by their own actions, most New York slaves had successfully accelerated the legislature's lackadaisical timetable. But to assert, as any number of usually complaining New Yorkers would in the 1820s and 1830s, that whites had generously bestowed freedom on their slaves, was not only a palpable and self-serving distortion of what had occurred but an all too typical erasure of the key role that blacks had played in determining their own destiny.

Although for a few uneasy, transitional decades masters continued to be able legally to do with their slaves pretty much as they wished, in these years the doomed institution seemed increasingly aberrant and anachronistic. In 1825 the slave Samuel Ford, who had managed to accumulate $53 in his account with the Savings Bank of New York, was suddenly "taken away by his master" to Washington. Soon after this, however, Ford's bank book and a power of attorney were presented to the New York bank's cashier and his money was withdrawn.[13] There is something very strange and anomalous in this story about a slave preparing for the obviously anticipated eventuality of his removal from the city by arranging for a power of attorney so that his wife could have access to his bank account.

The edginess that such legal and social ambiguities created showed up in many ways. In the early decades of the nineteenth century, an unprecedented number of masters were charged with treating their slaves cruelly. The New York Manumission Society in particular did its best to publicize such violence, and it was this Society that brought the most notorious case in the city's history to public attention. Early in 1809, Amos Broad, an upholsterer by trade and a well-known evangelist who had established his own church, and his wife, a milliner, were sent to trial for "assaulting and beating" Betty, their slave, and her daughter Sarah. The details of the case were little short of horrendous. Broad had repeatedly flayed his slave's naked back with a horsewhip, and on at least two occasions had then forced her outside in very cold weather and thrown water over her naked body. He had routinely locked the woman up for long periods without food and compelled her to eat a large bowl of Glauber Salts (a laxative) even though she was not constipated. On one occasion, after Betty had brought in an over-full teapot, Broad ordered her to hold out her hand and poured boiling water over it, saying "Am I not a good doctor to doctor negroes?" On occasion he had also lifted up three-year-old Sarah by her ears and carried her a "considerable distance," had literally kicked her across a room, and had made her stand up for hours at a time in the cold, severely beating her whenever she attempted to sit down. During the course of the trial the Broads "voluntarily" manumitted Betty, Sarah, and one other slave they owned, a tactic whose feigned magnanimity impressed neither jury nor judge. Both husband and wife were found guilty: Amos

Broad was fined $1,000 and sentenced to 120 days in the city prison; his wife was fined $250.[14] What was especially horrifying, as the New York Manumission Society pointed out, was that the case was far from unique. The Society had on its books "cases of almost equal enormity." New Yorkers who "in deliberate wantonness torture their [slaves'] feelings and lacerate their flesh" were, the Society announced, hardly a rarity.[15]

At least partly because of the Manumission Society's activities, white New Yorkers showed a greater willingness to bring charges against cruel owners. A white neighbor testified in court, in November 1814, that a Mr. Lavau of Varick Street savagely beat his slave Betty to the point where she was "entirely deranged." Lavau then decided to free the now valueless woman, telling her "to go & take her clothes with her or words to that effect." Phoebe Dodge, who lived in James Street swore that her neighbor, John Plume, a porterhouse keeper, continually kicked and callously beat his slave woman and on at least one occasion had knocked her senseless with a blow. Charles McLean, living at 293 Broadway in 1817, gave evidence that Jacob Brown, a resident in the same building, cruelly beat his eleven- or twelve-year-old black girl "without a good cause." From what he had seen, McLean opined, Brown was "an improper person to have a slave under his command." McLean's belief that slaveowners ought to observe proprieties was gaining increasing acceptance among white New Yorkers, but if the courts shared that general view, it is still clear that their own standard of what constituted acceptable behavior was very low: each of these owners was charged with assault and battery, and though there is little doubt that each had inhumanly treated his slaves, each was acquitted.[16] Slavery may have been on its last legs, but judges and juries remained extremely reluctant to interfere in the relationship between slaveowners and their human property.

Beneath the dry language of the court records, the mundane details of everyday, sadistic cruelty chill the soul and finally give the lie to the self-serving myth that slavery in New York was but a mild and relatively benevolent version of the South's peculiar institution. One owner arranged for a journeyman blacksmith to fasten a chain with a twenty-eight pound weight to a slave woman's leg. Eleanora Pienard almost daily beat her young slave Jack and a slave woman "in a cruell & inhuman manner not only with a cowskin but with the fire tongs & pieces of wood or anything that happened to come handy." She then had Jack's feet chained inside a box; in this position he was obliged to work seven days a week rolling cigars. On one occasion, Pienard had summoned another resident in the building and had her look at Jack's back, saying laughingly "I have made his back red instead of black." At several other times this neighbor had seen both of Pienard's slaves stripped and beaten "so that the blood runs down their backs." Yet the cover page of the papers relating to this case also bears the simple notation "acquitted."[17]

Masters of black indentured servants could be similarly cruel. In 1813 charges of assault and battery were brought against one John Towt. Nine years previously a very young mulatto girl named Mary Graham had been bound to Towt by the Commissioner of the Alms House, but for the past five years Graham had frequently absented herself from her master for days and nights at a time. When questioned by the authorities she admitted that "her time is not yet expired" and that she had run away seven times, but she also stated clearly that she did "not want to go home & serve as she is bound to do." The reason may be discovered on a separate fragment of paper in the file of this case, which bears the notation "complains of being unmercifully beaten, evidenced by the marks on her body." Unfortunately, the outcome of the indictment against John Towt is not clear from the district at-

torney's records, but it takes little imagination, as one pieces together the spare legal documents that survive, to understand why
Graham was so determined to avoid him.[18]

In these transitional decades before slavery ended, instances in
which slaves retaliated against their owners were also more frequent. Court records (voluminous, but anything but complete)
register this sharp increase, but, since slaveholders generally preferred to deal personally with their slaves, turning to the authorities only as a last resort, almost certainly the cases recorded display merely the tip of a very large iceberg. In 1805, the slave
Anthony not only attacked his mistress, Phoebe Stewart, with his
bare hands but repeatedly claimed that he was going to stab her, a
threat that she took seriously enough to seek relief from the authorities. Reveste Chaux claimed that her slave Jane had not only
"lately behaved herself very obstropulously," refusing "to obey
[her] lawful commands," but that in early May 1807, Jane had also
shoved and jostled her, laying "violent hands" on her. This had
prompted Chaux to file charges of assault and battery.[19]

The long-running struggle between Robert Warnock and his
slave Betsey Paulding showed how a contest between an owner
and a determined slave could easily turn into a very public and
doubtless embarrassing affair for the owner. In December 1816,
Warnock claimed that Paulding's behavior was becoming intolerable; she "was very insulting & refused to obey [his] reasonable
orders" and turned violent when he tried to stop her going out. In
April 1817, in a case that appears to have been instigated by the
slave, the owner was charged with assault and battery. A woman
who lived next door but one testified that on at least two occasions
Warnock had beaten Paulding with a cowskin whip (a particularly
painful experience). As was usual in such cases, the slaveowner
was acquitted. Sometime early in 1818, however, Paulding sought
help from the New York Manumission Society. According to the

Society's minutes, the slave had three times complained to the Police Office of Warnock's violent behavior, but on each occasion he had brought counter-charges on the grounds that she had repeatedly threatened him and his family. Apparently nothing was resolved at this time, because in September 1818 Warnock swore that Paulding had "so annoyed him by her conduct refusing to serve, being impudent and running away; cursing & swearing & beating & ill treating his children that he has no peace of life with her"; indeed, she had just that very morning told him "she would do as she pleased." Paulding was convicted, but a month later Warnock was still complaining that she had "behaved herself in a most obstreperous and outrageous manner" toward himself and his family, and continually disobeyed orders. This time she was not only convicted but sentenced to prison.[20] Doubtless there was legal merit on both sides of this dispute—Paulding wanted to be free and was proving a handful, and Warnock had resorted to violence to restore, as he saw it, proper order—but what is more important here is the way in which the previously generally understood relationship between master and slave could transmute into an openly raw contest of wills, not infrequently with violent results. As most blacks in the city became free, the slave system simply could no longer work as it once had.

As the slave system unraveled, fears of black-initiated violence came from other quarters. Urban areas, still predominantly built of wood, were highly vulnerable to fire, a situation which frustrated slaves could easily exploit. Expressing a general fear, one New York judge pointed out that arson was "among the most atrocious of human offences": "in the hour of repose," he continued, "what guard can shield us against the wicked purposes of those in whom we are obliged to place confidence?"—a clear enough reference to slaves. The best-known case involving the use of fire was that of Rose Butler. By 1818, Butler had been in the

Morris household, probably as some sort of bound servant, for three years. She continually clashed with her mistress over such issues as how much additional work could be expected of her as she prepared dinner. Questioned in court about her attitude toward her mistress, Butler stated that she "was always finding fault with my work, and scolding me. I never did like her." In the end, Butler had decided to torch the Morrises' house. She failed in the attempt, and no one had been injured; the fire had been extinguished after the stairs were burned down. But during and after her trial, Butler's demeanor was anything but contrite; she was "rude and offensive" to all, particularly to the clergy who visited her in her cell. Such behavior, however, was immaterial. Given the state of public opinion and the fear arson induced, her fate was all but sealed. While the Governor was considering whether to commute her sentence to a prison term, the *Evening Post* editorialized on the "salutary effect" the execution of a black man found guilty of the same crime three years previously had had on the number of house burnings. On July 9, 1819, Butler was marched up to the Potters Field, hanged in front of a large crowd, and buried a few yards from the scaffold.[21]

Rose Butler was not the only young black girl to seek this form of revenge. In June 1810, Jemima, a twelve-year-old slave in the household of the butcher William Wright, took a shovelful of embers from the kitchen fire and tried to burn the house down. She had done so at the prompting of Louisa Davis, a slave in the same house, who told Jemima that she "did not like Mr Wright or any of his family except James Wright one of her Master's little sons." Jemima, too, was convicted of arson. In another case, Charlotte, a very young indentured black girl, was whipped by her master "because I did something naughty"; she had "pulled up my petticoats before a little white boy which my Mistress had before forbidden me to do." Later that day Charlotte took a lighted candle into the cellar and set fire to some paper adjacent to several large casks of beeswax. The fire, however, was quickly put out. In a similar instance in December 1811, an eight-year-old black servant girl, having been whipped by her mistress, used a burning log from the kitchen fire to try and incinerate her owner's stables.[22]

Given New York African Americans' prominent role in the preparation of food, the threat of poisoning was even more worrying. In December 1806, a hired servant of Thomas Snell testified that nineteen-year-old Margaret and twelve-year-old Diana, slaves in the same household, continually talked about wreaking vengeance on their owners. Margaret stated that "she would not poison any but her old & young mistress because they whipped her." The plan was to put poison in the family's tea kettle and then burn the house down, thus destroying the evidence. Initially, Snell's servant dismissed the threat as idle talk, but when Margaret returned from an errand with a phial of pink liquid, the servant reported that fact to her employers. Margaret and Diana were convicted of conspiracy. In the same month, Eleanor Rankin, a fourteen-year-old black indentured servant of William Smith, put ratsbane in the coffee, killing her mistress and making several other members of the family very sick. The young black girl confessed that she had done it "because she did not like her said Mistress," adding, hardly reassuringly, that "she did not intend to kill her." Cases such as these, which touched particularly raw nerves, could easily prompt retaliatory violence. Luse, the slave of H. G. Livingston, garnished the crust of the family's meat pie with ground glass and pins. On discovering the potentially fatal nature of the meal, Livingston's father-in-law pummelled, kicked, and threatened Luse until he had extracted a confession. Only the quick action of his son-in-law prevented the angry and excited man from pulling the trigger of the blunderbuss he was flourishing under Luse's nose.[23]

The extent to which African American women, and very young ones at that, were involved in such violent actions is striking. Partly the reason lies in the city's demography—female slaves had outnumbered males in New York City for decades—but it is also likely that women had much greater difficulty than did men in negotiating a deal with their owners and in fulfilling its conditions. As slavery wound down in New York, slave women took the lead in violent resistance to the institution, playing out roles that people have commonly assumed were the preserves of males. This too must have further unsettled white New Yorkers. In October 1814, Bet, the slave of John G. Tardy, was brought before the courts, charged with larceny. In the course of investigating Bet's theft, it was revealed that she had not only "used the most abusive and threatening language" toward her mistress, but had also declared that "if she had money she would buy a small barrel of gunpowder & Blow up the House and everybody in it." Indeed, Bet had stolen a fifty-dollar note, an offense that must have given her owners some pause.[24]

Slave-initiated violence affected the course of freedom in New York City. The often desperate actions of Bet and other slaves may not have ameliorated their own misery—many went to prison and some were executed—but reports of their rebellious behavior had a wide impact. Stories of arson, poisonings, and of masters being bashed by their slaves, circulating to every corner of the city, formed a menacing backdrop against which New York slaves negotiated their freedom, sapping the determination of slaveowners to continue the struggle. If even ten-year-old girls were prepared to visit terrible havoc on those who oppressed them, was it worth hanging onto one's human chattels? How much easier to come to terms. In the long run, every slave in the city who managed to extricate himself or herself from the hated

institution before July 4, 1827, was the beneficiary of this violence.

The lives of New York blacks, whether bond or free, were affected by the decline of the northern slave system as well as by the
expansion of the southern one. The fact that any one of the thousands of blacks walking New York streets, if delivered to the slave
markets of New Orleans or Charleston, was worth hundreds of
dollars proved an irresistible lure to unscrupulous whites, and
even to some blacks. Kidnapping was highly profitable and relatively free of risk; once shanghaied blacks landed in the South,
who would believe their claims, unsupported by documentation,
that they were free? As a result, kidnapping was a constant threat.
Occasionally, participants in this nefarious trade were caught. In
December 1819 Joseph Pulford was convicted of kidnapping. He
had contracted with the captain of a Havana-bound vessel to deliver to him four or five blacks for $50 a head (when the buyer em-
phasized that these had to be "very black," Pulford had claimed
that "he could get them as Black as he wanted them"). Though
Pulford was arrested before he could fulfill his part of the bargain,
he had already inveigled Mary Henderson into turning up at the
dock by telling her that a "Gentleman" traveling in a vessel required a servant who would be paid $100 a month, a spectacular
sum.[25] As with most crimes committed against blacks, however,
very few people were ever charged with kidnapping.

By and large it was all too easy to isolate and secure a black and
return her or him to servitude. Blacks working "along shore" or
on the docks—and these were among the few jobs open to them—
were always at risk. Young children on the streets anywhere in the
city, too, were often in danger. In November 1829, for example,

the *New York American* ran a story under the caption "Beware of Kidnappers!" According to the paper, it was well understood "that there are at present in this city a gang of Kidnappers, busily engaged in their vocation of stealing colored children for the southern market!" Three or four children were already supposed to have been spirited away and secreted aboard a vessel in the harbor.[26] This sort of alarm was both common and very real.

Slave runaways, arriving in significant numbers from the South, also affected the lives of New York blacks. As the city's free black population mushroomed, New York became more and more attractive as a destination for fugitives. For some, the city was a large, anonymous place, where they could start over as free men and women; for others, New York was a way station to somewhere else, in many cases Canada. Occasionally the arrival of fugitive slaves was spectacular enough to warrant notice in the newspapers. As reported by the *Daily Advertiser*, at daybreak on July 23, 1829, a thirty-foot pilot boat quietly nudged up to the wharf at the end of Dover Street. As soon as the boat docked, six black men and one woman jumped ashore and disappeared into the city streets with "light hearts and nimble heels." According to rumor, this group of slaves had stolen the boat and escaped from the eastern shore of Virginia and were now hidden "secure from the search of the most vigilant."[27] Most runaways, however, quietly slipped into New York in ones and twos by land or sea.

Where runaways fled, catchers soon followed, and their attempts to apprehend southern absconders often provoked wrenching scenes: a Virginian slave dragged out of his boarding-house residence in an early morning raid; another Virginian slave, cornered in Hanover Square, desperately sticking Constable Hays in the leg with a knife in a futile attempt at escape; a young black man sprinting for his life down a crowded Wall Street with a couple of well-known slave catchers in furious pursuit. Such dramatic encounters constantly reminded all blacks of the precarious nature of their freedom in the young republic. When he arrived in New York in 1834, Moses Roper, a famous runaway slave, assumed he was now free "but I learned I was not, and could be taken there." There is ample evidence that demonstrates the correctness of Roper's surmise. On July 4, 1821, a young African American stood idly on the fringes of a crowd listening as soapbox orators in the park waxed eloquent about the Declaration of Independence. Suddenly, he was set upon by a man who later claimed to be his owner, thrown to the ground, tied with a rope, and dragged away. As this was taking place, the whites who were listening to speeches about liberty simply stood by, an irony pointed out by the *Spectator*.[28] But for African New Yorkers, long forced to rely on their own actions, the contradiction between professed ideals and practice would hardly have been news.

Few things were as likely to provoke African New Yorkers to direct action as was the threat that some in their midst—whether local blacks or recaptured runaways—were about to be consigned to a life of slavery. That had been so from the beginnings of the New York free black community. In 1801, rumors had swept the city that a Madame Jeanne Mathusine Droibillan Volunbrun was preparing illegally to ship twenty blacks to Virginia. A white West Indian émigré, most of whose capital was invested in the slaves, Mme. Volunbrun felt threatened generally by New York's abolition measure and more specifically by a New York Manumission Society suit claiming that her slaves were already legally free. Bankruptcy loomed unless she could do something to forestall it. The rumor of her proposed action galvanized a group of "French negroes," many armed with clubs, who gathered outside her house on Eagle Street to prevent it. By evening, the crowd, swelled now to 250, was threatening to "burn the said Volunbrun's house, murder all the white people in it and take away a number of Black Slaves." The black protesters were dispersed only after a pitched battle in the streets with fifty members of the watch. Twenty-three of their number were convicted of riot and sentenced to sixty days.[29]

In later years violent action tended to center on the area around the courts, the site at which slave catchers attempted to prove that the blacks they had captured were indeed slaves. In June 1819 a slave catcher took Thomas Hartlett to the Police Office, where Hartlett ultimately confessed that he was indeed the runaway slave of a Mr. Hall of Montgomery County in upstate New York. When Hall's agent heard that a crowd of blacks was gathering nearby, he requested a police escort to the wharf on the North River, but in Barclay Street the convoy was beset by angry African New Yorkers, who roughly manhandled one of the marshals and only just failed to effect the prisoner's release. A similar confrontation occurred in September 1826, when a very large crowd of blacks gathered outside the doors to City Hall, where the case against a family of allegedly runaway Virginia slaves was to be heard. The blacks belligerently jostled and harassed parties to the case and witnesses as they entered the building, and also abused the police. At about one o'clock the Mayor directed the constables to remove the protestors, but by four o'clock a much larger crowd of blacks had congregated in the park. When attempts were made to disperse them, showers of bricks and stones rained down on the police, the slave catcher, and not a few passers by. Newspapers reported that several of the blacks had been armed and that it seemed clear that the crowd had intended to use force to set the captives free.[30]

If African New Yorkers were outraged by the actions of white southerners or their agents in attempting to reclaim their "property," at least such behavior was to be expected; what was intolerable was the spectacle of blacks themselves selling out their compatriots. In July 1833 a "large collection of blacks" rioted in the Five Points district over several nights. According to the *Morning Courier and New-York Enquirer,* it appeared "that they had taken umbrage at one of their own color, for giving, as they allege, information relating to runaway slaves." On the night before the story appeared, the suspect had been caught, taken to a house, subjected to an extralegal trial by his captors, found guilty, and condemned to be whipped. News of these extraordinary events leaked to the authorities, and at the eleventh hour the prisoner was saved from his fate by a large contingent of the watch, a rescue that undoubtedly confirmed, for the makeshift jury, the correctness of their verdict. Another well-organized black action occurred in 1836, when a "gang" of armed African New Yorkers attacked the crew of the Brazilian brig *Brilliante* at midnight, caught them by surprise, and succeeded in freeing two of the five slaves who were on board. When the mate, awakened by a noise, ran up on deck, "one of the gang cocked a pistol at him and threatened to blow his brains out in case he interfered." This was less the action of an enraged mob than an efficient guerilla operation, the worst nightmare of those opposed to black freedom. Little wonder, then, that the *New York Journal of Commerce's* story was printed under the caption "Gross Outrage."[31]

For all the violence that accompanied slavery's last years, and notwithstanding the precarious nature of the freedom that newly liberated blacks enjoyed, New York acted as a magnet for both free blacks and fleeing slaves. Indeed, for a while, the black population managed to match the city's spectacular demographic growth, maintaining its share of slightly more than ten percent of the total number of inhabitants until 1810. In 1790 there were 3,470 blacks in the city; by 1810, that figure had almost trebled to 9,823. And although, over the next two decades, the black share of the population slipped to just under seven percent, this still represented a more than forty percent increase in the number of African New Yorkers between 1810 and 1830. By the latter date, 13,976 blacks lived in the metropolis.[32]

Little, if any, of this population growth could be attributed to natural increase; it would be many decades before black family life shrugged off the pall of slavery. As with the city as a whole, the black population's main source of growth was immigration. Initially, in the 1790s and over the first few years of the new century, most black migrants came from the Caribbean. Slaveowners, fleeing the great uprising on Saint Domingue, brought some of their slaves with them to America, and many of these refugees ended up in New York City, where they helped to shape the tenor of slavery's last expansion before it began to wither away. Slaves from the Caribbean—often French-speaking and from a culture decisively shaped by the African past (many were African born)—were considered to be fractious, often running away and becoming involved in, or at least being blamed for, much of the slave unrest that occurred in New York around the turn of the century.[33]

In 1803 an irate "Citizen" drew the attention of readers of the *New York Gazette and General Advertiser* to the "whole host of Africans that now deluge our city." Even as he wrote, however, the principal source of newly arrived blacks was changing. Slavery died hard in the rural areas of New York and New Jersey, but gradually the abolition measures of 1799 and 1804 had their effect, and, in a pattern repeated time and time again, rural blacks who managed to secure their freedom left the area of their enslavement and headed for the city. For blacks who longed to escape the constrictions of a society in which they would always be stamped as former slaves, New York City, holding the promise of anonymity and employment, had an almost irresistible attraction.[34]

Throughout the 1820s and 1830s the city continued to draw

blacks from the local region. Many were simply curious about life in a big urban center. In 1819 Tom Johnson, who lived in Fishkill, "came to this City last Monday," as he said, "to see it, the City." Other immigrants were fugitives from the South. In July 1826 the editor of the *National Advocate*, having declared the "increase of Negroes in this place . . . a subject of alarming observation," went on to complain bitterly that New York was "the point of refuge to all the runaways in the Union." Nor was it only slaves who left the South. In the course of her trial for theft in March 1833, Ann Beckett, a black woman, stated that she had been born free in Accomac County, Virginia, and that about four months earlier she had left, with "a cargo of other negroes, who, born free, like herself, were expatriated for the sin of being born free, and for fear of the contagion of their opinions and examples being communicated to the slaves." In the wake of the Nat Turner slave revolt in 1831, free blacks in Virginia had been subjected to much closer control, a circumstance which, the *Courier and Enquirer* suggested, could "explain the reason why so many free blacks from the south, are roaming our streets."[35]

In the early decades of the nineteenth century, black New York was a city not only of ex-slaves but also of migrants. Into the 1830s, a majority of the African Americans living in New York had been born elsewhere. Of course, the city was a booming port, which meant that at any one time there were black maritime workers from all around the Atlantic in town. But mostly the newcomers were migrants, blacks who grew up, usually as slaves, in the French Caribbean, in the often Dutch-influenced slaveholding areas of New York and New Jersey, or in Virginia and Maryland. James Pennington, a runaway slave from the South who arrived in New York in 1829, immediately "felt serious apprehensions of danger," but as he eloquently pointed out "I felt also that I must begin the world somewhere."[36] Migration turned the city's black population into a cultural mélange, a development that was to have a profound influence on the character of black life. The great cultural diversity of the city's black inhabitants, their optimism, their determination to start anew, yet at the same time their unwillingness to forget the still fresh scars of slavery—all these contributed to the emergence of the unusually lively and vigorous black urban culture that characterized New York in the first three decades of the nineteenth century.

But if New York's continuing ability to attract so many blacks suggests something of the appeal of settling down in a place where there were large numbers of their peers, it also says something about the limited range of options for African Americans in the young republic. The material realities of life for most of New York's black inhabitants were grim. Under slavery, many blacks had been owned by artisans and employed in their workshops. As the institution began its slow demise in the very early years of the nineteenth century, newly freed blacks found work in the occupations for which they had been trained, but the opportunities to earn a living as skilled tradesmen did not last long. In the 1810s and 1820s, most New York blacks were hired in piecemeal, short-term fashion, usually as domestic servants if they were female or as laborers if they were male. But even here they were often squeezed out of these meagerly paid jobs by the poor Irish migrants who were flooding into the city. In November 1833, a contractor building a row of houses on 8th Avenue hired both blacks and whites, whereupon the Irish refused to work with the blacks. The contractor's response was to discharge both groups of laborers. Each group blamed their sacking on the other and the inevitable result was a "pitched battle" in which two blacks were seriously injured.[37] This sort of pressure soon convinced most employers to avoid hiring blacks.

To be sure, there were African Americans who managed to operate small businesses, particularly those selling food and, most notably, oysters. In New York the oyster cellars were predominantly run by blacks and remained open until 3 or 4 in the morning (whereas in Philadelphia oysters were sold by white-owned businesses and shut down around 1 A.M.), but in the 1830s, the traveler Francis Grund noted, "clever white men" were beginning to take the business out of African New Yorkers' hands. The difficulties black shopkeepers faced in dealing with often inebriated white customers late at night are attested to by numerous cases in the court records and newspapers. Scuffles and worse broke out over customers' refusing to pay; patrons resented blacks for asking them to pay before eating; some even resented blacks for getting ahead altogether. Something of the nature of the problems African New Yorkers encountered is suggested by the wording of a small story reported in the *New York Spectator*. In 1827 David Ruggles, a black man who became a staunch abolitionist and publisher later in his life, moved from Connecticut to New York and opened a grocery store there. Just before Christmas 1829, his premises were broken into and partially burned; money was taken. To the *Spectator* the case was deserving of sympathy: the proprietor was "an industrious man" who overcame suffering "those prejudices which a dark skin presents" and had built a "desirable little business." Ruggles had achieved all this, the newspaper concluded, in a telling phrase, "by his conciliating manners."[38]

Despite all they faced, a few blacks did manage to get ahead and make a name for themselves. Thomas Downing, a free black who came to New York from Virginia in 1819, ran an elegant, up-market oyster establishment just off Wall Street. Pierre Toussaint, originally a slave from Haiti, became a prominent ladies' hairdresser.[39] The best known black entrepreneur at the time was probably Cato Alexander, who ran a hotel on the main road out of town near present-day Fifty-Second Street. For nearly fifty years fashionable young whites stopped off at Cato's for a drink while horseriding or sleighing. When the actor Tyrone Power called at the hotel in the early 1830s, he was impressed partly by the place but mostly by the demeanor of its proprietor, "who for courtesy and bienseance might serve as a model to most of his young friends." So well-known was this black man's hotel that the designation "Cato's" required no further explication if encountered, for instance, in a newspaper story.

But these were clearly exceptional cases. More obvious was the large number of unemployed and underemployed blacks. An anonymous Glaswegian visiting New York in 1822 was surprised by the "great many of the African race" in the city and could not help but notice that "they are generally in a most woeful condition." He was unable to "conceive from their lazy lounging conduct how the half of them find sustenance." The attitude of this visitor was judgmental, his language pejorative, but he was pointing to a very real problem: it was difficult for African New Yorkers to find employment that paid enough to enable them to support themselves in any comfort. As Peter Joseph, a black accused of grand larceny, put it in 1821, laconically describing his situation to his interrogator, "when he has money he eats & when he has no money he does without."[40]

New York's acute housing shortage made the situation worse. Under slavery, most blacks had lived in their owners' residences, in kitchen cellars or in garrets, but once free, an increasingly high proportion of African New Yorkers resided in black households. Unfortunately, these newly liberated blacks striving to establish an independent family life were seeking accommodation at a time when the city's population was exploding at an almost exponential rate, and when economic changes were transforming the way the metropolis worked. As production was divorced from the household and wage labor was introduced (rather than "room and board" being part of a worker's remuneration), laborers were forced into usually inferior rented places. In these years too the old mixed neighborhoods of the "walking city" were giving way to the more specialized spatial arrangements of the emerging indus- trial metropolis. More and more workers and their employers lived at some remove from one another. African New Yorkers be- gan clustering where they could get access to scarce housing, of- ten in basement cellars. To be sure, there were still many whites residing in these sections of the city, literally on top of the blacks in many cases, but some areas, such as Bancker Street and the lower west side around Chapel and Anthony streets, began to take on the appearance of identifiably black neighborhoods.[41]

From the beginning of New York's free black community in the 1790s and early 1800s, its people were forced into living quarters that were often appalling: cellars that filled with filth when it rained, back-alley shanties devoid of any amenities, and the like. But for all their obvious shortcomings, these primitive dwellings seem the almost inevitable result of pressures from the city's booming population. Sometime about the 1820s, however, there was a discernible change. For the first time, slum landlords who deliberately set out to exploit New York blacks appear with some frequency in the surviving records. Not only did these property owners jam more and more blacks into smaller spaces, but they also charged them higher rents. In 1820, a "gentleman" took "some pains" to ascertain the details of one building in Bancker Street: the house occupied almost all of the 20 feet wide and 70 feet deep lot, although an alley ran up the center of the two-story structure. Here lived 15 families numbering almost 60 people, virtually all of them blacks. The building and land were probably worth some $1,100, but the owner "extort[ed] from the miserable tenants" about $800 per annum in rent (payable either nightly or weekly). Further along Bancker Street, William Slam owned a run-down building worth less than $100, but by dividing it up into small rooms and renting it to blacks he was able to make $45 a week. That was in 1823. In 1827, neighbors complained about an area commonly known as the Duane Street Arcade. Here a landlord had converted a ramshackle "old shade" some 80 feet deep, which had been used as a distillery, into some dozen apartments, which he rented to black families. Needless to say the building contravened virtually every one of the city's building and health regulations. A couple of years later neighbors protested about a similar, albeit larger, structure in Ludlow Street. At this site a series of linked sheds sprawled out over several lots from the back of two houses. Not only had the owner, Barclay Fanning, "divided & subdivided these apartments into probably more than fifty rooms many of them very small," but he was renting them by the week, payment in advance, a strategy that had made them "sources of great emolument." At any one time anything up to a hundred blacks inhabited this slum. Inevitably, such areas became the haunt of petty criminals, prostitutes, and hustlers of all types.[42]

These dismal conditions were not limited to the Five Points, then rapidly developing an international reputation as the city's most notorious slum. They also prevailed in places with only local fame, such as Sebrings Alley, a bleak passageway off Anthony Street "tenanted by a wretched set of blacks," or Rotten Row, a set of frame dwellings behind the brick houses on Laurens Street.[43] And, small wonder, a continuous stream of blacks from these locales was brought before the courts on charges of larceny, often for stealing items worth pennies. Prison, the only "safety net" available, was hardly a soft alternative to life on the streets. If any sort of misadventure befell ordinary black men and women—economic downturn, a hard winter, illness or injury (common enough for manual laborers)—catastrophe was not far behind. James Fortune Barnes, found sleeping on a front stoop in Beekman Street and taken to the Police Office in August 1825, had been the victim of a misadventure. Four years earlier he had been kicked in the head by a Jersey horse, and, as a result, his cheeks were still disfiguringly swollen and his teeth all askew. Now age 22, he was described by the *New York American*'s court reporter as "a lounger about market" who "sleeps about in different places." As he had no money when he was picked up, Barnes was adjudged a disorderly person and sent to the penitentiary for six months.[44]

For many African New Yorkers life was hard and all too often short. Traces left by blacks who had fallen by the wayside in this most unforgiving of cities are easy enough to find in municipal records and newspapers. The coroner's report on John Richards, a black man found dead in New York in January 1804, noted succinctly that Richards had languished and died "from the Want of Bedding, Cloathing, and the Common Necessaries of Life and the too frequent use of Spirituous Liquors." For all their spareness, many of these stories still have the power to haunt. Early one July morning in 1829, a young black woman pawned a gown, her last possession other than the clothes she was wearing, for half a dollar, bought some rum, and, having drunk it, climbed to the top of a three-story house at 150 Anthony Street and jumped headfirst from a window. The small item in the *New York American* that recorded the event noted that the woman's head had been "completely dashed to pieces." In this case the coroner, accustomed to coping with many such bodies (more usually recovered from the East River), fell back on the well-worn, if hardly convincing, formula that the woman "came to her death in a fit of mental derangement."[45] Yet the chilling mixture of studied efficiency and hopelessness in this unnamed woman's suicide is suggestive less of individual mental instability than of societal disorder, and of the despair that many African New Yorkers must have known at least occasionally.

It would be wrong, though, to underscore too heavily the undoubted miseries that the city's blacks had to endure. They themselves certainly did no such thing. What mattered most to them during these transitional years was that more and more New York blacks were gaining their freedom, a development that was affecting virtually every facet of black life. Exactly what that freedom meant had still to be worked out, in piecemeal, ad hoc fashion, in day-to-day encounters between New York's black and white citizens.

It did not take long for infuriated whites to detect that blacks were treating them in new ways, ranging from insouciance through to contempt and outright aggression. At times black infractions of previously understood social codes were minor, almost comical. For whatever reason, in late December 1834 a black man named John Johnson climbed to the roof of the five-story Union Building and proceeded to shovel the fresh snow onto the heads of passers by. According to *The Sun*, Johnson had been "amusing himself," but he had also taken "particular pains" to throw off a full shovel load whenever a sleigh went by.[46] John Johnson sought little more than to puncture the pretensions to dignity of a few randomly selected whites; other African New Yorkers had more serious intent and more specific targets in mind.

In December 1807, Nancy, formerly the slave of jeweller Michael Souque, located her former mistress, beat her up, and threatened to take her life. Among the ex-slaves few had as much to be angry about as did Betty, the victim of the sadistic couple who had owned her, Amos Broad and his wife. They had been sent to trial for cruelty against her and her daughter, and, most unusually, were convicted. This case, notorious at the time, has remained a staple adduced by historians writing on blacks in New York; the sequel is less well known. According to the compiler of the pamphlet version of the Broads' trial, the court's punishment of Broad—the hefty fine and the period of imprisonment—gave "the most universal satisfaction." But, as it turned out, this was not so: far from being grateful about the outcome, Betty believed that, considering what Broad had done to her and her daughter, he had escaped far too lightly. She therefore began harassing the evangelist at his church in Rose Street, interrupting service by walking around inside, talking "loudly," and creating a considerable and, for Broad, an embarrassing disturbance. On at least one occasion she also arranged for some friends to throw stones and "other substances" through the window, which must have reduced the impact of Broad's sermons. Eventually, the evangelist was forced to resort to the law and have Betty indicted for rioting in a church, a charge which, ironically, was most commonly used against white rowdies who disrupted African American religious services.[47]

The boundaries of freedom were negotiated in the city's workplaces as well. African New Yorkers saw little point in gaining freedom if they continued to be treated as if they were slaves. White New Yorkers found black employees particularly sensitive on this point, quick to take umbrage and indeed legal action if they thought they had been discriminated against. On January 22, 1811, James Arden, a white merchant, hired Henry Lawson, a black man residing at 9 Cross Street, as a servant. Lawson, however, did not meet Arden's expectations—the merchant complained of "improper conduct, and absenting himself," probably an indication that this free black man refused to behave like the slaves Arden had previously owned—and after twenty days Lawson was discharged. Arden tried to pay his former employee for the twenty days of his service, but Lawson indignantly refused to accept the proffered amount, demanding remuneration for the whole month. A heated argument ensued, during which, according to Arden, Lawson "was quite impudent and made considerable noise." Arden "then without any Violence raised his flat hand to the said Henry Lawson's mouth merely with a view of preventing a disturbance in his family and not to strike or injure the said Henry Lawson," a claim that stretches credulity now, as it did in 1811. The aggrieved servant promptly took Arden to court, suing to recover his wages. He lost his case but proceeded immediately to the Police Office, where he filed charges of assault and battery against his former employer. Impeached by his own unconvincing account of what had happened, Arden ultimately admitted his culpability; the cover of the District Attorney's file on the case bears the simple notation "submits."[48]

Not surprisingly, many white New Yorkers found the changed social environment perplexing. In a voluminous series of letters written to his daughter Eliza, John Pintard, a businessman and establishment figure, revealed a few of the travails newly afflicting the servant-employing classes. In July 1818 Pintard declared himself "much plagued" with servants, acknowledging, however, that "the comfort of existence depends on domestics." The continued employment of eleven-year-old Betty, their "little black girl," depended, much to Pintard's displeasure, on the "caprice of her mother & she may be taken away at a moment." Working conditions were the sticking point in the protracted negotiations which finally broke down in late September. Not only did Betty's mother insist on what Pintard regarded as the "extravagant wages of $3 a month" for Betty, but she also expected "that her child shd be sent daily to school & have presents in the bargain." Nine months later Pintard complained that "our domestic comfort is once more unhinged." Hannah, the new servant, "had behaved very well," but only until her husband, a New Jersey slave, was emancipated. On the previous Saturday she had tried to take time off in order to go to Princeton with her husband (whom Pintard called "her troublesome boy"). Doubtless discouraged by Pintard, she had stayed at home "abed all day," but had conveyed to another of Pintard's daughters that "she was going to cook no more dinners for our family." On Sunday Hannah spent the day in church, and on Monday she arose at 4 in the morning and departed the Pintard household, only to reappear several days later "to demand her wages." "I discharged her," Pintard wrote, "for her conduct & ingratitude." But he was too late: now that her husband was free Hannah could quit her place of employment, and had done so days before she was fired. In principle Pintard opposed slavery and supported black rights, but in his own house he expected of his servants not only something very close to slavery at a very low wage but gratitude as well.[49]

A little over a decade later, and five years after slavery had ended in New York, the question of how blacks were to be treated in the workplace was still at issue. Two African Americans who worked "along shore," which is to say, laboring around the docks (a common occupation for blacks), were hired by a Captain Wilder to load a quantity of flour onto his vessel. One of the loading hooks slipped, and a barrel crashed down onto the ship, narrowly missing or possibly grazing Wilder. The enraged captain grabbed a piece of rope and struck a black laborer named Green on the head. The man sued for trespass and assault and battery. When the trial judge came to address the jury, he announced that if its members believed the testimony of one of Green's co-workers, a black, the case for assault and battery was made; if, on the other hand, they believed a white witness, who stated that "the blow was so slight that it would scarcely have made a child of two years old cry," then the charge was "rendered doubtful." Unsurprisingly, the jury took only a couple of minutes to decide that the captain had not committed an assault. Whether the blow was hard or not, what mattered was Green's reaction to being hit with a length of rope. Slaves had long been beaten with whips and ropes, but this free black man was no longer willing to tolerate such treatment. He had immediately downed tools and walked off the job, stating to all and sundry that he intended to sue. The actions of this ordinary black man evidenced a widespread, if mostly misplaced, faith in the New York legal system, but they reflected, too, an implacable determination of a free man against allowing anyone to manhandle him like a slave.[50]

At issue was the general question of how white New Yorkers would be prepared to treat the city's new black citizens, and the answer was not slow in coming. The proposition that free and independent black men and women should be able now to assert their rights as citizens was just about the last thing a substantial number of whites were willing to consider. The demeanor of free blacks—the way they dressed, talked, or walked down Broadway—offended these whites, not least because such behavior betrayed a lack of gratitude for what whites saw as their generous act in emancipating the slaves in the first place. Surely the recipients of such beneficence were obliged to reciprocate by comporting themselves in a decorous and appreciative fashion. There was a strange expectation among whites that the newly freed blacks would behave in a way slaves never had—namely perfectly—and hence a very personal sense of betrayal ensued when this idealized standard was not met. Blacks, by contrast, believed that freedom should bear no resemblance to slavery at all, and, to the disappointment and irritation of white New Yorkers, they acted accordingly.

Mordecai Noah, then editor of the *New-York Enquirer*, expressed himself on this subject with particular asperity, but the tenor of his remarks was hardly out of step with white public opinion. In August 1827, a month after slavery's end in New York State, Noah wrote that blacks generally were "an evil and a blotch upon the face of American society," and that New York's free blacks were "a nuisance incomparably greater than would be a million of slaves." Virtually everything about African New Yorker behavior on the city streets, from the "boisterousness of their manners" to the "disgusting indecency of their language," offended him. Most of all, though, he was irritated by blacks' ingratitude: "instead of thankfulness for their redemption, they have become impudent and offensive beyond all precedent."[51]

The old deference accorded whites was well and truly crumbling everywhere. Diana Dixon, an African New Yorker sentenced to six months in the penitentiary for stealing two teaspoons and a fan, angrily told the judge that "six months is nothing; I would not care if you added ten more to it." Eliza Hazard, a young mulatto convicted of theft, "set the whole court to scorn" by shouting out that she wanted the judge "to go to hell along with her." On hearing that she was to spend the next fifteen months at hard labor in the penitentiary, she burst out in "an audacious laugh" and retorted "Oh, but that is but a little while." After one morning's session in 1833, the *Courier and Enquirer*'s court reporter commented that, of the fifty people tried, "an unusually large portion of the offenders were young blacks, many of whom have been before the court on former occasions." What was even more noteworthy was that "not one of the number sentenced, exhibited the least signs of regret for their offences, or alarm at the extent of their punishment." Indeed, one young black man had grinned throughout the proceedings and on the sentence of six months being pronounced, had "burst out into a loud laugh, and remarked, that six months to him was only a breakfast spell." He then marched out of the court "with a lightness and levity more in character with one receiving favours than punishment."[52]

Just as insidious as brazen contempt was the verbal byplay between African New Yorkers and officials of the court; this, too, gnawed at the authority of the legal system. Many blacks were adept at a style of badinage seldom blatant enough to attract retribution but sufficiently guileful to convey disrespect. In March 1834 Joseph Edwards was hauled before the magistrate in the Police Office on suspicion of stealing two hens, one black and one white. When he was asked where he got the black hen, the following exchange ensued:

Prisoner. Git 'em? Got 'em where I did the white one.
Magistrate. Well, where did you get the white one?
Pris. Got 'em where I did the black one.
Mag. Where did you get them both, then?
Pris. Got 'em both together. [Laughter].
Mag. I'll make you laugh out of t'other corner of your mouth before you get through.
Pris. Well, massa—you ax me civil question, and I gib you civil answer. [Laughter].[53]

Such familiar and occasionally pointed exchanges were yet more evidence of the transformation in relations between African New Yorkers and whites.

In the first several decades of the nineteenth century, almost every assertive African New Yorker's action was met by a resentful and surly white reaction. After the incident in which scores of blacks attempted to free the runaway slaves at the court in September 1826, the *Enquirer* published an extraordinary letter from *"An Unfortunate White Man,"* which was immediately reprinted in numerous newspapers.

What is to be the result of all this? Are we to be governed by a mob of Negroes—I beg pardon, *ladies and gentlemen of color.*

> Are the Negroes—I mean the *ladies and gentlemen of color*, to
> be not only manumitted from slavery but to become a privi-
> leged order—privileged to interfere with the administration
> of the laws—to insult our magistrates, and pelt our citizens
> with brickbats? Truly, this is carrying philanthropy to the end
> of its tether.

The author's choking resentment over the black use of honorifics
and titles rather than "negro" or "nigger" (increasingly employed
in newsprint at this time), his suggestion that blacks were being
given favored treatment to the detriment of "us poor white people," would still echo over a century and a half later in complaints
about the use of the terms "Afro-American" and "African American" and in the diatribes against affirmative action.[54]

Given such sentiments, it is hardly surprising that some white
New Yorkers could see no point in allowing blacks to remain in
the city and made several organized attempts to get rid of them.
In September 1816 a man named Spencer tried to arrange for "a
number of coloured convicts" in the State Prison and the Bridewell to be released from jail on condition that they serve the rest
of their sentence on a southern plantation. Convinced that the inevitable fate of these blacks would be enslavement for life, the
New York Manumission Society investigated and found that the
information they had received about the plan was correct. But discovering that the "Governor of this State, the Judges of the Su-
preme Court, the Mayor of this City &c. advocate the measure &
that opposition will be unavailing," the Society was suitably in-
timidated and promptly discharged the matter from its books.
Eighteen months later the Society heard that a consortium of
three men and their lawyer had contracted with 23 blacks, pres-
ently being held in the City Penitentiary for vagrancy, to serve
three years in the Illinois Territory. In return, the prisoners were
to be set free from prison and paid $40 for each year's service in

the west. Again the Manumission Society was skeptical that anything other than slavery awaited these blacks, a majority of whom were female and many of whom were minors. But the Society found that there was no law preventing such a scheme and concluded there was little it could do to avoid "a constant repetition of the same thing by the city Police." Indeed, should its members try to warn these blacks against signing up, the Society itself would be liable to prosecution. The police, the secretary of the Manumission Society noted ruefully, were clearly "anxious to rid the city of the blacks," with remarkably "little concern for their future destiny."[55]

How many poor blacks were spirited away to the South and elsewhere in such schemes is unknown. Clearly, though, ordinary African New Yorkers regarded those responsible for these activities with all the enthusiasm they mustered for kidnappers, supporters of the Colonization Movement, and anyone else who tried to remove them from the city that was now their home. In early October 1818 a scuffle occurred down at the wharf at the end of Broad Street. One James Boardman attempted to escort two blacks who had signed indentures with him onto a vessel bound for Amboy and then Mississippi. A hostile crowd gathered to frustrate Boardman's efforts, while entreating the two men not to go. Although the indentured men finally boarded the ship, a white man and several blacks convinced one of them, Francis, to change his mind and come ashore. At this point Boardman returned to the dock and grabbed hold of Francis, only to be forced to release him by angry blacks, who warned him that "if he laid hands on the said Francis [in order] to put him on board" they would beat him up.[56]

White New Yorkers' concern over the presence and behavior of blacks in the city seemed wildly out of proportion to their numbers. According to city censuses, the percentage of African Ameri-

cans in the population in the early decades of the nineteenth century was not only low but was even diminishing; in the 1800s and
1810s the figure was about ten percent, in the 1820s and 1830s it
hovered around seven. Faulty statistics partly explain the dispar-
ity. Permanent black residents of the city were likely to be under-
counted; moreover, the census takers inevitably ignored transient
blacks (a large group as court records suggest) and residents of
the surrounding countryside, who continued to come into the
city markets just as they had in slavery times. Of far greater significance than their numbers, however, was their visibility: most
African New Yorkers were forced to live a very public existence.

For many blacks, the street became the place of employment.
Here they helped feed the city's white inhabitants, cleared the
snow from their paths, and cleaned up after them. Each morning
an "army of black sweeps" moved through the New York's thoroughfares trying to keep the city clean. This task was done early,
though not early enough for one white New Yorker, who complained that nothing could be worse, after finishing the "labors of
the toilet," than being forced "to march thro' a cloud of dust."[57]

Much of the work done by blacks was of a casual nature (typically unskilled manual labor). Thus besides working on the
streets, they spent a lot of time out on the streets seeking employment, often to the inconvenience of whites. At the Court-
landt Street wharf and around the Battery, where the steamboats
docked, up to thirty "lazy, thieving, vagabond rascals, mostly negroes" acquired "a sort of starving livelihood," undercutting the
licensed porters by up to half, or, conversely, hustling the odd
dupe for five or six times the usual fee. The crush after a vessel arrived was such that "ladies and gentlemen can scarcely pass without danger, even of being thrown overboard by their rude and ill-
mannered jostling." In the winter months, when the demand for
firewood peaked, the sawyers, most of whom were black, "com-

monly [took] possession of the side-walks" in order to cut up the logs, forcing pedestrians onto the street where they often got mired in mud and filth. Up near Hanover Square in October 1826, as one unhappy correspondent of the *New York American* noted, a number of blacks were out in the street shaking and beating carpets, filling "neighborhood stores with dust."[58]

Black petty entrepreneurs of all sorts were also an obvious and irritating presence on the streets. Among a whole list of complaints arising from a walk in the Bancker Street area in 1820, "Humanitas" drew attention to the "oyster stands and numerous tables of eatables" that rendered passage along the sidewalks all but impossible. But the most visible, and audible, were the street peddlers, those "smutty vendors who," as one querulous white observed, "roll out the long words—Cha-a-a-a-r-r Co-a-a-le . . . in varying tones upon each syllable as long as an Anaconda." From early in the morning until late at night—far too late by many accounts—their distinctive cries could be heard all over the city. Hollers such as "he-e-e-e-e-er's your fine Rocka-a-way clams" and, most famously, in the autumn months, the ubiquitous "h-a-u-t corn," "h-a-urt ca-irr-ne," formed a recurring and often disconcerting part of the city's soundscape.[59]

In the latter part of 1824, Samuel Jenks worked for several months as newspaper editor in New York. Originally from Nantucket, he was, judging by the entries in his diary, particularly sensitive to the barrage of sound that constantly assailed his ears in the metropolis. At four o'clock on an August morning he was awoken by "incomprehensible and barbarous outcries" coming from the street below. On peering out his window he discovered that the noise came from four blacks "armed with besoms" (brooms made of twigs) and "iron instruments resembling a short hoe." The adult, "wrapped in an immense mahogany-coloured shawl," was urging on three children, garbed in "ragged cloaks of the same hue": "Come, wy de debble don't you hollar?"—"Yes, missee—*Ek ho! yaw, ak hikko yek! E oh! yekko kik aw!*" "The long character in the shawl," Jenks observed, "was a strapping, she-negro chimney-sweep; and the smaller imps were her apprentices, thus compelled to proclaim their vocation in accents more dismal and appalling than those of Orpheus."[60]

Local knowledge was needed to decipher some of the more arcane calls, and those who lacked it entered the city's lore. New York's "most hideous and outlandish cries" were those of Jersey blacks advertising "but-Milk!" and "White Wine" in a Dutch-inflected accent. ("White wine," as the locals knew, was no alcoholic beverage but sour buttermilk.) One common story told of a "parcel of Communipaw negroes," who paraded the streets with a wheelbarrow and a Dutch churn "bawling out 'white wine,' as near as one can understand them." A country bumpkin (often that contradiction in terms, "the shrewd Vermonter") purchased a cup of "wine," tasted it, and, believing himself to have been deceived, "dashed the cup & its contents into the negro's face, and demand[ed] his penny back." For the Vermonter and many out-of-towners, the proffered "white wine" was nothing but pig swill.[61]

African New Yorkers were also a highly visible, if sometimes resented, presence at the various markets scattered about the city. Black "loungers" were usually in attendance at the market at Catharine Slip, where Long Island and Jersey blacks staged dance contests on raised shingles. This activity drew appreciative crowds of whites, who rewarded the dancers with eels and cash.[62] Whites were happy enough to applaud other black performers. In a ritual whose origins are obscure, whenever one of the Fulton Market butchers married, it was customary to hire a "negro who marched through the market ringing a bell" to announce the wedding, and for spectators to cheer the black man's progress around the stalls.[63] Less pleasantly, journeymen butchers had also invented a

ritual called "burying"—that is, approaching a person from behind, pulling his hat over his eyes and roughing him up—which
they employed to harass intoxicated blacks or those who would
not buy meat.[64]

Late at night another army of blacks, the tubmen, swarmed
over the city. The job of emptying the privies, which is to say, carrying the tubs down to the nearest dock and dumping the contents into the Hudson or East rivers, was virtually a black monop-
oly. Not only was the work hard, unpleasant, poorly paid, and
nocturnal, but whites constantly complained about the way it was
done. In 1817, twenty-two inhabitants of the First Ward peti-
tioned the city in an attempt to curb the "detestable cries" of the
"vagabond negroes" vying for this business. Nor was excessive
noise the whites' only complaint. As soon as they earned some
money, the black sanitary workers bought rum, presumably to try
and anesthetize themselves, and a few hours later were in such "a
state of intoxication" that invariably tubs were dropped in the
streets, accidents that, for hours the next morning, left pungent
reminders of the workers' passage. Mostly, though, it was the din
they made that irritated. Black tubmen usually worked in pairs, an
arrangement that resulted in raucous duets cutting through the
night air, and any request for quiet was greeted with "a torrent of
clamorous abuse." Indeed, it was not just "their savage yells" that
offended, but their "habit of bawling out such expressions as are
most shockingly indecent." A person standing in Franklin Square
could "often hear a dozen or twenty of them at once." Tubs were
not supposed to be emptied until after 11 P.M., a rule often broken
but also periodically enforced; in August 1819, for example, several blacks were prosecuted for emptying tubs as early as 9:30 P.M..
But even when the tubmen kept to the allowed hours, some people complained. A year later a writer to the *New York Evening Post*
decried the behavior of "the black scavengers who go around our

city at midnight emptying privies," driving their carts "through the streets down to the wharves in such a state that people are awakened from their sleep and before they can shut their window they find their houses filled with the stinking stench." Frequent spillages meant that "our streets show the broad track wherever they have passed, the next morning."[65]

Any unoccupied space in the city, but particularly the sidewalk, became a potential site at which African New Yorkers could spend their hours away from work. Their miserable housing conditions hardly induced them to stay inside unnecessarily. Similarly, convivial African New Yorker spaces such as dance houses and grog shops were usually cramped, crowded, and hot, especially in summer, so patrons often spilled over into the street. Again, blacks' often noisy intrusion into these public spaces caused resentment. Complaints to city authorities about black-inhabited buildings that were a public nuisance often included a few pointed comments about the number of inhabitants commonly loitering out the front. In a similar vein, the more than thirty signatories to a petition directed at premises on Lombardy Street, owned by William Slam, were offended by, among other things, the fact that "the walk in front of the house especially in the evening is generally incumbered with from three to six or eight of these worthless characters." There were protests, too, that the vacant lots opposite the Lafayette Circus on Laurens Street were taken over, particularly on Sundays, by "negroes and vagrant white boys" who spent the whole day "throwing dice and pitching pennies."[66]

Occasionally, the sources hint at the almost inevitable turf wars that occurred on the streets. In May 1812, the old Slip boys and the Whitehall boys (black gangs) clashed violently with whites in the vicinity of Broad and Beaver streets. Errant stones flung by rival groups struck passers by and damaged property. Subsequently, Leonard Emmons, a young black man who was "called Captain of one of the said mobs," was convicted of riot. Two decades later black gangs still ranged over the city streets, particularly late at night. According to the *Courier and Enquirer* in 1834, a "gang of juvenile thieves, all negroes," was making a habit of stealing meat and fish from "the shambles of Fulton market." Several of the young black men were arrested and claimed "they did not know the real name of each other, but that the captain of the gang was known by the name of 'Long Tailed Blue,' and lieutenant by that of 'Bloater.'" The spoils of their nightly raids were sold either to a white man in the Five Points district or to a black man living next door to the free school.[67]

At virtually any time of the day or night, then, there was a black presence on the city streets, so that incidents ranging, say, from the recapture of a runaway slave to the staging of a prizefight quickly drew large crowds. When one letter writer to *The American* passed the corner of Anthony and Little Water streets on an afternoon in August 1820, he observed a prize fight "between two blacks, who, I understand, are noted for their pugilism." The boxers stripped and commenced their bout in front of "an immense crowd," whose "volley of oaths and indecorous language" and loud shouts of "*Give room, enlarge the circle!* &c. [were] truly shocking." A decade later much the same sort of event was still a common occurrence: as reported in *The Morning Courier and New-York Enquirer*, "two ragamuffin colored 'gemmen of the ring' amused themselves and the admirers of the fistic art by a scientific prize fight on the Collect," for "50 cents a side." The bout was stopped by the authorities after thirty-six rounds.[68]

Most of all, blacks used the streets simply for walking. The years in which African New Yorkers finally gained their freedom were the same during which the sociability of the street, activities associated with what would later be called the "stroll," became established as a key element in an emerging and distinctive northern urban black culture.[69] As the *National Advocate* noted in August 1821, "their modicum of pleasure was taken on Sunday evening, when black dandys and dandizettes, after attending meeting, occupied the sidewalks in Broadway, and slowly lounged towards their different homes." A year earlier, "A New-Yorker," writing to the *New-York Columbian*, had drawn attention to the same phenomenon. On an August Sunday afternoon, he revealed, two "gentlemen" had "had the curiosity to count the number of negroes, male and female, that passed a house in Broadway, near Washington-Hall." In just under two hours no fewer than 1,480 blacks had strolled past, and in the course of the evening several hundred more went by. This was an extraordinary number, somewhere between one in six and one in five of the black inhabitants of the city. But it was more than just numbers that impressed this pair of white observers. These blacks "were all well drest, and very many much better than whites." Almost without exception, the males "wore broadcloth coats, very many of them boots, fashionable Cossack pantaloons, and white hats; watches and canes," the last-mentioned accessory being "flourished with inimitable grace to the annoyance of all." Further, these African New Yorkers "usually walk four or five a breast, arm and arm, with segars in their mouths, bid defiance to all opposition, and almost universally compel our most respectable citizens, returning from church with their families, to take the outside of the walk, and sometimes to leave the sidewalk altogether."[70]

"A New Yorker's" observations had a broader application, one that helps to explain the paradox of how a minority of blacks maintained a public profile out of all proportion to their numbers. If the sheer number of blacks on the city streets often seemed almost overwhelming, it was more than their apparently dominant physical presence that made them such a noticeable part of New York life. The larger-than-life style of African New Yorkers, the way they dressed, talked, and moved, often combining flamboyance and aggression, left a heavy imprint on observers' recollections of the city. Various reasons were advanced for this behavior, which so unsettled whites. A writer in the *National Advocate* sought to blame "discontented runaway blacks from the southern states," for such fugitives did "little more than corrupt the few good and make the bad worse."[71] But runaways were hardly a significant factor; unless exposed as such, they were, if anything, more inclined to keep a low profile than to flaunt their presence. The main reason for black New Yorkers' highly visible assertiveness was neither particularly complicated nor traceable to outside influences. As large numbers of African New Yorkers managed to win their freedom, they had also shucked off the petty restrictions of slavery, and that in its turn effected an exhilarating transformation that impelled them to test deliberately, consciously, and publicly the boundaries of their newly won liberty.

Travelers' observations register this transformation. To Henry Fearon, a visitor from England, the "striking feature" of the New York of 1817 was "the number of blacks, many of whom are finely dressed, the females very ludicrously so, showing a partiality to white muslin dresses, artificial flowers, and pink shoes." Fifteen years later, James Stuart, engaged, as many travelers continued to be, in making comparisons between New York and London, wrote that "one of the great novelties to us" was the "immense number of people of colour—many of them as well dressed as the whites." Stephen Davis, another visitor to the city (in 1832), "repeatedly saw coloured females in the height of fashion in Broadway." Although strikingly dressed African New Yorkers might be seen anywhere in the city, they were most prominent on Broadway and on the Battery at the southern tip of Manhattan. According to Carl Arfwedson, a Swedish visitor who recorded his observations in 1832, all classes promenaded along this public walk, but "particularly those of the sable cast, making a profuse exhibition of their finery." The dress of African New Yorkers, he declared, bordered on "extravagance": "the women wore bonnets decorated with ribbons, plumes, and flowers, of a thousand different colours, and their dresses are of the most showy description," while the men were attired in "coats so open that the shirt sticks out under the arm-pits; the waistcoats are of all colours of the rainbow; the hat is carelessly put on one side; the gloves are yellow, and every sable dandy carries a smart cane." Arfwedson found these fashion statements amusing: "it was with difficulty I could refrain from laughing, on seeing these black *beaux* (the name by which they generally go) doing homage to the black housemaids or cooks, known as *belles*." Another visitor to New York wrote of blacks that "a fashion to come up to their idea of taste, cannot be too outré; let it be ever so ridiculous, they adopt it immediately." When he was there, in 1833, "striped trowsers, kid gloves, three or four feet of guard chain for the watch, and gold headed canes, were the 'correct thing.'" On Sunday afternoons, when the city streets "appeared entirely given up to the African world, it was a high treat to witness the switching of canes and important strut of the one sex, and the affected dangling of parasols and reticules of the other."[72]

References to what seemed to whites to be African New Yorkers' extravagant and inappropriate clothing appeared, too, in the city's press. In December 1821 the *New York American* printed the counsel for the plaintiff's opening address to the jury in a case against Cox, a black defendant who "for some time past [had] cut a considerable dash in his mode of living." According to the counsel, Cox was "a first rate dandy, as you will at once perceive by the style of dress in which he appears before you; and, in addition to this, he keeps a horse and gig, and occasionally drives tandem through the city." In November 1829, the *Morning Courier and*

New-York Enquirer reported that police had come across a black man's trunk in the Five Points, whose "contents displayed an amusing list of the et ceteras necessary to finish off an ebony exquisite." The story ran under the caption "Nigger Cuffee's Wardrobe."[73]

Representations of dandified black men and women were also common in other genres. The caricaturist Edward Clay, best known for his *Life in Philadelphia* series, produced a similar series of prints for New York City. Clay's images of flamboyantly dressed African Americans engaged in various activities about town were the visual equivalent of the verbal descriptions of elaborately dressed blacks that appeared in travelers' accounts and newspapers. Similarly, the character Job Jerryson, a black servant in a contemporary play, was a black fop. (William Dunlap's *A Trip to Niagara* was first performed at the Bowery Theater in November 1828.) Against the remote possibility that the action and dialogue of the play failed to make clear how a white actor should play the role, the stage directions put the issue beyond any doubt. Paying close attention to what the *Courier and Enquirer* had labeled the "et ceteras" needed to finish off an "ebony exquisite," Dunlap repeatedly interpolated into Jerryson's lines such instructions as *"Puts up his snuff box," "Looks toward them through his eye glass," "Looking at his watch"* and *"Takes snuff."* White representations of the black dandy would reach their apotheosis in the minstrel show's figure of Zip Coon, a white actor in blackface who strutted vaingloriously about the stage. What made these caricatures effective for their various audiences was that they were merely exaggerated versions of the figures that whites claimed to see every day on the streets of New York.[74]

Zip Coon and similar creations were depicted as fools and played for laughs. If such representations picked up on the visually striking clothing of urban blacks and lampooned their language, what was largely leached from them was the bumptious and often intimidating behavior of African New Yorkers on the street. Yet this sort of behavior evoked the most vociferous and frequent complaints. Newspapers constantly protested against the way in which blacks shouldered "respectable citizens," meaning whites, off the sidewalk. In May 1815, the jurors of the State of New York nominated as a serious public nuisance "the unbounded licentiousness of the black and coloured women of this city," their use of "obscene and infamous language," particularly "profane oaths and vulgar epithets," as well as the aggressive way they conducted themselves on Sunday evenings, "crowding and jostling against the peaceable citizens of this city." A decade later, it seemed to "A Citizen," writing to the *New York Spectator*, that respectable New Yorkers had lost control of some areas of the city. It was no "longer prudent for decent and unprotected persons to pass thro' Catharine street to the market," because "crowds of female blacks" had taken "unmolested possession of the passageway, and render[ed] it both dangerous and unpleasant." These "vicious and abandoned wretches" evidently considered the area in question and the nearby intersection of Orange and Cross streets "as their exclusive property."[75]

Because of the fleeting nature of most of these street encounters, it was often very difficult for whites to apprehend those who had transgressed the accepted norms of behavior. There were some successful prosecutions, however. In May 1812 Isaiah Kip was walking down Broadway at about ten o'clock at night when four black women "spoke to him in a very vulgar obscene manner calling him Blue Bollocks," before shoving him to the ground and continuing to shout abuse. In this instance, Kip was able to obtain redress. A few years later, Henry Olmstead, who had been proceeding "peaceably" down Chatham Street, was shoved off the walk by two black men and a black woman. Apparently the action was intentional as "they laughed at & made considerable fun about it & went on." In this case, too, the offenders were apprehended. In another instance, Hannah Prior, one of a number of black women on Broadway who were "strolling up & down cursing & swearing & using very indecent language & shov[ing] people about on the walk," became the unlucky scapegoat nabbed by the watch.[76]

But successes of this kind were rare, and the aggressive behavior on the part of blacks continued to be widespread and to create keen resentment. One offended white pointed out in the *National Advocate* that the "daily complaints made by our citizens, especially the female part, of the insults and outrages committed by the colored gentry, who promenade through the principal streets in this city, (particularly Broadway) in large squads, insulting almost every person they meet," required action from the authorities.[77] Occasionally snatches of black speech, supposedly overheard by whites, signaled an apparently sinister intent behind such actions. In July 1822, three black women "tricked out in the height of fashion" came upon "a lady" (a term that meant a white person) outside St. Pauls. One of the blacks gave way to the "lady," whereupon another demanded in stentorian voice *"Louisa, why did you give the wall to that white woman?"* On Broadway, in similar circumstances, a black woman made the same kind of comment and was also heard to say "she wished the yellow fever would kill all the whites, that they [the blacks] might have the side walks to themselves." On another occasion a stout black man "was lately heard to exclaim, in a peevish tone, as he elbowed a lady out of her way, *'Damn these white people, there's no getting along for them.'"*[78] For many white New Yorkers, the world had truly turned upside down.

During the early decades of the nineteenth century, not coincidentally, the city's elite began to develop new kinds of housing, removed, both literally and metaphorically, from downtown city streets. As Elizabeth Blackmar has written, the "new domestic values" galvanized elite New Yorkers "to ensure dwellings against the social encroachments that they had encountered in lower Manhattan."[79] Recently freed and immigrant blacks, according to the newspapers, committed an overwhelming proportion of the social affronts inflicted on respectable white New Yorkers, especially women. Ironically, just as the newly refined development of slum housing was an important factor in fostering black street culture, the concomitant feeling among whites that they were losing control of parts of New York was one of the principal factors promoting a style of living among better-off whites designed to shut out the clamor of the city.

In the years before emancipation began in earnest, New York slaves had been an accepted part of city life, attracting for the most part surprisingly little comment. Once freed, however, and with numbers swollen by fugitives and migrants, the city's blacks were marked off as a separate group and increasingly demonized. This process was often expressed in body terms, blacks being an affront not merely to whites' eyes, but to almost the full range of senses. If the look of "dandified" blacks strolling on Broadway caused offense, so too did the touch of the black body that shouldered whites from the sidewalk, the "savage" sounds of black street cries or loud conversation, and, somewhat less frequently, the smell that black bodies were believed to emit. In June 1821, a writer in the *American* could barely restrain his sarcasm at the sight of usually disdainful Federalist Party gentlemen at the polls with their arms around the shoulders of potential black voters, whose support they sought: "We observed, however, that the young gentlemen for the most part wore gloves—and were compelled, after the introduction of each colored vote, to take a turn or two in the open air."[80] This forced intimacy was a momentary aberration that fooled no one, and merely highlighted the horror of most whites at public physical contact with African New Yorkers. In June 1823 one letter writer, protesting bitterly to the *National Advocate* about black behavior on the streets, concluded by pointing out that "they are so rude, and talk so loud, and smell so bad, what are we to do—to whom shall we apply, Mr Editor, to keep them more orderly?"[81] In large part, such unhappiness was caused by the deliberate actions of free blacks who declined any longer to remain quiet and unobtrusive. In reaction, whites developed new ways of perceiving the city's black inhabitants.

Increasingly, whites insisted on a physical separation from African New Yorkers in public, at first merely in fact, but later in law; indeed, the first attempts at Jim Crow segregation are to be found in the North rather than below the Mason-Dixon line. At the same time, New York blacks bore the brunt of an increasingly virulent racism, the strength and vituperativeness of which simply amazed many travelers. In 1829, a visitor from Montreal remarked that in New York all blacks "indiscriminately are looked upon with aversion by the white population." Blacks may have been free, but neither the legislature nor anyone else knew "how to talk or to act towards them." If "these 'Niggers' are on board a steam boat they dine together after the other passengers." If they attend church "they are crammed into some corner like a proscribed body." They were unable to join the army because whites did "not choose to stand shoulder to shoulder with a 'Nigger.'" In 1817, Henry Fearon could scarcely conceal his bewilderment at the fact that a black hairdresser who wished to retain his white clientele could not also service a perfectly respectable-looking black man. A few years later, J. S. Buckingham commented that, whereas in the South slaves would shake the hand of whites when they met, "at the North I do not remember to have witnessed this once." Not in "Boston, New York, or Philadelphia would white

persons generally like to be seen shaking hands and talking familiarly with blacks in the streets."[82]

Ironically, exclusion gave added impetus to the development of
separate black institutions, but, in a cruel twist, their very success
attracted harassment from surly and resentful whites. Black shopkeepers often faced violence from customers who did not like to
see them getting ahead. A similarly churlish impulse was directed
at any organized black activity. Black churches bore the brunt of
these attacks. White children and young men repeatedly threw
stones against the walls of black churches, trying to disrupt services, and hung around their doors on Sundays attempting to provoke scuffles.[83] During the 1820s the Callithumpian band, a mob
of young white men, celebrated New Year's Eve by running riot
through the city and damaging much property, often that belong-
ing to blacks. In 1827 they headed for the African church in Elizabeth Street, where the black congregation was holding a Watch
Night. The rioters smashed all the windows in the church, broke
down the doors, and destroyed the pews, before tying ropes to
the building and attempting to pull it down. Having failed, they
turned against the congregation, chasing its members in all directions and beating them with sticks and lengths of rope.[84] When
the city erupted into large-scale violence in the July 1834 riots,
the mob again targeted black churches and schools.

The black New Yorkers' organized uses of the street also af-
fronted their white fellow citizens. Excluded from most white parades and processions, African New Yorkers, to the discomfort of
many whites, held their own. As early as 1809, members of the
African Society for Mutual Relief decided to mark their first anniversary by a parade through the city. Decades later, James
McCune Smith, a prominent black doctor, remembered that Society members "had some very handsome silk banners painted,"
emblazoned with the motto "AM I NOT A MAN AND A

BROTHER?" Smith also recalled that "white friends" attended a meeting of the Society and "protested, begged, insisted" that they should cancel the march for fear of what might happen—but to no avail. "Secure in their manhood and will," Smith wrote, "they did parade, in large number, on the appointed day, easily thrusting aside by their own force the small impediments that blocked their way." Similar white entreaties followed the decision of African New Yorkers to celebrate with an annual march the official ending of the slave trade on January 1, 1808. In November 1809, the New York Manumission Society, concerned that the blacks' "method of celebrating the abolition of the Slave Trade was improper" and alarmed that they would "cause reflections to be made on this Society," sent a delegation of six members to inform the "people of Colour" that "both their Processions and Politicks in their Orations should be discontinued for the future." If the delegation expected grateful blacks meekly to follow such unsolicited white advice, they were disappointed. These African New Yorkers informed the representatives of the Manumission Society that they had already "incurred considerable expense in providing their standards and other things" and simply "could not think of relinquishing their proposed method of Celebrating the day."[85]

When, two decades later, celebrations marking the end of slavery in New York on July 4, 1827, were organized by blacks, much the same issues arose, only this time African New Yorkers themselves were split over what to do. Early on the editor of the *New-York Enquirer* suggested that if the blacks "will hearken to the counsels of their well-wishers," they should avoid any "manifestations of gratitude" over the granting of freedom. The Fourth of July was a day when the "passions of the lower orders come into fierce play," and a procession by blacks "with banners, devices &c." would likely lead to trouble. Some African New Yorkers agreed: after a public meeting they acknowledged that the point of a celebration was "to express our gratitude for the benefits conferred on us" and that in the circumstances and to avoid public disorder, it was better to "abstain from all processions in the public streets on that day."[86] In June, however, a rival group decided to hold a procession on July 5, distancing themselves from white interference, whether from drunks or well-wishers. "This is very foolish," opined the *Enquirer*'s editor; it was "disgraceful" echoed one correspondent to *Freedom's Journal*, the newly established black newspaper. Nevertheless the blacks' parade went ahead on the fifth, beginning a tradition that lasted for some years. Despite the entreaties of prominent blacks ("intelligent and prudent leaders," according to the *Enquirer*) to remain quiet, African New Yorkers in their thousands determined that the occasion should be properly marked. The editors of *Freedom's Journal* may well have thought "that nothing is more disgusting to the eyes of the reflecting man of colour than *one of these grand processions*," but on this issue they were out of step with a majority of their fellow black citizens.[87]

Not every black parade drew the *New-York Enquirer's* wrath. When, in March 1827, that newspaper's editor accidentally happened on a parade of black masons on one of the streets branching off Broadway, he was pleasantly surprised. Not only had these marchers "conducted themselves with propriety, obedience and intelligence," but most importantly they were also "well dressed, silent and decorous."[88] But there of course lay the problem. Not many African New Yorkers were much interested in marching silently along a back street. The parades they organized would be loud and lengthy affairs—the July 5, 1828, marchers had to be assembled by 9 A.M. even though they were not due at their destination until 2.30 P.M.—traversing all the major and many of the minor streets of the city. The Chief Marshall who led the parade, the marshalls bearing long staves who walked on each side, and the officers and members of charitable societies who often marched in contingents were turned out in various eye-catching uniforms. The main body of marchers too were extremely well dressed, with many of them carrying "neatly executed and appropriate" banners. A band usually accompanied the parade, and in the case of the July 5, 1827, procession, according to the *New York American*, as many as "four or five bands, comprising a great variety of instruments, played with much skill, as will readily be believed, from the acknowledged talent for music of the African race."[89] Anyone out and about on the city streets on July 5 would have to have been deaf and blind to have missed these proud companies of African New Yorkers celebrating their freedom.

The spectacle of large, well-organized, and joyous groups of blacks marching along major thoroughfares was rather more than many white New Yorkers could bear, and, perhaps inevitably, black processions became the target for both ridicule and physical abuse. In covering the July 5, 1827, parade, the *New York American* could not resist a "diverting" anecdote mocking black pretensions. On Greenwich Street a sudden downpour caused band and marchers to scramble for shelter under the awnings and stoops of the shops. The marshal and his aides were left in the front "without a single follower," until the marshal's appeal—"For shame, gentlemen—for shame! you behave like boys! form, and move on!"—persuaded the marchers to reassemble. The newspaper's claim that, in relating this incident, "we by no means wish to throw ridicule on the ceremony" was scarcely convincing.[90]

African New Yorkers required a steely resolve to parade through the city, ignoring the invective and worse heaped on them by some whites. Coachmen and carters were notorious for mean-spiritedly and often dangerously driving their vehicles through black processions in order to disrupt them. As some of these drivers found out, however, African New Yorkers would not

always accept such intrusions. In August 1825 Henry White, a
grocer, drove his cart into the middle of a black society's procession. White later maintained that he had nudged his cart out between the marchers and the walk, whereupon one of the blacks
had lifted his staff and, disregarding White's quiet request, struck
the horse, which caused the animal to "jump in partly among
them." When White got off his cart and demanded "to know why
they interfered with him," several blacks "surrounded" him and
proceeded to "beat him & bruise him considerable" until he was
rescued by a few white onlookers.[91] Another, perhaps more likely
version might well read that White had deliberately endangered
the marchers and had been roughed up for his pains.

It is difficult to convey the inspirational effect, on participants
and onlookers, of the sight of a considerable body of blacks brush-
ing aside the impediments and obstacles placed in front of them
and taking possession, if only for a short while, of the city streets.
Some of the exuberance of these liberating times is captured in
James McCune Smith's recollection, from the vantage point of
the 1860s, of the first parade to celebrate slavery's abolition in
New York, a description whose exhilarating language reverberates
down to us through the history of the civil rights movement:
"That was a celebration!" Smith wrote, "A real, full-souled, full-
voiced shouting for joy, and marching through the crowded
streets, with feet jubilant to songs of freedom!"

It was a proud day in the city of New York for our people,
that 5th day of July, 1827. It was a proud day for Samuel
Hardenburgh, Grand Marshal, splendidly mounted, as he
passed through the west gate of the Park, saluted the Mayor
on the City Hall steps, and then took his way down Broadway to the Battery &c. It was a proud day for his Aids, in
their dress and trappings; it was a proud day for the Societies

and their officers; it was a proud day, never to be forgotten by young lads, who, like Henry Garnet, first felt themselves impelled along that grand procession of liberty; which through perils oft, and dangers oft, through the gloom of midnight, dark and seemingly hopeless, dark and seemingly rayless, but now, through God's blessing, opening up to the joyful light of day, is still *"marching on."*[92]

The parades proclaimed both to African New Yorkers themselves and to a skeptical and often hostile white audience that blacks were no longer slaves and that as American citizens they, too, had a right to the streets.

This was the way most African New Yorkers wanted to be seen, assertive and proudly defiant. Many did indeed live from hand to mouth in terrible conditions, with the ever-present threat of white violence or, much worse, kidnapping and re-enslavement, but set against these anxieties was the unassailable fact that they were now legally free. Their freedom may have been precarious, but that very precariousness gave a distinctive cast to the cultural convulsion that accompanied emancipation. These turbulent years saw a veritable explosion of black dance and music all over New York, in venues ranging from underground dance cellars through Catharine Slip and formal balls. Dance became a vital element in a communal culture that, for all its flaws, was the creative and expressive response of ordinary African New Yorkers to their recently acquired and hard-won freedom.[93] It was in this context, too, when anything seemed possible, that in 1821 a small group of African New Yorkers made their extraordinary decision to form a troupe of black actors. Eventually the venture failed. But in the case of the African Theater, this was less a comment on the troupe's talents or enthusiasm than one more example, in a long list, of the damage fearful whites had done to African Americans.

Throughout much of African American history, black cultural production has focused primarily on performance: on the development and expression of distinctive African American aesthetic principles at some remove from those prized by the dominant culture. In part, such efforts have been a response to oppression, but, importantly, they have also been the result of choice. It was this process on which African New Yorkers embarked as they sought to shrug off their slave past and test the limits of their new-won freedom. The pageantry of a black procession, over a thousand strong, striding out down Broadway, flourishing banners and slogans; the style of a black dandy, immaculately turned out, leaning against a post on the Battery and checking the time on his fob watch with a nonchalant flick of his wrist; the spectacle of strikingly dressed black men and women alighting from their carriages in Orange Street as they arrived at the African Ball for the benefit of Greek Freedom; the theater of an insouciant black defendant ragging a pompous magistrate in the Police Office; the panache of a rollicking crowd of blacks moving to the relentless beat in a sweaty, smoky dance cellar—all these and more helped define the meaning of African New Yorker freedom through bold public display. To be sure, poverty imposed limits on black expressiveness, and the possibility of harassment by whites was ever-present, but whenever one probes beneath the surface in early nineteenth-century New York, it is difficult not to be impressed by the vitality of urban black life. That much of this behavior also annoyed, occasionally even incensed, many white New Yorkers was to some, at least, an added benefit. It was in these circumstances that members of the African Company launched their ambitious enterprise and appropriated Shakespeare to their stage in yet one more spectacular way of performing freedom.

2 | STAGING FREEDOM

On the evening of Monday September 17, 1821, in New York City, a newly formed drama company staged its first public performance. The circumstances of the debut seemed far from auspicious (the venue was a makeshift theater in a private dwelling in Thomas Street, a less than salubrious part of town), but the house was full, and as the actor playing Richard III limped out onto the stage, the audience erupted into wild cheering. An even greater burst of applause greeted the conclusion of his first speech. In reviewing the company's performance, the *National Advocate*'s theater critic indulged in a few obvious puns, but even his account (and it is the only one extant) could not obscure the glow of enthusiasm, the air almost of self-congratulation, that suffused the production. And with good reason, for virtually all present, whether members of the cast or of the audience, had either been born into slavery or at the very least were children of former slaves, and few among them could have been unaware that they were witnessing a bold black intrusion into the world of acting, an arena hitherto unthinkingly accepted as the exclusive and "natural" preserve of whites.[1]

The black theater company's choice of play was particularly apposite, for Shakespeare and his dramas were an integral part of American culture, and *Richard III* was probably the nation's most

often performed and popular play during the first half of the nineteenth century. The version seen by Americans had been extensively "revised" by Colley Cibber, an eighteenth-century English
actor and playwright. Much as a modern day writer might adapt a
novel for the screen, Cibber had not only pared back the drama's
structure, but had also purloined a few lines from *Henry IV, V,* and
VI, and added some of his own. According to the literary critic
Gary Taylor, these changes muted the tragedy's ambiguities and
rendered it "overtly melodramatic." As a consequence, while the
other characters shed some of their more unpleasant characteristics, Richard became, in William Hazlitt's words, "as odious and
disgusting as possible."[2] Yet the openly manipulative and ambitious protagonist of the play, physically weak, hampered by dis-
ability, and relying on his ingenuity and cunning to achieve his
own advancement, was not that far removed from the trickster
of African American folklore.[3] Certainly the complexities of the
juggling act Richard attempted throughout the drama must have
resonated with the torturous process of negotiating their self-
purchase that some of the actors and many in the audience had recently endured. A few years later, in 1825, the *New York Spectator*'s
theater critic commented with some irritation on the reaction of
the African American section of the audience to a performance by
the British actor Edmund Kean playing Richard III: "they relished the *sentiment* of the play so highly, that they could not contain themselves, and their applause was obstreperous."

The very ubiquity of Shakespeare in American culture had a
different meaning to blacks than it did to whites. Indeed, the body
of his work became an important part of the linguistic barrier that
whites used to hem in the recently freed blacks in northern cities
and thus to continue their subjugation. The great dramatist had
rapidly become, for blacks, a suffocating presence whose words
were frequently invoked to explain negative aspects of African

American behavior. In 1822, for instance, a white man in Norfolk, Virginia, believing that he and his wife were bewitched, killed a black man whom he blamed for his problems. The *National Advocate* reported that the white Virginian got these strange notions from a black fortuneteller, "this modern 'witch of Endor,'" a reference to Shakespeare's *Macbeth*.[4] In late 1818, the same newspaper related the story of a "gentleman" who retired for the evening in one of New York's main hotels and, supposedly, began to read *Othello*. At the point where "he was most interested with the bed chamber scene," he heard the sound of breathing in the room and cautiously looked under his bed, only to discover "a *gigantic black*, who had concealed himself there for the purpose of robbery, or something worse." "Here," the *Advocate* concluded, in a reference that could hardly be missed, "was *Othello* personified."[5]

Of course, *Othello* did its most significant cultural work in cases involving interracial sex. Apparently, any instance of a white woman being attracted to a black man was so horrible that newspaper editors were able to acquaint their principally white readers with its details only by borrowing from Shakespeare. In 1827 the *New York Evening Post* reported that an "*Othello* has been recently married to a *Desdemona*, who it seems considered him 'comely although he was black.'" In another case, a white woman was reported as having accosted her "better half," who was a "gentleman of colour," and "thinking herself slighted for some more favored fair one, sought redress with a case knife, which she attempted to bury in the heart of her faithless Moor." In the unlikely event that anyone had missed the point, the story was run under the caption "A Female Othello."[6]

Not only did editors borrow characters from Shakespeare; they also appropriated his language, fairly peppering their broadsheets with lines from the great bard's plays. In April 1820, the *National Advocate* ran a hostile account of a meeting of free blacks that had

been addressed by Garry Gilbert, a political hack who was seeking the black vote for New York Governor Clinton. The *Advocate*
captioned the piece "Black spirits and white," a quote from *Macbeth*.[7] This propensity to quote Shakespeare was most apparent in
the reporting from the city's courts. In the late 1810s and 1820s,
the newspapers began to take interest in the life of the city's lower
orders, particularly that of the black population, but at least initially writers seemed unclear as to what tone to take in writing
about them. The pattern that emerged was that writers would attempt to distance themselves from their subjects, archly dropping
in latinisms or larding their stories with quotes, often from Shakespeare. The *Sun*'s account of events at the Police Office in October 1834, the morning after "26 dark shaded 'Five Point' worthies
. . . of every shade of coloring from the blackest Ethiopian, to the
quarter blooded mulatto" had been hauled out of a gambling and
drinking dive on the corner of Leonard and Orange streets, began
thus:

> Black spirits and white,
> Blue spirits and gray,
> Mingle, mingle, mingle,
> You that mingle may.[8]

A few years later, whites who performed in blackface in the minstrel shows would parody this propensity, and of course perpetu-
ate it as well, by continually referring to the authority of Shakespeare: "you know what de Bird of Avon says 'bout 'De black
scandal an' de foul faced reproach!"[9]

All this helps to explain why the spectacle of a small group of
blacks performing *Richard III* on a warm September night in New
York would challenge whites' cherished cultural assumptions. The
entirely novel sight of African American actors declaiming the

words of Shakespeare on stage demonstrated that, regardless of the derision and sneers scornful whites would heap on them, they too were part of American culture, even while their distinctiveness remained obvious for all to see and hear. By laying claim to Shakespeare, they reaffirmed the famous dramatist's role in popular culture and refused to countenance any suggestion of his becoming the exclusive preserve of a white elite.

The creative drive behind the black drama company's first production had come from a black impresario named William Brown. Probably of West Indian origin, Brown had worked, in the 1810s, as a steward on the packets that plied between Liverpool and New York. The position of steward, usually filled by blacks, was a relatively lucrative one; according to the African American doctor James McCune Smith, "next to the captain" the steward was "the most important personage in the ship." Many who held this office became well-known figures in the world of the Atlantic. The most successful of the black stewards combined solicitude for their passengers' welfare—a "stately courtesy" attracted the best tips—with a certain flamboyance, creating what Smith referred to as "their style," a reference to the way they dressed and comported themselves, both on board ship and when they were ashore.[10] Inevitably, however, success came at a price: the ease and confidence with which this elite group dealt with whites and their tendency to see themselves as a cut above other blacks could grate with both racial groups. Hence stories about pushy stewards receiving their comeuppance became part of the lore of the Atlantic world. One such black steward, the story goes, while "exhibiting his well dressed person" to some compatriots in Orange Street, New York, in 1833, "had a trick played upon him which may tend hereafter to keep his vanity within proper bounds." As the man boastfully displayed a gold watch, for which, as he casually informed all within earshot, he had recently paid sixty-five dollars, a quick-fingered black in the throng managed to detach the watch from its chain and replace it with "a brass toy watch of the value of twelve and a half cents." By the time the steward discovered the substitution, the miscreant had disappeared. Even the police could do little more than "congratulate [the steward] upon his escape from the farther perils which awaited him, had he remained much longer in the society of his dextrous and covetous companions." It is difficult to work out who relished the incident more, the blacks who regaled all and sundry with the story, or the *Morning Courier and New-York Enquirer* which gleefully repeated it.[11]

If William Brown had heard such stories, he thought them of little relevance to his plans. At some time in the late 1810s, Brown had decided to quit the sea and settle in New York. Although at first he hung out a shingle as a tailor, in the summer of 1821 he launched an innovative venture: to offer an alternative venue to those blacks who so conspicuously strolled the city's streets but were denied access to its recreational facilities. To avoid public contact with newly freed blacks, white New Yorkers had refused blacks entry to the ice cream parlors and tea garden establishments then so fashionable in the city. Sensing an opportunity, Brown opened an entertainment or tea garden called African Grove, designed specifically for African New Yorkers, and before long crowds of well-dressed patrons were purchasing ice cream or ice punch (and probably, though illegally, alcohol as well) from his establishment, and enjoying musical performances in the crepuscular light of the city's summer evenings.[12]

Right from the start the press assumed an adversarial and derisory attitude towards William Brown's endeavors, as it did toward virtually anything African New Yorkers attempted. Most obvious was the hostility of the *National Advocate* and its editor, Mordecai Manuel Noah (1785–1851). This intriguing individual would be editor of several newspapers over his long career and had also been involved in democratic party politics. Indeed, thanks to his Tammany Hall connections, he was sheriff of the city in the early 1820s. Noah was probably the most prominent Jew in America at a time when Jews were a very small minority, barely one percent of the population, and was well known as a proponent of a plan to resettle persecuted Jews from Europe in upstate New York. He was also a playwright. Noah was a complex and fascinating man, defying simple categories, but it does seem likely that he projected the anti-Semitism he experienced in New York politics onto the city's newly freed black population. He was someone who understood stereotyping all too well, but for all that, or because of that, became obsessed with African New Yorkers generally and the African Company in particular.

The long story in the *National Advocate* on August 3, 1821, announcing that the tea garden had opened for business, began with this generalization: "People of colour generally are very imitative, quick in their conceptions and rapid in execution," but these characteristics were evident only in "the lighter pursuits requiring no intensity of thought or depth of reflection." Noah went on to describe in mocking terms some of the black dandies in attendance at the tea garden, and to render in crude dialect some of the conversations he claimed to have overheard there, before concluding that blacks "run the rounds of fashion; ape their masters and mistresses in every thing," and were "happy in being permitted to dress fashionable, walk the streets, visit African Grove, and talk scandal."[13]

Apparently the African Grove succeeded too well; on September 21 1821, the *National Advocate* reported that following complaints about excessive noise, the watch had shut the place down. Stymied in this attempt to provide entertainment for blacks, Brown decided to put on a play at the same site. The *Advocate's* gloss on what happened after the closing of the garden—the "imi-tative inmates of the kitchen and pantries" had been determined to have some entertainment, and "after several nightly caucuses, they resolved to set up a *play*"—is not particularly plausible, al-though staging a play may well have seemed a natural progression from the musical performances the African Grove had offered.[14] It is much more likely that the germ of the idea originated in the often transgressive currents eddying around the Atlantic world—New York, after all, was part of the ocean's littoral, and all manner of things washed ashore.

The production in Thomas Street was not the first to be staged by African Americans. During the War of 1812, sailors confined in Number Four, the section of the British Admiralty's Dartmoor Prison in Devonshire reserved for blacks, had performed plays for their own edification as well as for that of white prisoners. Some whites were impressed by what they saw; one diarist recorded that black actors "can perform as well as in any play House," and another recollected that "the blacks were pretty well in panto-mime—it seemed to be more natural to them." Others were less appreciative—one told of watching "a tall strapping negro, over six feet high, painted white, murdering the part of Juliet to the Romeo of another tall dark-skin"—but in the dreary context of prison routine any sort of novelty, even the disturbing spectacle of a cross-dressing black in whiteface, was a welcome change.[15] After their release, hundreds of black inmates of Dartmoor returned to sea, and doubtless stories of these performances entered seafaring lore. As he plied the trans-Atlantic run in the immediate after-math of the war, William Brown could hardly have avoided hear-ing of what had taken place in Dartmoor's Number Four.

There was only one dramatic performance in the house in Thomas Street, but over ensuing weeks the black company took to the stage every Monday night at new premises uptown, at the corner of Bleeker and Mercer streets, a few yards from the one mile stone on Broadway. Judging by the early playbills, the troupe continued to expect to perform before an audience of African New Yorkers. The playbill for September 24, 1821, for example, announced that "Mr. Brown has spared neither time or expense in rendering this entertainment agreeable to the Ladies and Gentlemen of Colour, being the second attempt of this kind in this city by persons of colour."[16]

Mr. Brown may have been trying merely to run a small theater on the edge of town for the edification of his fellow African New Yorkers, but his venture proved provocative to whites, to whom the very idea of a black actor was still shocking, perhaps even dangerous. It did not take long for the newspapers to focus attention on the fledgling enterprise. In early November 1821, the *New York American* revealed that Charles Beers (also known as Charles Taft), "lately a *principal actor* in the African *corps dramatique*," had been tried and convicted of grand larceny. Beers, "a mink-black little negro" by this paper's description, had entered a house through the coal shute and carried out Thomas Drumgold's trunk full of clothing and a little over $100 in cash. Under suspicion—in part because he had been seen around in new clothes—Beers promptly fled to Newark, but an angry Drumgold pursued him and had him arrested there. He was brought back to New York and sentenced to ten years' hard labor in the state prison.[17]

Beers was the first African American actor to garner notoriety, albeit fleetingly, and extensive press coverage, though in the circumstances he probably could have done without it. The *City-Hall Recorder* noted that "several black gentlemen" prompted by "a laudable emulation" had "organized a dramatic corps, at the head of which was the prisoner, who actually appeared on the stage, several times." The *Commercial Advertiser* gave Beers a more enthusiastic notice, commenting that he had "amused, and very probably delighted his sable brethren and sisters, in performing the difficult part of Richard 3d." But the emphasis in most of the coverage lay elsewhere. As far as an intrigued press was concerned, Beers's story was freighted with moral import. The *American* noted that "it has been suggested that his passion for his new pursuit led him to the deed for the purpose of obtaining funds to purchase new decorations for his theater." In the *National Advocate*, Noah surmised that the erstwhile actor's motive had been more selfish: "it seems he wanted cloathes to dress in the character of Richard the 3rd, and therefore stole them." For the *City-Hall Recorder*, the whole sorry case was something to be "submitted to the sage consideration of the *lovers of drama*, and the *members of the manumission society*," a wording that neatly concealed which of these groups the *Recorder* considered to be the more disreputable.[18]

Quite possibly Beers did steal for the benefit of black acting, though the *American*'s "it was suggested" and the *Advocate*'s "it seems" imply that the editors were recording the stories of the case which white New Yorkers had told to one another, rather than anything Beers had said. It was a reassuring and typical way of looking at the recently freed black population. By framing the story in a fashion that clearly linked the crime to the theater, the white press reduced something extraordinary, an African American actor, to a more manageable and mundane figure—the black criminal. This would be a recurring strategy of those wishing to belittle African New Yorkers who took to the stage, and the press would always seize on it with relish. Blacks might mimic whites and even become professional actors, but the changes were only superficial and could not conceal what whites saw as the essential nature of blackness.

As recounted so far, the story of Charles Beers is basically a gloss on the tale white New Yorkers told one another, and, hardly surprisingly, in that tale the black protagonist remains for us out of focus. In fact, the white storytellers could not even get his name right. When the defendant was a slave he had been called Beers, but on gaining his freedom he had named himself Taft. Charged with the theft of Drumgold's clothes and money, he had signed his statement, filed in the District Attorney Indictment Papers, as Charles B. Taft, yet the case was recorded in the Minute Book of the Court of General Sessions as *The People v. Charles Beers*.[19] Similarly, the defendant was Beers in all the newspaper accounts, Taft not even being mentioned as an alias. And yet as much as white New Yorkers ignored, or denied, the possibility that Taft had a mind of his own, some of the detail recorded in the documentation of the case allows us glimpses of his private and public worlds.

Charles Taft had been born a slave. In the 1810s he had been owned by a Thomas Hodgkinson, who ran the Shakespeare Hotel at the corner of Nassau and Fulton streets. At the time of his conviction in 1821, the *American* reported that the defendant had been "for years an approved waiter" in the Shakespeare, "a most respectable porterhouse and tavern." It is particularly interesting that from the 1810s to the 1830s the Shakespeare was the haunt of the New York literati, frequented by such luminaries as Washington Irving and James Kirke Paulding.[20] Given the course of future events, what the young slave saw and overheard while bussing tables likely had a considerable impact on him. It is not known how Taft became free, but as the legislation of 1817, which applied to slaves born before 1799 (almost certainly the case with Taft), would have freed him only in 1827, he had probably come to some sort of private arrangement with his owner. It also seems that freedom changed the complaisant waiter's behavior, a not uncommon transformation and one that created tension between Taft and his former master. Not only did the former slave announce his new identity by changing his name, but the once "approved waiter" was, according to the statement of Drumgold, "turned away for his bad conduct" and was now "idleing about the Streets apparently without any visible means of livelihood."[21]

The details of timing in all this are infuriatingly vague in the sources, but it is tempting to see a close linkage between Taft's achievement of freedom, his new and more assertive persona, and his taking on of the role of Richard III in a black theater company. The liberating power of these black stage performers was ineluctably tied to their own and their free audience's often boisterous exploration of what freedom actually meant. White New Yorkers certainly saw this as well, though they were less sanguine about the change in blacks' attitudes. Taft's hopes for freedom were, not surprisingly, bound up in his slave past. Attracted by the life of the artist, as he had observed it, this African New Yorker pursued his unusual goal with the same impressive determination that would characterize the efforts of the other black actors. Scarcely any of the New York literati that Taft had waited on in the Shakespeare could support themselves on the proceeds of their artistic endeavors; many were also lawyers, merchants, or physicians, lucrative occupations that were closed to blacks. Taft chose to steal to support his acting career, was rather easily caught, and given a punitive sentence.

With the removal of Taft (or Beers), James Hewlett, another black actor, came to the fore and before long was completely dominating the bill, singing most of the songs and playing the most important roles. James McCune Smith claimed that, like Brown, Hewlett had come from the West Indies, but according to an article in the December 22, 1825, issue of the *Brooklyn Star,* the black actor was "a native of our own dear Island of Nassau, and Rockaway is said to have been the place of his birth." The latter account seems the more likely—Hewlett was a not uncommon name in Rockaway—and he probably moved to New York along with many freed blacks from the surrounding countryside. Apparently he was quickly drawn to the theater and spent a considerable amount of time watching performances from the gallery. The *Star* also stated that Hewlett was the "servant boy" of George Frederick Cooke and Thomas Abthorpe Cooper, two famous English actors who performed in America in the early 1810s, and from whom he received his "histrionic education." But for all this writer's appreciation of Hewlett's abilities—he acknowledged that the black performer "must have had a natural talent for theatrical performances, and an excellent voice withal"—the idea of a black actor was still so startling that he felt compelled to denigrate him, asserting that Hewlett was not simply influenced by Cooke and Cooper but that he "*stole* their actions and attitudes in moments of recreation or recitation."[22] There are faint traces of Hewlett's activities in New York over the next few years. In October 1813, a "black man" named James Hewlett was found not guilty of assaulting an African American sweepmaster named Simmons. In September 1815, the *National Advocate* carried a theater advertisement announcing a forthcoming benefit performance for "Hewlett and Diego."[23] In all likelihood, James Hewlett picked up work at sea but hung around the theater whenever he had the chance; he may even have been employed there when he was in town. Hewlett had performed as a singer in Brown's entertainment garden. He was probably not in the city for the opening performance in Thomas Street, but very soon thereafter assumed the leading role in the company.

The meager evidence we possess suggests that African New Yorkers attended theatrical performances with some frequency, even though many must have found it galling to do so. Theaters, notorious the world over for their crush and inadvertent body-contact, were among the first institutions to be segregated in New

York. Blacks were relegated to the gallery up near the roof, distant from all but the most disreputable whites. Thomas Hamilton, a traveler, recounted the story of a young Haitian's tribulations in New York in the 1820s. The well-dressed young man—in fact, he was something of a "dandy"—was turned away from not only the best hotel but from all the hotels and forced to "take up his abode in a miserable lodging-house kept by a Negro woman." That evening he went to the theater and tried to pay the doorkeeper to gain admittance to the boxes, but his money "was tossed back to him, with a disdainful intimation that the place for persons of his colour was the upper gallery." According to Hamilton, the humiliated young man left New York by the first available conveyance.[24]

For the most part black patrons went unnoticed, other than by those counting box office receipts, but every now and again they made their presence felt. In 1820 the famous English tragedian Edmund Kean had declined to go on stage in front of a sparse Boston audience, a display of hubris that ruined his immediate prospects of success in the United States and forced him to decamp across the Atlantic. Five years later Kean returned to a Boston still uninterested in his apologies: a baying crowd shouted him down and pelted him with refuse. When Kean performed in New York, however, black theater patrons, possibly empathizing with him because of their own hostile treatment by whites, decisively took the actor's part. The *New York Spectator* sniffed that "the most ludicrous part of the affair, was the interest manifested for Kean by the blacks in the upper tier." A black man in the audience had led his compatriots in chants of "Kean, Kean!," had wittily put down a white heckler, and made sure to drown out any further opposition. According to the *New York American*, when the black yelled out "Hurra for Kean" the "whole gallery instantly responded to their leader."[25]

Very occasionally one can find references by blacks to their attendance at the theater. In December 1823 four young black men were indicted and, with the usual alacrity, convicted of grand larceny. From their testimony in the legal proceedings, we can piece together a fascinating account of their varied activities over the couple of days before their arrest. Twenty-nine-year-old Richard Brown, only three months free of his third stint in the penitentiary (his statement to court officials that he "expects this will be the fourth time" hardly helped his cause), had spent Monday night "at the Theater & from there went & stayed with a girl whom I met at the Theater," and left her bed the next morning sometime between seven and eight o'clock. Brown later added that he "went to the Theater drunk," and while there had bumped into Bow Jackson, Mary Spencer, Harry Foster, and Eliza Williams. Jackson and Foster, also somewhat the worse for wear, then had a disagreement and, according to Foster, had left the building to settle their differences "but returned again without fighting." Bow Jackson did not even mention this incident; his principal memory of the performance was that he had "got a sleep." In fact, Jackson had "slept till the People were all out of the Theater." What is interesting here is that going to the theater is casually mentioned as an ordinary part of these African New Yorkers' lives. These denizens of Bancker Street, men at the very bottom of the city's hierarchy, frequented the theater; it had become a social site for them, just as it had for white patrons. As well, in any history of the theater there should be room for the unforgettable image of Bow Jackson's somnolent shape, remaining sprawled all over his seat until it was time to lock the building up.[26]

At any rate, African New Yorkers did attend the theater and did support their own theatrical venture. Whites who came uptown to view black productions were "welcomed" in much the same way as blacks were at the Park Theater. In late October 1821 the *National Advocate* noticed that the "gentlemen of colour" were putting on another play and "have graciously made a partition at the back of their house, for the accommodation of whites." Legend has it that, in a handbill, Brown justified this separation on the grounds that "whites do not know how to conduct themselves at entertainments for ladies and gentlemen of colour," although no copy of the broadside survives.[27] At a time when the State Constitutional Convention was debating whether or not blacks should be completely excluded from the vote, and when African New Yorkers were increasingly being segregated from whites, the "gentlemen of colour" gave tit for tat, reversing the "natural" order of things and pointedly signifying on the actions of the dominant culture. Banishing white patrons to lousy seats at the back of the theater may have been a small, largely ineffectual protest against white behavior, but it was one of the very few ways in which blacks could register dissent.

William Brown soon realized that black patronage alone could not support his theatrical venture. Within a few weeks of the opening, he and the theater company changed tack completely, seeking out white patrons and aggressively enticing customers away from the most important theater in the city. Sometime in December, Brown daringly hired space in the Hampton Hotel next door to the Park Theater, thus returning his company to a downtown site not far from its Thomas Street beginnings. As the *National Advocate*'s editor Mordecai Noah noted, "the sable managers, not satisfied with a small share of profit and a great portion of fame, determined to rival the great Park Theater."[28] At this time the Park was run by Stephen Price, an impresario who had business connections in other northeastern cities and with the theatrical establishment in England. Price was in a vulnerable position. The Park Theater, rebuilt at considerable expense after a fire, had reopened only a couple of months earlier, in September, and Price was not about to tolerate a motley crew of upstart blacks commencing operations next door and eating into his receipts.

In the first week of January 1822 a dozen members of the watch halted Brown's company in mid-performance and hauled the actors off to the watch house. Perhaps it was mere coincidence, but at the annual theatrical dinner several days beforehand, Stephen Price had, "after an appropriate complimentary address," presented Sheriff Noah, in his capacity as playwright, "with two splendid silver pitchers, as a testimony of personal esteem, and of a sense of the benefits derived from his productions." In the pages of the *National Advocate*, Noah then decided to cast the police break-in as comedy. According to the *Advocate*, a watchman interrupted Richard III (played by Hewlett) in the middle of one of his soliloquies with "Hallo you, there—come along with me," whereupon Richard replied, "Fellow begone—I'm not at leisure." As Richard and the cast were taken into the watch house, Hewlett "dropped his character and assumed Macbeth":

> "How now you black and secret
> Midnight hags—what are you about?"

At last, wrote Noah, the black actors had "pleaded so hard in blank verse, and promised never to act Shakespeare again, that the Police Magistrates released them at a very late hour."[29]

The editor smugly assumed that the officious intervention of the watch had succeeded and that the black troupe would quietly disappear. Other newspapers came to the same conclusion, albeit with less obvious relish. According to the *Republican Sentinel*, the "African Theatre," which had "recently made some *noise* in this city" (the writer interestingly continued to associate black actions with irritating sound), "is no longer permitted to be opened for the amusement of the public." The *Sentinel* noted that "the Police found (or *thought*) it necessary to interfere," a qualification suggesting at least some ambivalence on their part.[30] As it turned out, however, Noah's death notice for the black company was premature. Within a few days the city was plastered with posters announcing that "Mr Brown has been obliged to remove his theatrical corps to the old place, corner of Bleeker and Mercer streets." Amused at Noah's misreading of the situation, the *New York Spectator* commented that the black company was "not so easily to be driven from the field in which Shakespeare, Garrick, Cooke, and our right worthy and jolly Sheriff have reaped such harvests of glory."

An extract from a contemporary poster printed in the *Spectator* makes it absolutely clear who, according to William Brown, was to blame. Brown "respectfully informs the public, that in consequence of the *breaking up* of his theatrical establishment, there will be no performance this week." Further, he "believes it is through the influence of his *brother Managers* of the Park Theater, that the police interfered." Their reasons were obvious: "There is no doubt that *in fear of his opposition*," the said managers "took measures to quell his rivalry." In spite of these "jealousies," however, his company would continue in its old premises up in Mercer Street.[31] Such a public verbal assault by a black on a white man, let alone one as prominent as was Price, was unprecedented; it was yet another sign of the liberties free blacks were now taking. But if the fury of the barely masked attack on Stephen Price revealed the white heat of Brown's anger, his choice of *The Fortress of Sorrento*, written by Noah, as the play the company would perform on its return showed a more controlled and devious intelligence. This was not the first of Noah's plays the black actors had staged—*She Would Be a Soldier, or the Plains of Chippewa* had been put on a little over a month previously—but *The Fortress of Sorrento*, written and published over a dozen years earlier, when Noah was a callow youth of twenty-three, had never been performed on the New York stage.[32] For all the unabashed nastiness of Noah's gratuitous comments about African New Yorkers generally and Brown's company in particular, there was always something more complex about his racism. At the very least Noah's newspapers gave the fledgling actors free space and publicity, much more so than did any other publication, and, it seems, over the years the editor developed a sort of affection, albeit a very grudging one, for Hewlett in particular, probably based on their shared and genuine love of the theatrical world.

The Fortress of Sorrento was but one part of the night's entertainment. After that item "an entire new play" was to be staged, "written by Mr. Brown (the sable manager), [and] called *Shotaway; or, the Insurrection of the Caribs*, of St. Domingo. King Shotaway, Devillee." This was the first African American dramatic production, an event that elicited from the *Spectator* the comment that "it seems that these descendants of Africa are determined to carry into full practice the doctrine of *liberty and equality*, physically by acting plays, and mentally by writing them." The newspaper applauded that "they are so patriotic as to give a preference to the productions of our own country," yet remain not "insensible to the beauties of Shakespeare." Indeed, "with a laudable spirit of independence, and a taste that cannot be too highly commended, they wander through the gardens of imagination in both hemispheres, and cull the choicest flowers, no matter whether they bud upon the banks of the Avon, or bloom upon those of the majestic Hudson." These lines are difficult to decode. The overblown language continually teeters on the edge of sarcasm, but there is also a note of genuine appreciation of what the black actors were doing. At the very least, the *Spectator* seems to have understood the core of the whole matter, discerning the link between the Company's existence and the assertion of black freedom.[33]

Shotaway intrigues. The insurrection of the Caribs was in fact the Second Carib War of 1795–96, which occurred not on St. Domingo but on St. Vincent. Some writers have chosen to set the drama within the tradition of the "stage Indian," suggesting that Brown was at the cutting edge of a trend that, by decade's end, would produce *Metamora; or, the Last of the Wampanoags*, giving the remarkable actor Edwin Forrest his signature role.[34] There is considerable merit in this view. But when one reads the few surviving shards of evidence concerning *Shotaway*, this is not the notion that first springs to mind. In the context of New York in 1822, the spectacle of black actors portraying a struggle for freedom inevitably conjured up images of slavery. Brown was certainly aware of that connection and played it for all it was worth. Placing the drama on St. Domingo rather than St. Vincent, as the playbill for the first performance had done, was an unlikely geographic error for a native of the Caribbean. Moreover, at the play's second performance eighteen months later, the producer claimed that the drama was "written from experience." The great slave rebellion on St. Domingue, of course, was the specter that had haunted the eastern seaboard for nearly three decades, a constant reminder not only that slave revolts did occur but that sometimes they also succeeded. Within six months, the Denmark Vesey Conspiracy was unearthed in Charleston and given extensive coverage in New York, with transcripts of the trial consuming swaths of newsprint. When the company next staged the play in June 1823, Brown sensibly muted the overt reference to the slave revolt and corrected his "error," relocating the drama to St. Vincent. If anything, the correction and the new circumstances probably made the resonances between *Shotaway* and the slave system even stronger.

No text of the play has ever been found; it is doubtful whether anything but the most rudimentary skeleton of the drama was ever put down on paper. On both occasions on which the play was performed, William Brown was specifically credited with its authorship. Earlier in January, when the *Republican Sentinel* announced the demise of the American Theater, Brown had been described as "a dramatist who wrote for this establishment."[35] Yet several months later, when he came to sign assault charges, he could only mark the papers with an X, usually a sign that the person in question was incapable of writing. Possibly his writing arm had been injured in the assault, but the chances are that Brown could not, in the usual sense of the word, have written *Shotaway*. It seems likely that the play was improvised, blocked out roughly in rehearsal, and allowed to take its course on the night. This was a much more collaborative process than the designation "author" usually allows for, and must have involved the whole cast, particularly Hewlett, the principal actor. The announcement of the second performance claimed that the play was "Written from experience by Mr Brown," but in all likelihood it was not so much Brown's experience of St Vincent in 1795, but Brown's, Hewlett's, and other cast members' experiences—and they of course were mainly of American slavery—that shaped the performance of this first African American drama. There was at least an element of this sort of improvisation present whenever the black actors were on stage, even where a printed text of the play was available.

After several months of silence Brown reappeared in the newspapers. On July 22, 1822, a small notice in the *Advocate* declared that "MR. BROWN, most respectfully informs his friends and the public, that he has spared neither pains or expense in erecting a Theater in Mercer-st" and that at opening night on the following Tuesday he wished for "that patronage he has in former times received from a generous audience."[36] Not only was the Mercer Street establishment, by decades, the first theater built by and for blacks, but it also must have been one of the largest investments made up to that time by any African American entrepreneur, and certainly the most conspicuous. Among the few contemporary descriptions of the theater that survive is one by someone known simply as Twaites, who had observed the construction work on his walks down Mercer Street. The Pit, Twaites wrote, "was just what it should be, and what its name indicates, a deep hole"; the "Boxes, or rather Box, there being no partition to impede the circulation of the air, was extremely agreeable, although built upon an entirely different plan from those very convenient benches in the side boxes at the Park"; and the Gallery was "well conceived" if indifferently built, there being very little headroom.[37] Another early visitor published his scurrilous observations in a small pamphlet entitled *Sports of New York. By Simon Snipe*. According to Snipe, the theater was "particularly well suited for the warm weather, as it let the breeze in plentifully between the crevices of the boards," although not in sufficient measure to dissipate "the offensive perfume" emanating from the audience. But even Snipe had to concede that the new venue was a "tolerable well built house."[38] James McCune Smith described the building as being "of wood, roughly built, and having capacity for an audience of three or four hundred."[39] Although this last seems exaggerated—the lot was only one hundred feet by twenty five—there is no doubt that the theater company's new premises were more expansive than its earlier accommodations had been.

When Brown and his black actors made their initial foray into theater, their intended paying audience was other African New Yorkers. From the start, there was a decidedly commercial aspect to much of the culture of newly freed New York blacks. This was hardly surprising; opportunities for making a living were limited, so participation in leisure-time activities must often have been prompted less by the desire for aesthetic display than by the need to supplement one's income. The black theater provided one such sphere of employment; the burgeoning black dance culture supplied another. Black musicians were paid for their services; black dancers at Catherine Slip collected eels or cash from appreciative onlookers; black entrepreneurs who staged dances and balls charged for admission. Frequently, dances were occasional, staged in someone's house, precursors of the much better-known Harlem rent parties of the 1920s, but some were more organized. In the mid 1820s, William Molineaux, a black barber, hired a room in Mulberry Street, paying $120 rent for the year. Here he put on dances on his own account, charging patrons one shilling for admission. For this price they received either one or two glasses of liquor and the right to listen to the music or dance. On other occasions Molineaux hired the room out for five dollars a night to someone prepared to take the risk of putting on the entertainment. Clearly, there was income to be earned from such activities. Two decades later the journalist George Foster wrote about Pete Williams, owner of a well-known dance cellar in the Five Points, as "a middle-aged, well-to-do, coal-black negro, who has made an immense amount of money from the profits of his dance-house."[40]

The African American drama company's decision to build its own theater was a step away from this black economic milieu, and New York's black population simply could not support an enterprise of this size. Posters advertising productions were no longer directed specifically at "Friends of Colour" but at anyone willing to pay the price of admission. More and more Brown was positioning himself with African New Yorker entrepreneurs who depended on white patronage for their living, such as Thomas Downing, owner of an upmarket oysterhouse. That strategy substantially increased potential revenue, but it also forced the actors as well as the businessmen to deal with often boisterous and inebriated young white males, whose pride was easily pricked by perceived affronts from blacks.

An incident involving Cato Alexander, owner of the fashionable tavern at the four mile stone, three miles further out from the city center than Brown's theater, illustrates this point. The actor

Tyrone Power may have remembered Alexander as exhibiting a remarkable "courtesy and bienseance" toward his white patrons, but the tavern owner was also a tenacious defender of his property. The almost inevitable concomitant of being a black man of any prominence at all in New York in the early decades of the nineteenth century was that sooner or later he would find himself involved in some sort of an incident, usually violent, that would end up in court. In 1819 Cato Alexander was convicted of violently assaulting and beating Abel Wheaton, a white blacksmith, at the corner of Middle and Old Harlem Road, probably as a result of some dispute arising from his business, although no details survive in the record. Seven years later Alexander appeared in court to testify against one John Ryan. Ryan, nineteen years old, white and unemployed, had deliberately disabled Alexander's water pump in the hope of being hired to repair it, an offense which earned him a conviction for petit larceny. The incident fits into a larger pattern which showed at least some whites regarding obviously prospering blacks as fair game.[41]

The most violent incident involving Alexander occurred in late January 1831. Near midnight on a Thursday, eight or nine males and two females, the latter variously described as "lewd women" and "Girls of the Town," demanded entry to Alexander's establishment, on the pretext that one of the women had fainted. A suspicious Alexander tried to turn the group away but they pushed past him, made their way into the "Bar Room," and threw him backwards over a chair, "at the hazard of his life," as he later claimed. The black proprietor was held down and struck on the head. Aroused by the racket, Alexander's pregnant wife burst into the room, only to be thrown heavily to the floor. At this point, the innkeeper, "exasperated at the violence used to his wife in her delicate situation made a rush upon the whole gang & after great exertion expelled them from the store."

Matters could hardly end there. Rumors of reprisal quickly spread around the city, some of them reaching the well-connected Alexander. The violent intruders had later hung around Luke's Store (which one of them ran) at the corner of Greenwich and Beach, and their loud talk had been overheard. Andrew Luke had declared that "he had struck him [Alexander] between the eyes or on the forehead" and "boastingly said that he [Alexander] would not get over it in some time." John Priest, his head wrapped in a bandage, "took a pistol from under his Coat, took out the ramrod and measured the quantity of loading he had in the Pistol which was about an inch and a half charge using profane language at the same time and said that no such damn negro should live." Cato Alexander learned that the group planned to come out to his house, call for a room, "produce a Quarrel & Kill this deponent [Alexander]." On Friday, the day nominated for the attack, Alexander feigned illness and shut up at nine o'clock, much earlier than usual. Between ten and eleven the white toughs arrived in sleighs. Frustrated in their designs, they tried to force their way into the house, "beating the doors and windows with great violence, [and] using lewd profane and riotous language." Three more times that night, presumably fortified with alcohol, they returned, firing shots and throwing rocks through windows. They destroyed the outhouse, broke the corn crib and granary, and, on at least one occasion, fired shots through the window of Alexander's bedroom. In the circumstances, Cato Alexander's belief that "it was the intention of the said persons and their associates to have taken his life" and that if they had broken in to his tavern "some or one of his family would have been murdered" seems well founded.[42]

In a general context in which African New Yorkers were negotiating their freedom and whites mostly attempted to condemn them to continued inferiority, Brown's building of a permanent home for his actors was a clear enough statement to Stephen Price (the impresario who had tried to run him out of business), indeed to the entire white entertainment industry, that he would not be cowed or driven away. Anticipating trouble, he named his new building the American Theater, but this attempt to wrap his enterprise in the flag probably only added fuel to the impending conflagration, which, in the event, was not long in coming.

About two hours into the performance, at 9 o'clock on the night of August 10, a group of young white men ("a gang of fifteen or twenty ruffians"), bought tickets, entered the pit of the theater, and started a riot. Some clambered up into the boxes and cut the rope holding up a large circular frame containing lights and candles, which crashed into the pit. Others smashed the remaining lamps, broke the benches, slashed the scenery, tore down the stage curtain, stripped the costumes from actors (doubtless roughing them up in the process), and shredded their garments, scattering pieces everywhere. A member of the watch, who arrived in the midst of the ensuing chaos, recalled "great . . . noise and confusion." All in all, according to Brown, in excess of two hundred dollars' worth of damage was inflicted on the luckless black company. The rioters also took particular care to beat up William Brown, and one of their number, George Belmont, struck the theater manager in the face.[43]

New York audiences were as boisterous as their counterparts in other cities on the North Atlantic rim, if not more so. A few months previously, the New York City Recorder, in sentencing a couple of young men for creating a disturbance at the Circus, felt compelled to point out that many New Yorkers were in error "as to the extent of the rights which they claimed in a Theater or place of public amusement." A ticket purchased a seat "to witness the performance, and you are at liberty to express your pleasure or disapprobation at the exhibition in the customary way, by applause or by hissing." Audiences, that is to say, were not expected to be polite and decorous; demonstrative behavior was expected, but not to such an extent that the theater became "a scene of riot or confusion," in which case the managers were authorized to turn the culprits out. But this city official at least "was happy to say that these scenes were rarely exhibited in New York."[44] Perhaps, however, times were changing faster than the Recorder appreciated. A few days after the sacking of the Mercer Street Theater, a serious disturbance occurred at the Circus. As the melée erupted, the police officers present called for assistance from the audience, following which plea the cry of "out with your knives" was "heard on every side." Evidently the whole affair had been staged to mask the activities of pickpockets.[45]

Black actors were perfectly capable of handling ordinarily unruly patrons, but what happened on the night of August 10th was different. A conspiracy had been organized to put the theater out of business by sacking the building and thereby warning off future audiences, and it is difficult to believe that Price was not in some way involved in it. The only coverage of the affair in the newspapers came in a letter, signed by B., printed in the *Commercial Advertiser*. According to its author, "one or more" of those arrested was or were Circus riders, who had entered the theater "with full intent, as is understood, to break it up root and branch; and the vigor of their operations is reported to have corresponded fully with their purpose." At this time Stephen Price and the Park Theater were in a close business relationship with the Circus, staging some productions at its facilities, and in the following year Price became the Circus's owner. The second paragraph of the letter to the *Commercial Advertiser* began by pointing out that "the matter should not be spoken of in the spirit of *badinage*," a reference to the "jocular" manner in which Noah and the *Advocate* had described the previous travails of the black actors. The writer went on to suggest that theater as an institution was "indeed of questioned utility; but when theatricians themselves boast so loudly of the ennobling influences of the drama, to refine, ennoble, and exalt the soul, will they deny those benign influences in awakening the mind of the poor African from the dormitude of ages?"[46]

The August 10th assault on the Mercer Street Theater fits into a larger pattern of violent harassment, by people associated with the theater, of both the black actors' productions and of the actors themselves, a campaign that had begun with the January closure by the watch. Three weeks earlier, on July 19th, Ira Aldridge, then just five days short of his fifteenth birthday, had been violently assaulted on a street in the sixth ward by James Belmont, another Circus rider and brother of George Belmont who would attack Brown on the night of August 10th. Aldridge (1807–67) eventually became the most famous black actor of the nineteenth century, enjoying a stellar career in Europe. He had been educated at the African Free School (by comparison with most of the signatures in the court records his was strikingly confident and clear), was at the time of his attack associated with the African New Yorker actors, and may have already played a minor role or two on stage. On December 2nd, a few months after the beatings of Aldridge and Brown, James Hewlett was assaulted in the Park Theater. (Charges were brought against the assailant but were dismissed.) Seemingly, trouble of some sort or another was never far from the black actors.[47]

What is also interesting is the virtual silence that surrounded both the opening of Brown's American Theater and the violence that ensued. The *National Advocate* carried an advertisement in its July 22 issue announcing the beginning of Brown's venture and commented nastily the following day that it was "rather hazardous to open the African Theater [the writer refused to countenance the new name] with the Thermometer at 85."[48] B's letter to the *Commercial Advertiser* was reprinted in the *Spectator.* But with these exceptions, and in spite of the fascination Noah had previously evinced concerning the activities of black actors, nothing else was printed. This silence was matched by the inaction of the legal system. For all the faith African New Yorkers continued to place in the courts, these institutions provided absolutely no redress for the black actors. The charges against the rioters on the night of August 10th were dismissed; those against the Belmonts for the beatings of Aldridge and Brown were not, but nothing ever happened; seemingly the cases were lost in the city's chaotic paperwork. Of course, many cases were never resolved, but it would not be overly conspiratorially minded to suggest that those who violently assaulted the black actors were protected by someone important and powerful.

In 1849 a literary work entitled the *Memoir and Theatrical Career of Ira Aldridge, The African Roscius* was published in London. Although the book was written in the third person, Aldridge was, at the very least, heavily involved in its creation.[49] His account of the events of the summer of 1822 was succinct. Stephen Price, "a manager of some repute, became actually *jealous* of the success of the 'real Ethiopians,' and emissaries were employed to put them down," whereupon "riots ensued, and destruction [fell] upon the little theater." Yet "there was no protection or redress to be obtained from the magistracy (for, unhappily, they were whites)." As a result, "the company dissolved," much to the "chagrin" of the African Americans involved in it, "who declared that *nothing but* envy prevented the blacks from putting the whites completely out of countenance."[50] Aldridge here telescopes events—the African New Yorker company would limp on for a while longer—but his analysis of what had happened seems sufficiently close to the mark.

*   *   *

Perhaps it is appropriate to pause at this involuntary lull in the black theater's history in order to try and see what all the fuss was about. What was the black theater like? As was the custom, patrons were most definitely presented with a full night's entertainment, usually a play, a comic afterpiece of some sort, and interludes of singing and/or dancing interspersed throughout the evening's offerings. On the night of October 1, 1821, for example, the bill began with ten mostly traditional English or Scottish songs, seven of them sung by Hewlett. These were followed by the performance of *Richard III*, and the evening ended with a rendition of the pantomime *Asama*. But moving beyond a mere listing of a theater company's repertory and cast members is not easy. How is one to recover even the bare outlines, let alone the textures, of past theatrical performances? Finding scraps of evidence from black spectators on this and other matters of importance is all but impossible. Most viewers were white, however, and fragments from the writings of travelers and locals allow occasional glimpses of black theatrical style.

Much as would happen a century later, when Harlem was in vogue, visitors to New York in search of the exotic often found it in the black areas of town. After viewing several performances by the black actors, Peter Neilson, a Scottish traveler who lived in New York for several years in the 1820s, commented that "it really is worth one's while to go there for a few nights for the novelty of the thing."[51] Some of the comments by whites are more closely observed than were Neilson's, but, unfortunately, most of them also are swathed in a miasma of racist utterances and arch attempts at humor. Writers heaped ridicule on the way stage mechanics failed to operate, how the stage curtain was likely to be hauled up on only one side at a time, how black actors missed their cues to appear on stage, and most of all how black actors often forgot their lines. Yet such mishaps were hardly restricted to the black theater. After a performance of *King John* at the Park

Theater, in which at one time several key players had remained mute for what seemed like an eternity, Fanny Kemble, the famous English actress, was moved to write in her diary "What a cast! what a play! what botchers! what butchers!"[52]

One of the things that made a night at the American Theater distinctive was the character of the music and dancing that was part of the evening's fare. As slavery wound down in New York in the 1810s and 1820s, a creative explosion of black music and dance occurred at public sites such as Catharine Slip and smaller places such as dance cellars, where black men and women congregated to dance the night away. Dance was the major expressive medium of ordinary African New Yorkers in these years, and black musicians and dancers took what they found around them and infused it with African influences, creating something new: dynamic, unruly music and dance forms that anachronistically we can label as "hot." This music's powerful attraction filtered into and shaped musical performance at the balls, then popular among more well-to-do blacks, and in the black theater; at the same time, its very pervasiveness and the ubiquity of African American musicians meant that more and more white New Yorkers became accustomed to, and indeed grew to like, its distinctive sound. That was not, however, true of theater critics who attended performances by the black actors. On seeing that the American Theater's orchestra contained only four members, Twaites "felicitated myself greatly" as he was "very fond of harmony, but detest[ed] a great Oratorio kind of noise." To his horror, though, instead of playing "simply four parts," the musicians played "that precise number of [different] tunes." The unhappy critic added bitingly that "no words of mine can do [the music] justice" and, ladling on the sarcasm, declared that "it was a thing to be heard, in order to be appreciated." Furthermore, when a violin player snapped a string in the middle of a solo, "the best ear could not distinguish any difference in the air." On the night on which he attended the African Theater, the vituperative Simon Snipe was even less impressed by the music, "if it may so be called," issuing from a three-piece orchestra, two of whose members, interestingly, were white. So great was the din emanating from the group that the clarinet "could scarcely be heard, except now and then it would burst out like a quaking duck or a yelping dog."

To the modern reader, Snipe and Twaites demonstrate an almost perverse refusal to hear or appreciate what was going on. It is more likely that what Twaites heard was not four separate tunes, but four musicians improvising in and around the one tune, creating dense and complex rhythmic patterns and a sound that was a precursor of the jazz of a century later. Even the fact that one of the violin players broke a string suggests that the black musician was playing the instrument percussively (rather than bowing in the European way) in a distinctively African and African-American fashion. Similarly, Snipe may well have been witness to solos from a white or a black clarinet player who was a forebear of a Barney Bigard or a Benny Goodman. This, after all, was a virtuoso performance that, Snipe conceded, had "greatly diverted" a *"variegated"* audience of "black, copper-colored and light brown," and also of his fellow whites, most of whom were more appreciative of the display than was he.

In attempting to convey the apparent discordance of the music, both Twaites and Snipe likened its sounds to those of machines, a comparison that allowed full play for a heavy-handed and unpleasant humor, but also revealed the alienation they felt. Twaites recommended that in future the black theater should "have this music go by steam," adding that the black players "might collect enough, and that of a strong kind in the house." For Snipe, the orchestra's version of Rolla's march was "no more like it than Yankee Doodle is to the Knight Errant!" a huge discrepancy that brought to his mind "The Cattee Piano." This instrument, supposedly, was a contraption within which a dozen cats, ranging from a kitten to an old ram cat, were placed with their tails deliberately caught in the crevices between two boards. When pressure was applied to the top board, "their voices will make an *excellent* symphonia."

Twaites was similarly nonplussed by the dancing intervals between the evening's main attractions. A young lady had danced a hornpipe "with a vigor seldom surpassed," continuing her performance not only "until some time after the music had stopped," but "until she was quite black in the face." She "was loudly applauded," Twaites decided, because of her "desire to please." In that belief, he was surely mistaken. At this time New York City was a hothouse of dance, and the chances were slim that an audience capable of appreciating complex combinations of dance steps would cheer mere enthusiasm. Presented with skill, Twaites had been prepared to acknowledge only "vigor" and had even resorted to a tired pun on color, all to achieve an ironically detached tone. Even the usually venomous Snipe was forced to concede that the woman who danced the hornpipe on the night he attended "really danced it well," because, as he confessed disingenuously, "I must give praise where it is due." He then went on to heap scorn on a second dancer, who had exhibited all the grace of "a butcher's bull dog" and had been driven from the stage by a shower of peas and potatoes.[53]

The most remarkable aspect of the entertainment Brown's troupe provided was the very idea of seeing blacks on stage acting in otherwise familiar plays. Although throughout the 1820s more and more white New Yorkers and visitors to the city became accustomed to this novelty, a white individual's initial encounter with the spectacle could still come as a bit of a shock. According to Peter Neilson, the Scottish traveler, a "black Douglas, with a kilt, makes a most preposterous appearance." Neilson was prepared to concede that "Othello may pass, and another character or two," but he believed that it was "too much for frail flesh and blood to see an absolute negro strut in with much dignity, bellowing forth" lines from *Richard III*.[54] Speaking from the vantage point of mid-century, Ira Aldridge suggested that such a view had been common among white New Yorkers at the time: the idea of there being "an Ethiopian Juliet to an Ethiopian Romeo" had been too much to bear. Indeed, "certain Yankees, with a degree of illiberality peculiar to *some* 'Liberals,' had no notion of such indulgences being allowed to 'niggers,' whose 'tarnation conceit and considerable effrontery licked natur slick outright.'"[55]

If the sight of black actors shocked many white theater-goers, their speech only added to those patrons' feelings of disorientation. According to Neilson, an excursion to the black theater compelled one "to hear the king's English murdered." Later in the decade, an anonymous visitor declared "the pronunciation" of black performers to be "ludicrous," although he did add, rather more perceptively, that the actors were speaking "Negro English."[56] Exactly what that label signified in the context of the New York of the 1820s is, of course, difficult to establish.

Blacks who crowded into the metropolis in the early nineteenth century had started out from places as diverse as Africa, the Caribbean, the South, as well as Dutch-dominated rural areas of New York and New Jersey. Some spoke French and a few Spanish, but the vast majority used English. No matter in which language these migrants were fluent, however, most spoke a creolized version of it, shaped both by their (however distant) African past, and by the vernacular speech of the area in the Americas from which they had come. Travelers to New York tended to comment only on those forms of black speech that seemed distinctive; on his arrival in the city in 1827, the Englishman Basil Hall was driven to his hotel from the dock by a "mulatto, whose broken lingo reminded me of the West Indies." After his sojourn in New York, James Stuart spoke more generally about the "broken English" that was "universal among the coloured people."[57] Overall, then, black New York was a city of linguistic diversity in which could be found a wide spectrum of speech forms. At one end were African New Yorkers who could utter only a few heavily accented words in English; arrayed in the middle was the vast majority of those who used Black English; and at the other end were those who, when they wanted to, could probably speak the language in a manner almost indistinguishable from that of their supposed racial betters.

Freedom, and the concomitant increase in the city's black population, allowed African New Yorkers more scope for the creative use of language. Some characteristics of black speech, undoubtedly present in slavery, became more open and more obvious. Perhaps the most frequently commented on example was "fancy talk," or the use of an embellished, almost ornate language in the set-pieces associated with formal or semi-formal occasions. White observers usually categorized this talk as merely hilariously inappropriate, yet one more example of blacks failing in their mimicry of refined white ways, but what these outsiders almost certainly missed was a sense of knowing playfulness, of a pride and a joy in the artful marshaling, often with striking effect, of words that rolled pleasurably across the tongue. This elevated black speech style was most apparent to whites on northern city streets, which had rapidly become established as one of the major arenas of black sociability. There, on meeting each other, finely dressed blacks exchanged "stylish compliments." John Palmer, a traveler to America in 1817, recounted a conversation between two well-dressed blacks that he had supposedly overheard on a Philadelphia street, an exchange that could just as easily have occurred in New York:

Mr. Quashi Ah, Mrs. Sambo, I hope I have the felicity of seeing you well this morning.
Mrs. Sambo Oh, Sir, yes, thank you, Sir; I hope your family are in good health.
Mr. Quashi Thank you, quite well; but how is your amiable daughter Miss Sambo? has she quite recovered from her late alarming indisposition?[58]

It takes little imagination to see that the formality of this language, the use of the titles "Mr" or "Mrs," were welcomed dimensions of the dignity freedom had brought and an explicit rejection of the enforced familiarity of slavery. For whites, of course, these speech forms were affectations, in and of themselves absurd—something else to laugh uneasily about.

Other formal occasions elicited similar linguistic displays, on which white observers were also quick to comment. In February 1822, a mulatto named Ross charged "a sensible honest looking black fellow" named Jordan with the theft of a pair of pantaloons and fifteen dollars in cash. His subsequent appearance in court as a plaintiff was an important event for Ross, who not only dressed up for the occasion but also brought along his best language. It was this, rather than his showy apparel, that impressed the court reporter for the *Commercial Advertiser,* who commented that, on the witness stand, Ross "afforded the most laughable display of *consequential cuffee*—of the ludicrous distortion of language, into which he runs when attempting display, that has been witnessed for a long time." The reporter rendered a brief excerpt from Ross's speech:

"Stop, Sir," [he said] to the Counsel, "hear me a minute, I tell you he points situate, derakly, and you wish hear him. Sir, you, not interrupt me sir,—That woman, not my wife sir. She was Indian woman, and Indians always tassicating in liquors, Sir."

According to this white observer, "the dandy went through his brief oration in *style*, while the court and audience were convulsed with laughter." From the reporter's perspective, the derisory nature of the plaintiff's performance was only increased when it was easily demonstrated in court that "Ross had flatly and flagrantly perjured himself."[59] The whole incident merely confirmed for the *Commercial Advertiser*'s man, and doubtless for most of his readers as well, an all-too-easy connection between foppishly dressed blacks, fancy language, and obfuscation if not prevarication.

Cultural differences in the creative use of language were further demonstrated by black preachers, archetypes of the black man-of-words. In August 1823, an anonymous Glaswegian attended a Methodist camp meeting in Westchester County. After recounting at considerable length details of the white worship, the Scotsman related how he heard a "prodigious noise" coming "from the bottom of the camp, where the blacks were assembled." Caught up in the throng of whites moving in the direction of the commotion, he eventually "got within sight of a black orator who was standing on the stump of an old tree, and expounding with great vehemence and invective." The preacher railed at his audience, telling them that "they need not expect to get to heaven with their upright backs and starched strict necks for they must bow, and carry the cross on their backs." Here, to render his image palpable, the black man picked up "a huge chair" and "placed it over his shoulder." As the bemused but fascinated onlooker noted, the "chair became the topic of illustration, its weight was discussed, then with outstretched arms it was flourished in the heavens, to show how it would be glorified and draw up those who carried it to heaven." The drama of this performance, uniting the language the preacher used with the way his entire body was caught up in the delivery of the sermon, elicited starkly different reactions from his racially mixed audience. Whites were laughing openly at the preacher's "shouting and mechanical sermonizing" (note the metaphor of the machine to describe African American sounds), and it "was the sport of all around." On the other hand, his "negro auditors," tears of joy streaming down their faces, were shouting out "God be praised!" and "Glory! Glory!"[60]

Again, whites who, for whatever reason, ended up sitting through the services at any of the black churches springing up in the city were also quickly reminded of the cultural differences between black and white. In May 1828, the *New-York Enquirer* reported that Isaac Wylie had been charged with disturbing a black service. The white man "admitted the charge alleged against him by the sable orator, but added that he was drunk, and the man was preaching nonsense." Apparently, some of the "figurative expressions" the black preacher used "rather shocked Mr Wylie's ideas of locality and dimension," a fact he made clear in an interjection "which savoured more of profanity than decency." Five years later, in December 1833, a slightly inebriated John M'Searley visited the Seventh Avenue African Church "for the purpose of witnessing the black people's worship." According to the *Sun*, when one of the congregation exclaimed "hallelujah," M'Searley bawled out "hal-ali-lo-li-lujah," further exaggerating the already pronounced African American elongation of the word. The intruder was "appealed to as a white man, as a gentleman—and as a Christian—not to disturb the congregation," and for ten minutes he complied with this request. But when one of the black church members next yelled out "Hallelujah!" he "was responded to, in a long-drawn, comical-sounding 'halle-lo-li-lujah' by Mr M'Searley." The watch had to be called and the unrepentant heckler was hauled away.[61]

A few whites did sense that more was involved in such instances than an inept attempt by blacks to imitate white speech. Far from hesitating or stumbling when they spoke, many blacks used language with extreme fluency, and with an artfulness that was widely appreciated by their peers. In a piece entitled "NEGRO ELOQUENCE," a writer in the *New York Transcript* in July 1834 acknowledged that blacks were "as fond of set speeches as professional orators." Although he condemned these black "harangues" for being "verbose and tautological"—missing the importance of the flights of linguistic fancy that blacks valued—this writer was willing to concede that a degree of conscious artistry was involved. Buried within what he thought of as the excesses of these speeches, "we meet, if not good argument, at least that which resembles it, and even supersedes its necessity—that is to say, acute illustration." If a black wished to warn of the folly of taking unnecessary risks, he would do so not "by mode and figure; but will at once say—'Crab what walk too much go 'na pot.'" Similarly, to express the idea that after death people are soon forgotten, he will say—"When man dead, grass grow at him door."[62]

Even at camp meetings, noted for the dramatic and highly emotional nature of preachers' addresses, some whites reacted with appreciation rather than scorn. By the end of the 1820s such meetings, organized on occasion by blacks for themselves, were a commonplace all around New York, in Westchester County, New Jersey, and Long Island. Some of these events were huge, attracting thousands of African American participants and denuding the city, for their duration, of thirty or forty percent of its black inhabitants, quite a logistical achievement given that Manhattan is an island. The traveler James Stuart, having carefully observed a black evangelist perform in front of three or four thousand African Americans, most of them from New York City, at a camp meeting in Flushing, Long Island, in the early 1830s, noted that although the preacher spoke in "broken English," he still "possessed a great deal of natural eloquence, and was not at all deficient either in matter or manner."[63]

As a perusal of newspapers and other sources from the 1810s and 1820s will readily show, newly freed blacks were using their own version of the English language, and whites were paying a good deal of attention to the ways blacks spoke. To be sure, it is easy enough to find eighteenth-century examples of whites' attempts to render Black English, but in the early decades of the nineteenth century a virtual avalanche of such material appeared. Occasionally it took the form of little filler items. In 1828 the *New York American*, seemingly apropos of nothing, printed a supposed black account of the origin of the white man. After Cain had killed Abel,

> de massa cum and say—"Cane, whar your brodder Abel?"— Cane say—"I don't no, massa." But de niggar no'd all de time. Massa now git mad, cum gin; peak mity sharp dis time. "Cane, whar you brodder Abel, you niggar." Cane now get friten, an he turn *wite*; and dis is de day de fus wite man cum pon dis yerth! an if it hadn't been fur that plaggy niggar Cane, we'd never ben tubled wid dese sassy wites, pon de face ob dis circumblar globe.[64]

For all the verisimilitude of this story (it is similar to other documented African American accounts of genesis; moreover, the dismissive attitude exhibited toward whites fits in so well with the prickly mood of black New York in the 1820s), the language in which it is recounted seems less an attempt to render the sound of

Black English than a strained effort to demonstrate difference, clearly equated with inferiority. Who, after all, does not pronounce "know" as "no" or "mighty" as "mity"? Much the same demeaning techniques were used in the reporting of blacks' court appearances, accounts of which provided the press with its most frequent opportunity to render black speech and became the very foundation on which numerous parodies of blacks were based. These burlesques, often quite lengthy pieces, were printed in the newspapers but were most commonly disseminated by handbills.

As one plows through the surviving written record of these years, the amount of material in dialecticized black English is quite striking. Clearly, many blacks were using black English, and it was different from the English spoken by whites, but whites were exaggerating those differences to create what rapidly developed into an accepted caricature of black speech. The reasons for this deliberate distortion were bound up in the ambivalent attitude of whites to the realities of black freedom. What particularly unnerved many white New Yorkers were the similarities between black and white. Too often, as far as they were concerned, black men and women could now speak and comport themselves like whites. Inserting an often ludicrously distorted, dialecticized language into black mouths was a way of reassuring white New Yorkers that blacks really were as different as whites wished to believe. This went hand in hand with another linguistic innovation, the use of the term "nigger" in print. All such devices were designed to remind everyone that although African New Yorkers might now be free, they were anything but equal.

Occasionally this newly conventional way of rendering black speech puzzled strangers who actually encountered African New Yorkers. A Mrs. Felton from England, for example, after conversing with many black females in the city, commented that "they generally express themselves in good language, and with an enunciation, as bold and as clear as any Englishman." "This struck me with surprise," she continued, "as I had formed my judgement of their conversational capabilities, from the dialogues given in broken English, that I had met with in the course of my reading."[65] Mostly, though, people heard what they expected to hear, and the caricatured speech perpetuated through newspapers, handbills, and the like was insidiously effective in demeaning blacks, as it has been down to our own time.

Thus, when the ex-slave Charles Taft, bedecked in the garb of Richard III, limped out on to the makeshift stage on the African Theater's opening night in September 1821, the few whites who were present probably had clear expectations as to what they were about to hear. Mordecai Noah's expectations were certainly met. According to his account in the *National Advocate*, the first words Taft uttered were: "Now is de vinter of our discontent made glorus summer by de son of New-York." Noah added unnecessarily that "it was evident that the actor had not followed strictly the text of the author."[66] Over the years, this version of the opening of *Richard III* became something akin to a trademark, signature lines that visitors to the theater often remembered. It was not unknown for white actors to insert a local allusion or two into their lines, and, seemingly, it was impossible for a white to pen more than two lines about blacks without punning, usually badly, but when a black actor made what by comparison was quite a clever play on the word "York," it was expected to be read as yet more evidence of the risibility of allowing African Americans on stage.

Noah proceeded to give other examples of the way in which the black actors changed lines in *Richard III*. Lady Ann, for example, said:

Would they were brass candlesticks
To strike de dead.

Here "candlesticks" was a replacement for "basilisk," a legendary creature that can kill by looking at its victim. But Noah was hardly the only person to note this trait. A few months later, in January 1822, the editor of the *Commercial Advertiser* commented that "the colored corps dramatique have made some very happy improvements in the hitherto approved readings of Shakespeare." Indeed, a few nights earlier, in a rendition of *Macbeth* the actor had changed "Lay on, Macduff, and damned be he who first cries hold." Macbeth held back the last word in this line "until after he had fallen in the fight; and while kicking and writhing upon the floor in the agonies of death, he turned up the whites of his eyes . . . and cried out *'enough!'*" "This," the *Advertiser* added, "is certainly equal to any improvement in reading made by Kean."[67]

It was well known that white actors omitted, changed, and, in the view of chagrined authors, mangled their allotted lines. Suddenly struck dumb for whatever reason, a nimble-footed performer could usually cobble together some verbiage to fill in the void until rescue, either by the prompter or their memory, arrived. On occasion, actors could even feel confident in their ability to give impromptu performances for rather longer periods of time. Late in the season of 1822, the troupe at the Park Theater had a new play foisted on them, *The Grecian Captive* by Mordecai Noah. In his memoirs, Joe Cowell, one of the main actors, remembered that as far as he and the rest of the cast were concerned, learning their parts for one night only "was out of the question." Cowell determined that he would "speak the meaning of the part after what flourish my nature prompted," an act of mutilation that did no great disservice to drama, as the play was one "that the author himself could never wish should see daylight." Halfway through the first scene, set in a Turkish garden, and with everyone happily making up their lines as they went along, one of the other actors whispered in Cowell's ear, "Dam'me, Joe, look at the books." It turned out that Noah had had the play printed and distributed to those in the boxes; other patrons could purchase copies if they wished. As the actors delivered their freely improvised lines, utterly perplexed members of the audience could be seen thumbing through the text, whispering to their neighbors as they tried to ascertain the place the actors were up to, and, very frequently, shaking their heads in despair. It must have been a memorable night, for that was only the beginning of the cast's problems. Some of the stage fighting got out of hand, resulting in one actor being flattened by a fist that "bunged up" his eye, and in the last scene, the "real elephant" introduced, in Cowell's felicitous phrase, "an unexpected hydraulic experiment" into proceedings. Next day a young critic informed an unimpressed Cowell that he had *actually sometimes cut out a whole page at a time.*[68]

Cowell's amusing story is quite revealing of the limits allowed to improvisation. The white audience had clear expectations of what they would see on stage, expectations which, in this instance, the Park Theater actors had manifestly failed to fulfill. It seems probable that plays were interpreted somewhat differently at the African New Yorker theater, and likely that, over time, the predominantly white audiences grew accustomed to those differences, for all the carping of the theater critics. The most telling account of acting practice at the black theater is contained in a letter that Twaites wrote to the *Commercial Advertiser.* After his visit to the American Theater to see the *Poor Soldier,* he commented that "most of the actors did not know their parts," but added that "instead of pausing or hobbling on" as did the cast at the Park Theater, the black actors had done something completely novel in Twaites' experience. The actor or actress "who had the best memory, struck in some distance in advance" and then, "in order to do the audience and author justice, they would uniformly play the scene backwards." After one player who had forgotten a line had left the stage, "with a propriety seldom equalled at the Park, he returned and corrected himself." Twaites confessed that "I do not know that I have ever witnessed this familiar play with more interest since I first saw it represented; for so artfully was it managed, that with all my ingenuity, I found it impossible to tell what would come next." Certainly, this critic was using the occasion to get in a few digs at the Park Theater, and his comments were leavened with a certain amount of sarcasm, but, for all that, his puzzlement at the performance was both genuine and based on close observation. The issue certainly gnawed away at him, for Twaites returned to it at the very end of his article, proposing that for future material the black company could turn to "the popular dramatic poem of Odofried," which, in shortened form, "would answer extremely well." This just published piece by Samuel B. H. Judah was already notorious for its incomprehensibility. Indeed, Twaites knew "from experience" that the poem "will read as well backward as forward."[69]

Another characteristic of the black performances that whites found disconcerting was the actors' habit of inserting material drawn from other sources. On the opening night, Noah sarcastically noted that "Eveleen's Bower," a popular song, "was sung well in the third act, by Queen Anne, although we could not but consider it rather inappropriate." This ploy would famously be sent up in Charles Mathews's spoof of the "Niggers' (or Negroes') theatre." When the actor playing Hamlet uttered the words "oppose 'em" it sounded like "opossum," prompting the audience to demand that the actor sing "Opossum up a Gum Tree." Soon after he had finished this performance, the actor strutted down stage, with "arms a-kimbo," and bellowed out "Now is de winter of our discontent, made de glorious summer by de sun of New York," upon which someone in the boxes told him "he should play Hamlet, and not Richard the Third." The actor replied, "Yes, him know dat, but him tought of New York den, and could not help talking about it."[70]

This jazz-like promiscuous sampling invoked both a world of associations and a sense of surprise that especially delighted black audiences. The result was familiar, yet another facet of an African American cultural aesthetic observable in all manner of things, from slave clothing styles and quilts through to the way slaves preached, but probably most obvious to white commentators who listened carefully to slave music. Four decades later, Colonel Thomas Higginson, the white commander of the First Regiment, South Carolina Volunteers, wrote of his black troops' singing as they marched along, that "for all the songs, but especially for their own wild hymns, they constantly improvised simple verses, with the same odd mingling—the little facts of to-day's march being interwoven with the depths of theological gloom, and the same jubilant chorus annexed to all."[71] That Shakespeare received much the same treatment as did the content of the hymn book should have come as no great surprise.

Occasional, almost offhand comments from even the most trenchant critics suggest, however grudgingly, that they saw at least moments of merit in the black productions. After viewing an African New Yorker performance of *Julius Caesar,* one anonymous white writer decided that "the acting was such as to show that the performers did at least here and there catch the spirit of the poet." The more dramatic, action-filled scenes were most likely to attract the critics' approbation. For Noah, who reviewed the company's first performance, the tent scene of *Richard III* was the "chef-d'oeuvre." Indeed, "the darkness of the night, the black face of the king, the flourish of drums and clarionetts, the start from the dream, the '*Gib me noder horse,*' and finally, the agony of the appalled Richard, the rolling eye, white gnashing teeth, clenched fists, and phrenzied looks, were all that the author could have wished." For all his knowing winks at African American stereotypes, Noah does here seem to be acknowledging a certain power in the black performance. Twaites was less ambivalent about the acting he saw on the night he went to the American Theater, declaring that "the fighting was admirable: it was preceded by a good deal of action, and loud declamation; and when it really began, wore the air of dread reality." He had never seen "any actor at the park, lay about him with the fury of Don Juan" and "expected every instant, to see a real death."[72]

Attempting to judge audience reaction to the spectacle on stage is difficult. Commentators whose notes have survived were usually striving for comic effect, their efforts frequently assisted by the antics of an unruly audience. Snipe depicted one such audience, which, incensed that *Othello* had been "transformed into mimic burlesques," pelted the stage with "chestnuts, peas, apple-cores, &c." At times, however, though with obvious reluctance, he conceded that some of those present may have enjoyed what they saw and heard. Toward the end of the evening, the critic's "ears were saluted" by song almost certainly performed by Hewlett:

> Is dare a heart dat nebber lub'd
> Or felt soft woman sigh;
> Is dare a man can mark unmov'd
> Dear woman tearful eye?

"When this song was finished," Snipe recorded, "peals of laughter came from all parts of the house, some laughed, perhaps, because it was sung well; others because it was an excellent song, but the principal part of the audience laughed at the pronunciation."[73] Years later, Ira Aldridge commented that the African New Yorker actors had achieved "considerable notice." Patrons "who went to ridicule, remained to admire, albeit there must have been ample scope for the suggestion of the ridiculous."[74] Like whites who commented ambivalently about the way slaves dressed or about the music they created, white theater-goers must have found this a disconcertingly different theater experience, but acknowledged that it was not without a certain appeal. Perhaps most tellingly, this small band of part-time black actors clearly drew sufficient white patronage for the theatrical establishment to consider them enough of a threat to warrant a concerted effort to shut their enterprise down.

Following the depredations wrought by white thugs in August 1822, the American Theater's black actors evidently managed to repair the site to the point where they were able to reopen, although for how long remains unclear. With two small exceptions, the press's pall of silence surrounding their endeavors continued for over six months. In the midst of a devastating yellow fever outbreak besetting the city, a short notice in the *National Advocate* announced on October 12, 1822, that, because of the epidemic, the "African Company have closed their Theater." But again defying white expectations that they would fold at the slightest obstacle, the black actors took their show on the road, playing, at the very least, in Albany. The *Advocate* went on to note, in a rare and probably inadvertent acknowledgement of equality between black and white theatrical companies, that there were "three *corps dramatiques* now in the north; two white and one black."[75]

The second brief mention of the African Company occurred in the *National Advocate*'s account of the January 1823 term of the city's Court of Quarter Sessions. Three black women—Martha Green, Mary Ann Tomkins, and Eliza Hays—who lived in a house in Theatre Alley, were convicted of receiving stolen goods from one Ann Vanderbilt and sentenced to sixteen months in the penitentiary. At the end of the item was the sentence: "It is said that some of the above parties belonged to the African Theatre—now no more!!!"[76] Again, the passive voice probably indicates that this was white scuttlebutt circulating around the court house; none of the cast lists in the company's surviving playbills mentions any of the women involved in this case. Whether or not the rumor was true, once again the press had conflated black acting and criminality.

The degree of relish, signaled by the three exclamation marks, with which Noah celebrated the assumed demise of the black actors' enterprise suggests that the African Company may not have reopened on its return to New York, possibly because of Brown's increasingly straitened financial circumstances. Life must have been tough for the participants in this theatrical venture. For all their tenacity, their fledgling company could hardly pay them anything like enough to live on, even in the brief periods during which they were able to perform regularly. How most of them survived can only be guessed at.

We do know, though, that during the African Company's abeyance James Hewlett, its principal actor, began a new venture in a rather different field. In early March 1823 he opened what he called his Clothes Dressing Emporium in Warren Street, near its intersection with Broadway. Advertising the new enterprise in the *New York American*, Hewlett claimed that his "mode of Dressing Coats, Pantaloons, &c. by Steam pressing" extracted "all kinds of Stains," allowing him "to dress Clothes so that no person can scarce distinguish them from new." Not only was the fabric "improved in appearance," it was also "uninjured"; indeed, his was the best method of cleaning clothes "that has ever been invented." Hewlett's shop also did tailoring work, altering and repairing "Gentleman's clothes in the neatest manner, and on reasonable terms."[77] In the parlance of the 1820s, Hewlett was running a scouring shop, something much like a dry-cleaner's establishment today.

When Hewlett launched his new venture, scouring was an occupation dominated by blacks. As "A SUFFERER" wrote to the *National Advocate* in 1826, "every black who can beg or borrow ten dollars . . . sets up a 'Scouring Establishment,' without any knowledge of the business or the materials he uses," which sounds like an accurate enough description of the level of expertise Hewlett must have possessed when he opened his shop several years earlier. If something went wrong in the cleaning process, expensive clothes were easily ruined, a circumstance that drove this irate letter writer to demand that no one should be permitted "to set up the trade hereafter unless the 'professeur' had served his regular apprenticeship to the business." The close association in white minds between blacks and scouring showed up in humorous stories of gentlemen's foibles that circulated at the time. Thus a guest in one of the city hotels, on encountering a black thief walking down the corridor heavily laden with an armload of coats, had asked "What are you doing with those coats, you black rascal?" "I'm jist 'gwine to take 'em home to scour 'em," the black adroitly replied. "Oh, you are, ha?" said the guest, "well, here take mine and scour it too."[78]

For whites, scouring was not only a menial occupation, but, partly because of its association with blacks, a somewhat unscrupulous or shady one as well. To African New Yorkers, by contrast, it represented one of the few businesses that could provide a substantial income. Proceedings of a court case in 1821 revealed that a scouring shop owned by a black man named Cox (he claimed it was the first to be opened in the city) was "so profitable that he has not only laid up money, but also for some time past cut a considerable dash in his mode of living." Another black man named Jennings secured "the exclusive right by patent" from the United

States government and opened a rival shop one door down from Cox's, on Broadway. Cox, who had long declared that he would brook no competition, did not react well to this intrusion. He first defaced Jennings' signs in public houses and then destroyed the sign outside his rival's shop by throwing oil of vitriol (sulphuric acid) on it. Jennings sued Cox for damages. The next day Cox, having slightly damaged his own shop sign with aqua fortis (nitric acid), took out an advertisement in the *New York Gazette* offering a reward for the apprehension of the villain responsible. Jennings's counsel concluded his statement to the court by observing that "such artful management to conceal and cloak his depredations" on his client's property "for the purpose of monopolizing this profitable business" proved Cox to be dangerous, malicious, and "highly deserving of punishment." The jury agreed and awarded the plaintiff, Jennings, damages of fifty dollars.[79]

There are tantalizing links between Hewlett and Cox, two of the better known blacks in New York. Although Hewlett opened his Emporium in March 1823, the thanks he extended to his "employers for the favors he has heretofore received from them, in the line of his profession," suggests that he may already have been engaged in the business for some time. In the *National Advocate* of July 9, 1822, Noah had run a rumor from black New York: "It is whispered in the fashionable world, that two black dandies, celebrated in this city as coat scourers, have had a serious dispute, which is likely to terminate in a duel," almost certainly a reference to the prickly Cox and possibly to Hewlett. A few months later, on December 2, 1822, Cox beat up Hewlett in the Park Theater. Perhaps Hewlett's plans for his Emporium were already known, and Cox was overreacting again to the news that another black competitor was setting up a scouring shop nearby. Doubtless Cox's financial success and life style appealed to James Hewlett as something to emulate. He certainly emulated Cox's advertising;

his notice in the *New York American* announcing the opening of his business venture can only be described as a plagiarism of earlier notices placed by Cox. One can imagine that the pair's conflicted history prompted Hewlett to indulge in a certain piquant satisfaction by appropriating his assailant's words and encroaching on his business as well.[80]

Later in March 1823, at the theater on Mercer Street, Hewlett staged what appears to have been his first solo performance. The evening's entertainment was divided into three parts. Hewlett began by singing twelve songs, four in imitation of Thomas Phillips, a popular singer who had recently been in New York, and one in imitation of John Braham, said to have been the inspiration for Phillips. In the second and main part, Hewlett performed in *La Diligence*, from a series of very popular monologues (or "monopologues," as the author called them), the "At Homes" by Charles Mathews (1776–1835), which the English actor performed on both sides of the Atlantic. In the final part of the show—called Recitations—Hewlett gave renditions of famous actors in their most famous parts. Thus he imitated Edward Kean delivering one of Richard III's soliloquies, John Philip Kemble as Rolla, and Mathews playing Goldfinch in *The Road to Ruin*. The playbill also announced that Hewlett "at the particular solicitation of his friends is induced once more, before his departure for the Southward, to make his appearance in this city."[81] It seems that Hewlett, for the first but not the last time, had decided to try his luck elsewhere.

A couple of months later the African Company reformed, without Hewlett, and, on June 7th, 1823, staged what it advertised as the "Musical Extravaganza" of *Tom & Jerry, Or, Life in London*. The choice was an auspicious one, for by that time the play—William Moncrief's adaptation of Pierce Egan's *Life in London, or The Day and Night Scenes of Jerry Hawthorn, Esq., and his Elegant Friend*

Corinthian Tom, accompanied by Bob Logic, the Oxonian, in their Rambles and Sprees through the Metropolis (1821)—was well on its way to becoming the theatrical sensation of the early nineteenth-century Anglo-American world. Not only was it fast-moving and colorful, much like a modern musical, but it also gained a generous degree of satirical pointedness by being set in a recognizably contemporary London, rather than in the more usual historical past.[82]

Reviewing the play's first American performance at the Park Theater on March 3, 1823, the *New York Evening Post*'s drama critic found it "full of whim, mirth and good humor, really . . . one of the most amusing entertainments ever presented on our stage, [it] is of a perfectly novel kind here." *Tom and Jerry* was immensely popular wherever it was put on, a success that led, according to a worried correspondent in the *Post* nearly a year later, to the "almost total neglect of the legitimate drama." "[C]omplaints are made against the managers for introducing such trash," the *Post* observed, "but the reply uniformly is 'if this be a fault, it rests with the public alone, whose taste leads them altogether that way.'"[83]

Inevitably, *Tom and Jerry*'s influence permeated American urban culture of the 1820s and 1830s, and traces of it can be found in all manner of places. The play probably affected the behavior of young white males; it certainly influenced the language with which newspapers recounted this behavior. The public took an increasing interest in what the lower orders, and more usually the young, were doing on the streets at night, and much reporting of this, particularly from the courts, was laced with slang taken from the nation's most spectacular musical and dramatic hit. In February 1827, for example, the *New York American* noted that "On Saturday night five Corinthians sallied from the La Fayette Theater, determined in true 'Tom and Jerry' style to have a 'swell.'"[84]

One of the reasons for the play's popularity was the ease with which its almost nonexistent storyline—a naive country boy is shown the ways of the city by Corinthian Tom and Bob Logic—could be adapted to local circumstances. (Within a few years an adaptation was being performed in as remote a place as Sydney, Australia.) Partly because no printed version of *Tom and Jerry* existed for several years, which meant that the African Theater's actors' experience of it was limited to their having seen the Park Theater's production, the black players were among the first to appreciate the flexibility possible within the play's accommodating structure. Certainly, the African Company's production bore little relation to the original, or even to the earlier Park Theater rendition—twenty scenes were reduced to eight; there was a smaller cast; and whole sections of the already scanty plot had disappeared. More importantly, the company added a completely new scene, "Life in Limbo—Life in Love," set in the Charleston slave market. Perhaps it was just a way of acknowledging the changes they had already made, but for their next performance the following Monday the black actors simply retitled the whole performance *Tom & Jerry, or Life in New York*, and also promised an additional scene, "Life in Fulton-market!!!" These adaptations marked the beginnings of a whole range of dramatic productions centered around life in the city; they would prove immensely popular over the ensuing decades, culminating in *New York As It Is* (1848), one of the most popular plays ever performed on the American stage.

Of all the performances put on by the African Company, *Tom and Jerry* must have been among the most disconcerting for white members of its audience. Whether the action was ostensibly set in London or not, both black and white theater-goers would always expect the representations of the lives of the lower orders of a modern metropolis, acted out by blacks, to be about African New Yorkers. Contemporary struggles over what forms of behavior were appropriate for newly freed blacks disporting themselves on city streets can only have given a deeper resonance, a frisson of self-recognition, to what unfolded on the stage.

The play's relevance to a society slowly relinquishing slavery was emphasized by the provocative and remarkable decision to include a scene set in the Charleston slave market. Almost certainly, this was the first time African Americans had publicly represented the rituals of the auction block—rituals that were central to the dominant culture's dehumanizing mythologization of blacks and that portrayed in graphic form this most traumatic moment in the slaves' lives. Surviving details are frustratingly scanty, but the scene's title—"Life in Limbo—Life in Love"—does strongly suggest that the plot, such as it was, featured a slave couple threatened by the auction with separation, a standard motif of antislavery literature. Whether this was the case or not, the holding up to scrutiny of one of the "peculiar institution's" central events, and, moreover, the telling, from a black perspective, of the story of human beings offered for sale, of relationships brutally sundered, was a sharp retort to the still considerable segment of the city's white population which continued to believe that only through the institution of slavery could black people be controlled. What authorized the transaction in the slave market was the difference in skin color between the seller and the saleable human property. But when, on the stage, a black actor took the place of the white vendor, the contrast in skin color could no longer validate the event. The assumed distance between masters and slaves, whites and blacks, and the denial of African American humanity were obliterated, and the absurdity, injustice, and outrage inherent in the act of sale itself, and in the system of which that act was a central feature, were presented in stark relief.

From today's perspective, the daring manner of staging *Tom and Jerry* was one of the company's moments of triumph, particularly for Brown, who had succeeded in pulling the whole production together without Hewlett, his most talented actor. But for African New Yorkers in 1823, the event probably seemed more like a brief moment of respite in the company's inexorable slide towards bankruptcy and disintegration. Indeed, the performance of *Tom and Jerry*, with its numerous expensive scene changes and the unusual pressures it placed on the company, could well have assisted in this process. For one thing, the staging of this production usually elicited complaints about its "unchanging pictures of low vice, without a single redeeming quality of humanity or virtue"; moreover, its difference from the more usual theatrical fare often fomented ructions among the actors. As William Wood, for many years a theatrical manager, remembered, "the chief peculiarity of this piece" was "that the under characters are in effect the leading features, and almost entirely the objects of amusement or interest, and are thus rendered of dangerous importance." Since theater companies were overtly hierarchical enterprises, "placing the auxiliaries fully on the same footing as the principal performers, led to a total and most injurious change." Bit players "were at once invested with an unlimited power to make themselves conspicuous and to engross the largest share of applause," elevating them suddenly to a "false position" and creating unrealistic expectations that could not be met by their subsequent roles. Inevitably, according to Wood, "a neglect of order and propriety" amongst the actors "became painfully evident."[85] It would be surprising if the financial pressures on the African Company had not produced some tensions, and likely that Hewlett's total domination of all the previous productions had also engendered resentment and jealousy. For his part, Hewlett was hardly likely to have regarded the staging of *Tom and Jerry* with any degree of enthusiasm; at any rate, he was then engaged elsewhere.

A few days after the performance of *Tom & Jerry, or Life in New-*

York, a new playbill, posted up around town, announced that "The performers of the African Company have kindly united their services [a form of wording suggestive of disintegration] in order to contribute a Benefit to their Manager, Mr. Brown." "For the first time," Brown was throwing "himself on the liberality of a generous public," a ploy undoubtedly forced on him by financial necessity. Theatrical notices were notoriously obsequious, but there was a hint of desperation in the remainder of this one: "Mr. Brown trusts that his unrelinquished exertions to please, will be justly considered by the Gentlemen and Ladies of this City, as on them depends his future support, and they can declare whether he is 'To be—or not to be—That is the question?'"[86] For this occasion, Hewlett returned to act with the company for, as far as we know, the last time, reprising his role of King Shotaway in Brown's drama of Caribbean insurrection. Indeed, Hewlett was the only actor who could readily have played the part. Very early in July 1823, the company was still performing, though there is no record of what it was performing and whether Hewlett was in the cast. The inimitable Noah, in the *National Advocate*, gave a listing of the entertainments available on July 4, which proceeded through nine venues before concluding: "and last and least, the African Theater."[87]

Finally, then, Noah's hopes for Brown's theatrical enterprise were about to be realized. However much the benefit performance raised, it was too little, too late. On July 19, 1823, a William Brown filed for bankruptcy.[88] "William Brown" was not an uncommon name in New York and it is not certain that this was the man in question. What is certain is that from this time the black theatrical manager disappears from the record. In a little under four turbulent years, Brown had risen faster and further than most, but after the final curtain he must have seemed to whites a pushy black seeking to storm the bastion of a distinctly white theatrical world. From today's perspective, his fate, in a city struggling to sort out issues of racial etiquette in the wake of slavery's slow demise, looks almost preordained. But Brown's fall was some time coming, and he had left his mark on the metropolis.

The final productions of the full company highlighted some of its distinctive achievements: the staging of the first play written by an African American, for example, and the adaptation of *Tom and Jerry* to American circumstances and its consequent infusion with a distinctly antislavery tone. One of the viewers of these last performances was Elias Ball, eighteen-year-old scion of a South Carolinian slaveholding family. In a letter to home dated July 23, 1823, Ball wrote that the "Black gentry of New York have opened a Theater and tell fine stories about their brethren at the South in the Cotton and Rice fields." Perhaps the critical slant on the customs of his native state that had privileged him so much unsettled the young man. At any rate, the humor in the rest of his brief account sounds somewhat forced: "I wish that some of them were in Carolina [where] they would learn to play on the Hoeboy, which would be a useful accompaniment."[89] Ball would not have needed to search too far to find like-minded white New Yorkers, citizens who believed that a stint on the end of a hoe on a slave plantation would be of benefit to some of the city's more independently minded former slaves.

A surviving playbill, dated August 8, 1823, advertises an African Company performance of *Don Juan*, with *Obi; Or, 3 Finger'd Jack* as the afterpiece, on a Friday, and *Forty Thieves* on the following Monday. Hewlett is not listed in the cast and for the first time Brown's name is no longer on the poster.[90] Then there is silence until December 1823, when it seems that the company tried to restore its fortunes by touring. There is a suggestion that the black players performed in Albany and that they also tried their luck further afield in Providence, Rhode Island. A brief item in the

Providence Gazette noted that a "corps of black comedians from New York" applied to the city council for a license to perform but were turned down, so that "they were not permitted 'to strut their hour upon the stage.'" According to the *Gazette*, the company's spokesman "was a very good Othello without paint, [who] expressed much regret at his want of success; but finding that the council could not be softened into compliance with his fair speech, made a dignified and respectful exit."[91] Again the form of words used by the newspaper, replete as it is with puns and the inevitable references to Shakespeare, conveys something of the obstacles the African Company continually faced. On this occasion, Hewlett may have been the spokesman. Whether that was so or not, in a playbill for a performance at the Mercer Street Theater in January 1824 he was listed as the "Manager of the Theater," and was also stated to be the only performer on a quite extensive bill.[92] By this time, that is to say, James Hewlett had well and truly embarked on his solo career.

3 | SHAKESPEARE'S PROUD REPRESENTATIVE

Two prominent and public figures, both of them white, are inextricably entangled in black actor James Hewlett's story. The first, Mordecai Noah, newspaper editor, erstwhile playwright, and ubiquitous character-about-New York, was the source of much of the information relating to Hewlett's activities and those of other black actors in the 1820s, giving them much needed publicity at the time and also helping to shape the way in which they have been represented since. Although this prominent New York Jew was intrigued by Hewlett and had personal dealings with him throughout most of the 1820s, ultimately Noah's racist assumptions prevented his taking the black performer as seriously as he deserved. The second significant public figure in Hewlett's professional life was the English comedian Charles Mathews, whose dramatic success alerted Hewlett to the commercial and artistic potential of a solo career.

Although Mathews started out as an actor, his chief fame stemmed from his series of one-man shows, beginning in 1817. His "At Homes," as they were known, displayed Mathews's remarkable talents as storyteller, singer, and especially, mimic. Typically, an "At Home" saw Mathews undertaking a journey—to Paris, for example, during which he would encounter persons displaying a diverse range of accents, which he would then skillfully imitate. The performance would climax with a rapid-fire conversation (he called it his "monopologue") between several characters, each with a distinctive persona, each played by Mathews. But after five years, the constant pressure to create similarly novel entertainments led Mathews to travel to America in search of fresh material and in the expectation of making a lot more money than a season in London could bring. In August 1822, therefore, the forty-six year-old actor embarked for the United States, where he was to remain for almost nine months, touring extensively. In the event, his financial hopes were disappointed, but Mathews was feted everywhere he went and made a lasting impression on American theater.[1]

As well as fulfilling acting engagements, Mathews closely observed the idiosyncrasies of the persons he encountered, collecting the material he needed for his stage entertainments. His correspondence is full of commentary on accents that intrigued him and snatches of dialogue that caught his fancy. "I shall be rich in black fun," he wrote in late February 1823 to his friend James Smith. "I have studied their [African Americans'] broken English carefully." Mathews then included for Smith's amusement a lengthy rendition of a black Methodist preacher's sermon, a comic turn that he could hardly expect actually to perform because "I dare not touch upon a preacher."[2]

On March 25, 1824, several months after his return to England, Mathews opened at the English Opera House in *A Trip To America*, a production which displayed him at the very height of his powers. Early in the performance, Mathews depicted himself attending the "Niggers (or negroes) Theatre." *Sketches of Mr Mathews's Celebrated Trip to America*, a twenty-four-page pamphlet rushed out to take advantage of the show's popularity, contained one anonymous observer's summary of this soon-to-be famous scene:

Here he [Mathews] sees a black tragedian (the Kentucky Roscius) perform the character of Hamlet, and hears him deliver the soliloquy "To be or not to be, dat is him question, whether him nobler in de mind to suffer or lift up him arms against one sea of hubble bubble and by opossum (oppose'em) end em." At the word opossum the whole audience burst forth into one general cry of "opossum, opossum, opossum." On enquiring into the cause of this, Mr Mathews was informed, that "Opossum up a Gum Tree," was the national air, or sort of "God Save the King" of the negroes, and that being reminded of it by Hamlet's pronunciation of "oppose'em," there was no doubt but that they would have it sung. "The opossum," continued Mr M's informant, "is addicted to climbing up the gum tree, thinking no one can follow him; but the raccoon hides himself in the hollow of the tree, and as poor opossum goes up, pulls him down by the tail, and that's the plot—the cries of opossum, opossum, increasing, the sable tragedian comes forward, and addressing the audience, informs them that he will sing their favorite melody with him greatest pleasure, and accordingly sings it. The following is a translation from the original Indian:—

SONG
AIR—"Negro Melody."

Opossum up a Gum Tree,
    Tinkey none can follow:
Him damn quite mistaken,
    Racoon in de hollow.
Opossum him creep softly,
    Raccoon him lay mum,
Pull him by de long tail,
    Down opossum come.

Jinkum, jankum, beaugash,
   Twist 'em, twin'em, run:
Oh de poor opossum,
   Oh de sly raccoon.

Opossum up a Gum Tree,
   Raccoon pull him down
Tink him got him snugly,
   Oh de poor raccoon.
Raccoon in de hollow,
   Nigger down below,
Pull opossum's long tail,
   Raccoon let him go.
Jinkum, jankum, beaugash,
   Twist'em, twine'em, run,
Oh de cunning Nigger,
   Oh de poor raccoon.

Opossum up a gum tree,
   Raccoon in de hollow;
No beat cunning nigger,
   Though him cannot follow.
Nigger him so clever,
   Him so sly and rum;
Pull him by de long tail,
   Down opossum come.
Jinkum, jankum, beaugash,
   Twist'em, twine'em, run:
Oh de poor opossum,
   Oh de sly raccoon.

Finishing his song, this versatile genius retiring up the
stage comes strutting down with one arm a-kimbo, and the

other spouting out in front, just for all the world like a black teapot, bellowing out—"Now is de winter of our discontent made de glorious summer by de sun of New York." And on a person in the boxes telling him he should play Hamlet, and not Richard the Third, replies, "Yes, him know dat, but him tought of New York den, and could not help talking about it."[3]

Several slightly differing renditions of Mathews's performances of *A Trip to America* were printed, none of them doing adequate justice to a man "whose plastic power could model even old forms anew, and warm them into spirit and motion." Mathews's wife dismissed out of hand the published accounts of her husband's shows, claiming that "it is quite impossible that Mr Mathews's entire entertainments can ever appear in print," and adding in italics that *"They never have been published."* She certainly had a point. Summaries reported in the third person inevitably flatten out a performance, all shading and nuance being lost. As Mrs. Mathews justly observed, "The extraordinary links, which his genius supplied, holding the whole together, are wanting."[4] Yet these barebones summaries of Mathews's performance, along with the reviews of critics, are all we have. They were also all that his contemporary Americans had, until an aging and sick Mathews returned to the United States a decade later.

News of Mathews's *A Trip to America*'s opening began to filter back to the United States in late April 1824. The *New York American* published an English reviewer's account of the production, mentioning in the process the scene in which Mathews visited the "Negro Theatre." "The *Hamlet* of the chief black tragedian was too excellent not to be remembered," the writer declared, "and we are presented with an amusing recital of what Massa means for *To be, or not to be!*" The reviewer went on to note that the "strange alterations in the text are most ludicrous; but the play is soon interrupted and the exhibition concludes by Hamlet's singing a 'real Negro melody.'"[5] Cut to the quick by what he had thus learned of Mathews's London performance, and feeling betrayed by someone he regarded as a fellow actor and an acquaintance, if not a friend, an aggrieved Hewlett penned a lengthy response to the English comedian's portrayal of black actors. He also turned to Mordecai Noah for help, visiting him at the *National Advocate*'s office, where, as the editor put it, he "entreat[ed], as an act of justice, that we would publish his [Hewlett's] letter of expostulation to Mr. Matthews." Noah did so, introducing Hewlett's letter by reprinting the lines quoted above about *A Trip to America*, and noting that they had "given offence to Mr. Hewlet, the chief performer of the African Theatre." He then editorialized that the black actor's response contained "so much easy imprudence in it—such an air of familiarity and good nature, that if it serves only to extract a smile, it will do no harm."[6] But for all of his belittling comments, which rendered it unlikely that the *Advocate*'s readers would consider Hewlett's words with anything like an open mind, Noah did at least publish the letter, a letter which, the paper's editor must have realized, revealed its writer as anything but a stereotypical black, the usual prompt for white "smiles."

Hewlett began his rebuttal familiarly with "My Dear Mathews," before chiding the English actor because he, Hewlett, had "not been honoured with a line from you since you left our happy shores, your pockets lined with golden eagles and your face puckered with smiles." From the newspapers, Hewlett had learned that Mathews had been "reciting your travels in this country, doubtless with all that wit and gaiety, that whim and humour, that genius and gusto for which you are so eminently distinguished." As Mathews had amused Americans with his "inimitable hits at John Bull," it was only "fair" that he should reciprocate in "good old England." But, Hewlett continued "in your new entertainment, I lament to say, you have given me cause of complaint." It was clear from the program of Mathews's performance in London that the English actor had "ridiculed our *African Theatre in Mercer-street*, and burlesqued me with the rest of the negroe actors, as you are pleased to call us—mimicked our styles—imitated our dialects—laughed at our anomalies—and lampooned, O shame, even our complexions." "Was this," Hewlett asked reproachfully, "well for a brother actor?" Especially "chagrined at your sneers about the Negro Theater," Hewlett upbraided Mathews for his ungenerous behavior.

> Why these reflections on our color, my dear Matthews, so unworthy your genius and humanity, your justice and generosity? Our immortal bard says, (and he is *our* bard as well as yours, for we are all descendants of the Plantagenets, the white and red rose;) our bard Shakespeare makes sweet Desdemona say,
>   "I saw Othello's *visage* in his mind."
>   Now when you were ridiculing the "chief black tragedian," and burlesquing the "real negro melody," was it my "mind," or my "visage," which should have made an impression on you?

Having eloquently asserted the English dramatist's universal relevance, Hewlett proceeded to quote more of the playwright's words at Mathews (revealing in the process a somewhat roseate view of race relations in England).

> Again, my dear Matthews, our favorite bard makes Othello, certainly an interesting character, speak thus:
>   "*Haply*, for I am black."
>   That is as much as to say, 'tis happy that I am black. Here

then we see a General proud of his complexion. In our free and happy country, custom and a meridian sun hath made some distinctions and classifications in the order of society relative to the complexions, "'tis true, 'tis a pity, and pity 'tis, 'tis true;" but in England, where these anomalous distinctions are unknown, nay, where international marriage and blending of colors are sometimes seen, what warrant can you have for lampooning our complexion?

Mathews, Hewlett continued, had the black actor's "entire good wishes," but should remember "when you next ridicule the "tincture of the skin," not to forget "the texture of the mind." The letter was signed "affectionately and respectfully yours, HEWLETT."[7]

Hewlett's missive is a remarkable document, fully consonant with the expansive yet prickly mood of the newly free African New Yorkers. There are mistakes—"haply" means "by chance," not "happily," a misunderstanding which caused the self-educated Hewlett to confuse Shakespeare's intention—but for all that the letter is a lucid, powerfully argued retort to Mathews's depiction of black actors in *A Trip to America*, one in which, hardly incidentally, American society is found wanting for its lack of racial tolerance. Just as William Brown and the rest of the black theatrical troupe had refused to back down in the face of physical threats, Hewlett also refused to acquiesce meekly when he considered that he and his colleagues had been slighted by one of the biggest dramatic stars in the trans-Atlantic theatrical world.

What rankled with Hewlett, what gave his letter a brittle edge, was the recognition that Mathews had been, in a sense, his model and had encouraged Hewlett in his solo career. "At your earnest and pressing solicitation," Hewlett complained to Mathews, "I performed several of my best parts; was perfect to a letter; and although it was a hazardous experiment, I even attempted your celebrated Mail Coach, which met with your unqualified approbation." In all likelihood, this is a reference to Hewlett's first solo performance (as far as is known) at the American Theater on March 24, 1823. "At the particular solicitation of his friends," the playbill for that night announced, "Mr Hewlett will be At Home" for a last time before "his departure for the Southward."[8] This was the point at which Hewlett left the struggling company while it put on *Tom and Jerry*, although he did return for the performance of *Shotaway*, one of the troupe's last hurrahs. At that first solo outing, and at another in January 1824, by which time the black theater company had disintegrated, Hewlett's performances, at least according to the playbills, were completely dominated by material that originated with Mathews; even several of the songs he performed were "as sung by Matthews." Little wonder that news that Mathews had had London audiences in gales of laughter at his expense stung the black actor so sharply.

In the letter of protest to the *Advocate* of May 8, 1824, Hewlett had identified himself thus: "Chief performer at the African Theatre, Mercer-street, which will be opened one night only for my benefit" and "tailor and coat scourer, John street." Always keenly aware of the power of publicity, Hewlett took advantage of Noah's largesse in opening the pages of the *Advocate* to him to advertise both of the ways in which he made his living. Presumably, over the ensuing months, he ran his shop and possibly even gave another performance or two, although no record of any shows survives. In late September or early October 1824, he headed for London. A small item in the *National Advocate* announced that "Mr Hewlett chief tragedian of the African Theater, Mercer-street, has sailed for Liverpool, in one of the packets, for the purpose of having a hit at the metropolis." The actor intends to "give entertainments after the fashion of Matthews, and calculates to make a few sovereigns by the trip." Noah then added one final curious sentence to the story: "We hope he may not die like Rhio Rhio, king of the Sandwich Islands, as he is a very clever man for his complexion."[9] It was almost as though Noah wanted to acknowledge Hewlett's talents but could not resist the racial qualification to what should have been a straightforward statement, beside adding a strangely inept comparison between Hewlett's trip and that of a Hawaiian king, which had ended tragically.

Hewlett never lacked audacity. Not only did he, a black man, travel to Mathews's home turf in order to imitate him, but he also, apparently, sought a personal confrontation with the famous English performer. In a letter to his wife from Liverpool, dated January 1825, Mathews wrote that "Hewlet has been here, and gave an 'At Home.'" Hewlett had also gone "to London, as he said, to challenge me, for ridiculing him in a part he never played." Mathews had tried, without success, to "find any body who saw him," although Hewlett had "performed here [Liverpool] two or three nights."[10] Nothing further is known about Hewlett's trip, but the silence suggests that he neither managed to settle scores with Mathews nor made much money through stage appearances. By late January he was back in New York.

The year 1824, marked by the collapse of the African Theater and the psychologically scarring treatment he had received from Mathews, had not been a happy one for James Hewlett. If anything, 1825 would be more miserable, though most of it was spent at some remove from any theater. His new troubles began with losing a bet. Nine months after this misfortune, Hewlett began his testimony in the ensuing court case by stating that he had taken the job of steward on the vessel *John & Edward* because of a "wager." The lengthy voyage had turned into a nightmare, the details of which should rudely puncture any still lingering notions concerning the romance of early nineteenth-century shipboard life. Initially, the vessel had spent several months cruising the Caribbean, docking in Havana, "Campeachy" in Mexico, and "Laguira" in Venezuela, before heading across the Atlantic to Marseilles. Nothing is known about conditions on the *John & Edward* on this part of the voyage, but the 77 days from the middle of August when the ship left Marseilles until November 4, 1825, at which time the relieved crew and passengers disembarked in New York, were a near disaster. The captain, Jonathan M. Ropes, had sold a considerable portion of the ship's stores in Marseilles without bothering to detail anyone to check the quality of the food left on board. As the crew and passengers soon discovered, it turned out to be "not fit for hogs." There were only two passengers on board the *John & Edward*, Frederick Tregear, an Englishman, who sued the captain at the end of the voyage, and one Devereux, a somewhat unbalanced and overly patriotic American. Devereux had determined, spuriously as it turned out, that Tregear was "unfriendly" to American "institutions" and proceeded to make the Englishman's life a misery, continually abusing him and eventually driving him out of the cabin and onto the deck. Devereux tried to force Tregear into a shipboard duel, assaulted him "openly on deck" several times, and, indeed, minutes before they disembarked, broke his cane over his unfortunate victim's head. As soon as Tregear had recovered sufficiently to go ashore, he promptly filed suit against the captain, complaining that the conditions for the duration of the voyage were unconscionably bad, and that the master had not only failed in his duty to protect his passenger but had befriended Devereux, even seeming to encourage his outrageous behavior.

As steward, Hewlett was well aware of the condition of the provisions and of the long-running drama involving the two passengers. Testifying against a captain, which he subsequently did, was hardly the way to get ahead in the maritime industry, but Hewlett saw himself as only a marginal figure in it. Indeed, as the report of his testimony in the *New York Evening Post* shows, he began by stating that he was a "comedian," and although he had been "employed as a steward on board packets and other ships before he took to the stage," he had only ended up on the *John & Edward* because of the happenstance of a wager. In a matter-of-fact manner the black steward related that after 17 days at sea the bread and flour had become infested with weevils; after 30 days the beef and pork, previously "middling," had "smelt strong"; and 60 days out the "tea, sugar and potatoes ran out." As well, when the ship left Marseilles, it lacked salt, pepper, and candles. Most of Hewlett's testimony, however, concerned the way in which Devereux had violently and dangerously hounded Tregear while the unconcerned ship's captain merely looked on. Hewlett depicted Tregear as a "gentleman" who was "very amiable in his manners to all," but the overwhelming image he must have left with the court was of a wan Englishman, sitting by himself on deck, morosely picking the worms out of a piece of bread. As the *Evening Post* reported, "the witness [Hewlett] and the hands pitied his situation"; indeed, none of them had ever seen "a gentleman so used before." The court found for the plaintiff, and awarded the ill-treated English gentleman $60 damages.[11]

Hewlett's shipboard sojourn apparently confirmed his belief that his future lay on a stage rather than beneath deck, and the black actor quickly recommenced his career. But his run of illluck continued, and within a fortnight of testifying against his former captain, his name was in the New York papers again. Hewlett had advertised that he was to provide "a grand entertainment for one night only, prior to his return to London to fulfil his engagement at the Coburg." On the night of November 30, 1825, the ballroom in Herring Street, Greenwich, where the performance was to be held, was packed—indeed it "had never before been so crowded"—with a very large audience "consisting of the flash and blood of the city." But the crowd, which included quite a few who had gatecrashed to avoid the entrance fee of fifty cents, quickly became boisterous; several songs into the performance a couple of individuals began heckling, and before long an all-out brawl had erupted. The *New York Gazette and General Advertiser*'s man on the spot, still wedded to the argot of *Tom and Jerry*, reported that in the fight "peepers were closed, and vast quantities of claret uncorked." Eventually, the floor collapsed and the pugilists, a becostumed Hewlett, "Richmond, the base drum, fiddles, flutes, musicians and audience" plummeted some fifteen feet into the carpenter's shop in the cellar underneath. No one was seriously injured, but in their reporting of the event the newspapers were able to have some fun at the performer's expense.[12]

Though hardly auspicious, this event did mark the beginning of Hewlett's concerted effort to establish himself as a solo performer. Accustomed as we are today to a great variety of one-person shows, it is very easy to lose sight of the newness of what Hewlett was doing. In England, before Mathews became a fixture on the London stage, a few actors had made some sort of a living out of one-person entertainments, but the genre was virtually unknown across the Atlantic. The English comedian's solo performances in 1822 and 1823 were a revelation for American audiences. In a gushing review, the theater critic for *The Baltimore Patriot* declared: "If the experiment had not been fully tried, it would be considered incredible, that any one man, by the variety of his tones, the extent of his theatrical reading, the flexibility of his countenance, and the rich humour of his style and manner, could satisfy raised expectation, and keep his hearers either in a roar of applause, or in a state of tranquil pleasure."[13] Today, hardly anyone realizes that the American pioneer of the one-person show, the forebear of a host of entertainers ranging from Lenny Bruce through to Robin Williams, Anna Deavere Smith, and Richard Pryor, was James Hewlett.

In his early solo shows in 1823 and 1824, Hewlett had been virtually a Mathews clone, but his estrangement from the English entertainer and innate creativity led him to redefine the embryonic genre in more innovative ways. He still gave skits drawn from Mathews's repertoire, but they soon became only part of a performance that included singing and imitations of a variety of well-known actors. It also seems that at this time the ever-controversial Edmund Kean took the central place in Hewlett's pantheon of theatrical heroes. In the fall of 1825, the great English actor was in the midst of an American tour during which he encountered a good deal of hostility (having slighted a Boston audience some years previously). To the irritation of many present, African New Yorkers in the audience at Kean's November 14, 1825, performance at the Park Theater had loudly sided with the embattled English performer. It is difficult to believe that the drama-starved Hewlett, just disembarked from a seemingly interminable voyage across the Atlantic, was not among the blacks sitting in the third tier cheering the beleaguered star. In the event, the partisan support of the blacks had little effect; the constable read the riot act and Kean had to be smuggled out the back door. A contrite Kean had a notice printed in the *New York Evening Post* acknowledging that he had "committed an error" and promising to go to Boston "to apologize for my indiscretions." He also stated that, on his previous visit, "I was an ambitious man, and the proud representative of Shakespeare's heroes."[14] Within little more than a week of Kean's capitulation to American public opinion, Hewlett had handbills plastered all over town announcing that *he* was "Shakespeare's proud representative," a label which stuck and by which the black actor would still be known fifteen years later.[15] It was a catchy title, and an obviously provocative one for a black man to assume. It was also a description that suggests that the ambitious and prickly Hewlett venerated the unreconstructed Kean, the one who had as yet failed to apologize to the white Americans he had so annoyed.

In December 1825 Hewlett performed at the Military Garden in Brooklyn, and in early January 1826 he gave three performances in Philadelphia, at a venue simply called the School Room on South Fourth Street.[16] The most important consequence of the Philadelphia venture was that through it Hewlett met Frank Johnson, easily the best known African American musician in the years before the Civil War. Johnson (1792–1844) had probably been born on Martinique, but had migrated to Philadelphia in 1809, and by the 1820s was well known as the leader of a dance orchestra. According to one white writer in 1819, Johnson was "inventor-general of cotillions; to which add, a remarkable taste in distorting a sentimental, simple, and beautiful song into a reel, jig, or country-dance," a description which suggests that the black musician was infusing a white cultural form with an African American beat.[17] The bill for Hewlett's third performance announced that "Mr. Johnson's Band have kindly volunteered their services for this evening." The favor was to be returned a few days later; *Poulson's American Daily Advertiser* carried a notice in which "Mr. Francis Johnson respectfully informs the public that Mr. Hewlett has kindly volunteered his services for the benefit of his New Band." The proposed program was that Johnson would accompany Hewlett's singing, that Hewlett would imitate several famous actors, and that Johnson would play variations on the kent bugle. For some unknown reason, however, the concert did not take place.[18]

In early February Hewlett returned to the Military Garden in

Brooklyn, and later that month he performed at the Grove Hotel in Spruce Street, New York. There are records of performances at the Grove Hotel every month or so for the rest of the year.[19] As well, he may have visited Boston in April, and probably went to Saratoga Springs in August 1826, this last engagement having been secured by Frank Johnson. For years the well-connected bandleader had played each summer at such fashionable resorts as Saratoga Springs in New York, Cape May in New Jersey, and White Sulphur Springs in Virginia. A notice in the *New-York National Advocate* in April 1826 had advertised that "Mr. Hewlett will appear, for the benefit of Mr. F. Johnson, at Saratoga Springs, 14th of August, for services shown Mr. Hewlett, by Mr. Johnson at Philadelphia." This event was probably a replacement for that fourth show in Philadelphia.[20] Early in November 1826, Hewlett was performing in Albany.[21] The following year he changed his New York venue, using the Military Hall in Duane Street for shows in January and then again in December.[22] In the intervening months he continued to tour, although only a few traces of his activities have surfaced. In May 1827, he gave an appearance or two in York, Pennsylvania, where he occupied a temporary stage in the courthouse.[23] Rather more surprisingly, in March 1827 he was performing in Alexandria—this is the only documented appearance of Hewlett in the South of which I am aware.[24]

Undoubtedly there were other performances in this period—it seems likely that for two years from late 1825, Hewlett extensively toured the Northeast and possibly even the South—but detailing these is of little moment. Much more important is the task of attempting to recapture something of Hewlett the performer, to breathe life into this bare-bones itinerary of his solo career, and to do so from sources that are fragmentary and frequently opaque.

At some time in 1824, a pamphlet containing a brief account of a performance of "Hewlett at Home" was published under the name of Simon Snipe, the same pseudonym as that used by the writer of the scurrilous description of the African Theater in which the clarinet playing was compared to a "quaking duck or a yelping dog." This account is nowhere near as offensive as the earlier one had been, but, ironically, it is also nowhere near as detailed or sharp in its observations of black performance, the author being more caught up in his own attempts at humor. Apart from a supposedly droll account of Hewlett's swordplay with Bates, a performer from the African Theater who occasionally played Hewlett's foil in some earlier skits, and a description of Hewlett's singing as being "a tarnal sight better than some of the white folks there," Snipe's pamphlet conveys little sense of Hewlett's stage presence or dramatic skills.[25]

In late December 1825, when Hewlett was shucking off the influence of Mathews and developing his own act, the *Brooklyn Star* printed an extremely favorable review of a performance by Hewlett earlier in the week at a venue in Brooklyn (the *National Advocate* reprinted it a few days later). After recounting a few bare details of Hewlett's early life, the writer suggested that the Rockaway-born black had "a natural talent for theatrical performances, and an excellent voice withal." Not only were Hewlett's songs "excellent, and his style, taste, voice and action such as would have done credit to any stage," but "his imitations of Kean, Matthews, Philips and others were recognized as correct, and evincing a nice discrimination and peculiar tact on his part," all of which should "recommend him to every lover of pure acting." Hewlett had "raised himself by the force of innate genius" and should be encouraged in his efforts. "His color is a serious impediment," the reviewer admitted; indeed, if it were not for his color, "he might rival some of the proudest who now tread our boards."[26]

A few months later in April 1826, "A Friend to Merit" wrote

glowingly of Hewlett in a brief notice for the *New York American.* "Admirers of talent," he declared, "will have another opportunity of witnessing one of the most astonishing phenomenas of the age: a young man, who notwithstanding the thousand obstacles which the circumstance of complexion must have thrown in the way of improvement, has, by the mere dint of natural genius and self-strengthened assiduity, risen to successful competition with some of the first actors of the day." Those who had seen his imitations "must have been convinced, by the accuracy and tact of his performance, that they were listening to no common individual." Indeed, when "the many difficulties he has had to encounter, the few opportunities for improvement, the unjust prejudices his complexion has produced" were considered, New Yorkers had to "acknowledge that his claims to patronage are neither few nor inconsiderable."[27]

Favorable comments like these, as well as the duration of Hewlett's career, do suggest that he was unusually talented. But for all their enthusiasm, these writers did not go much beyond recognizing the obstacles the black actor had had to overcome. Their accounts are flat, slighting the actor's art by focusing on the color of his skin. For me, at least, a far more revealing depiction of Hewlett on stage was contained in a couple of lines printed under the head of "Theatrical" in the *National Advocate* in November 1826: "Hewlett is at Albany. In one evening he played in forty-nine tragedies and seventeen comedies, besides singing snatches of more than a hundred songs. So it is said."[28] Exaggerated and dismissively sarcastic, to be sure, this description, particularly when combined with a glance at any of James Hewlett's surviving programs, bursting at the seams with songs and sketches, suggests something of the speed and energy of the black actor's performance style, and of the timing and skill that were deployed in holding it all together. Its tone—slightly bewildered, slightly askance—also hints at the originality and freshness of Hewlett's art, precisely the spark that was so exciting to the new audience he was attracting, and that helps to stake his claim to being the progenitor of a whole range of twentieth-century solo performers, from vaudeville entertainers to stand-up comedians.

In retrospect, the most striking aspect of Hewlett's theatrical endeavors was the way in which he was free to innovate, or to introduce and rework new developments. At least partly, this was because of his peculiar status as a black performer in a white milieu. He was certainly keenly aware of whatever was happening on other stages about town. The same had been true of the African Company. After all, *Tom and Jerry*'s vision of contemporary urban life, let alone the spectacle of black actors incorporating apparently extraneous songs into performances of Shakespeare, were at some remove from the carefully structured and heroic drama of the waning, if tenacious, neoclassical tradition. In Hewlett's case, his entire act depended on the changes that were taking place in the theater by the emergence of the "star system."

The beginnings of the star system, the move away from performances entirely put on by local companies toward performances by an actor of renown supported by locals in the lesser roles, is commonly traced to the arrival of George Frederick Cooke in New York in 1810. William Dunlap, a playwright and later a historian of American theater, claimed that Cooke's coming "caused a greater sensation than the arrival of any individual not connected with the political welfare of the country." Later performers did not receive quite so enthusiastic a response, but Cooke was at the head of a long procession of famous English actors who came to America, often in their declining years, in search of applause and money. Not only did Hewlett commence his theatrical education with Cooke's American tour (according to the *Brooklyn Star*, he was a servant to both Cooke and Thomas Cooper), but his solo career depended upon a continual stream of fresh material he obtained by observing the visiting "stars." Although Hewlett certainly did also imitate local actors, there can be little doubt that he was principally known for his renditions of Mathews, Kean, Cooper, and Macready, or that it was this part of his act that brought his audience back for more.[29]

Perhaps the best example of how Hewlett exploited the current stage sensations (his clever mimicry provides a litmus test for what was exciting local audiences) was the way in which he expanded the musical component of his show to incorporate opera. During November 1825, the month in which Hewlett returned from his lengthy shipboard sojourn, Kean was not the only international star to be treading the boards of the Park Theater—the Garcias and their opera company also gave their first American performance at this time. Originally from Spain, fifty-year-old Manuel Garcia, together with his wife and children, had forged a successful career singing opera in Paris, Naples, London, and elsewhere in Europe. Concerned to see (away from the spotlight of Europe) whether his two eldest children had the makings of stage performers, and attracted by the prospect of making a lot of money, Garcia made the novel and intrepid decision to take his company to America. On November 29, 1825, the night before the floor fell out from underneath Hewlett at the ballroom in Greenwich, the Garcias performed Rossini's *The Barber of Seville* at the Park Theater, in front of an audience of nearly two thousand people. Although English opera had been staged occasionally in America before, this was the beginning of Italian opera in the new nation. Over the ensuing nine months, the company gave seventy-nine performances of nine different operas in New York City, grossing $56,685 in box office receipts. Many New Yorkers must have found watching *Don Giovanni* or *Il Barbiere*, staged in Italian, a strange experience. Not merely the language of the opera, but the very idea of a drama or comedy conveyed in a musical form was novel for many spectators, and some members of New York society were prepared to mystify it even further. One local wrote to a newspaper asking how they should dress for the opera "in the European manner," and what was "the correct etiquette during performances." Right from the start there was an element of privileged display associated with operatic events, but the medium proved to be too popular with ordinary Americans for such motives to predominate. Not for some time would opera be sacralized as the preserve of the cultural elite.[30]

Part of the reason for opera's popularity with ordinary Americans was the role played by such cultural mediators as Hewlett. The Garcias performed only in New York, forcing some opera lovers in the Northeast to travel considerable distances to see them, but within weeks of their debut at the Park, Hewlett was offering "Imitations of the Italian Opera Troop" to Philadelphians willing to come to his show. Back in New York in late March 1826, Hewlett performed imitations of "Signior Garcia" in scenes from the *Barber of Seville* and *Otello*. Ten days later he was imitating Garcia in *Tancredi* and in the last scene of *Otello*. As well, Hewlett gave his own interpretation of the role of the operatic Otello, "in which character he will sing the favourite Melodies of Deh Calmo Oh Ciel."[31] Usually Hewlett only performed as himself in scenes from *Richard III*, so that this departure from his routine may well hint at the black actor's frustrated ambitions; if only in the operatic version, and then for just a few minutes, James Hewlett slipped into the most powerful role created for a performer of his color.

It was not only in opera that Hewlett functioned as a cultural middleman; his performances raised his audiences' awareness of theatrical developments throughout the North Atlantic world. In the 1820s Hewlett traveled extensively, certainly more so than most New Yorkers, and wherever he happened to be, the black mimic made sure he spent his free evenings observing other actors and singers. Everything was grist for his mill. While he was in Philadelphia in January 1826, he performed "imitations of all the performers at the Park Theater," and, on his return to New York, his first performance, across the East River in Brooklyn, opened with "imitations of *Wood*, *Warren*, and *Jefferson* of the Philadelphia Theater."[32] The black actor had learned well from Charles Mathews, his former hero, that travel presented numerous opportunities for collecting material that could be incorporated into his productions.

Hewlett gathered impressions from all his trips, abroad as well as to other American cities. He would perform scenes in the manner of Macready and the lesser known John Vandenhoff well in advance of these actors' arrival in America. Given the precision with which Hewlett delineated the characteristics and mannerisms of his fellow actors, he must have observed them at several of their performances. In the case of Macready and Vandenhoff, this observation presumably occurred in London or elsewhere in England. Even Hewlett's miserable nine months on board the *John & Edward* provided him with material. While the ship was in Marseilles in early August 1825, where the captain was busily trying to make extra money by selling off the supplies, Hewlett traveled to nearby Toulon to take in the local theatrical troupe. Five months later, in the second week of 1826, he was in Philadelphia performing "imitations of the principal Performers at Toulon, in France." Hewlett's version of French theater was part of his act in New York for a while; there the troupe he was imitating was described as being from the "Theatre Royal, at Toulon, in France."[33]

Yet for all his cosmopolitan sophistication, clearly on display every time he took to a stage, no one, least of all James Hewlett himself, was ever able to forget that he was black. Even "A Friend to Merit" and the writer in the *Brooklyn Star*, both of whom intended to laud Hewlett, soon slipped back into detailing how the black actor had overcome the obstacles confronting him because of his "complexion," suggesting that he should be encouraged on this count.[34] Almost invariably in his own advertising Hewlett made it clear that he was the "Coloured Comedian," possibly in an attempt to discourage those who would find this fact intolerable.

Every facet of Hewlett's theatrical life must have been made more difficult by his race. The indignities and often enough the dangers confronted by black entertainers and musicians traveling in twentieth-century America are now well known. There is little reason to think that finding accommodation or a meal in a strange place would have been any easier for Hewlett in the 1820s. This after all was the time when the North was inventing the system of Jim Crow, and it is not difficult to imagine what sort of mean lodgings the touring performer must have been forced to accept when in Boston, Philadelphia, or Albany, let alone York, Pennsylvania, or whenever he ventured into the South. Hewlett, along with Frank Johnson and his band, were pioneers who lacked even the extensive word-of-mouth knowledge that would allow later performers to get by in an unforgiving environment. The historical record of the early nineteenth century does not clarify these difficulties, but other problems are more clearly visible. For example, Hewlett seldom managed to perform in an actual theater, mostly treading the boards of a temporary stage set up in a hotel in New York, a school hall in Philadelphia, or a court house in York. The inappropriateness of some of these venues for the size of crowd Hewlett could attract was spectacularly demonstrated by the collapse of the floor of the ballroom in Greenwich Village, halfway through the show.[35] As a black man, Hewlett held a marginal position both in a theatrical establishment that was, apart from him, entirely white, and in a northern society that despite having ended slavery, could not be said to welcome the presence of free African Americans in its midst. For him, the simplest of things must often have been a challenge.

Hewlett's act was surely novel, but that alone was not enough to generate the publicity needed to attract a continuing stream of paying patrons and provide steady work. Decades later, after the Civil War, Charles Barney Hicks, another pioneering black theatrical entrepreneur who ran one of the first minstrel companies composed of African Americans, would achieve considerable renown for the ingenious way he publicized his troupe's appearances. He was acknowledged as one of the best advance men in the business.[36] Operating in the rather different circumstances of the 1820s, Hewlett never received similar recognition for his originality in this area, but he too developed an impressive repertoire of techniques for drawing attention to his shows. Financial survival depended on such efforts. Like Hicks, Hewlett had to entice white audiences to put their money down to watch blacks perform, and to get them to do this in the face of strong social prejudice against black achievement in any realm.

Few places can have been as hard for Hewlett to work as Saratoga, New York, then just beginning to establish its reputation as a ritzy resort town that attracted the fashionable from as far afield as the South. But where other acts distributed paper fliers around the foyers of the hotels, Hewlett, James McCune Smith remembered, distinguished himself by ensuring that his announcements were "thickly scattered around," and, even more noticeably, by having them "tastily printed on white satin." Smith recalled a few lines from one of these satin handbills:

JAMES HEWLETT

Vocalist, and Shakespeare's proud

Representative

Will give an entertainment

IN SINGING AND ACTING

In the Large Room of the United States Hotel.[37]

Satin handbills were only one of Hewlett's innovative marketing devices. In early December 1827, his engagement at the Military Hall in New York was promoted in a daringly different fashion. Tickets were to be sold by subscription, "and no gentleman [was] to be admitted in the room, without having his name on the subscription list." Intending patrons had to turn up earlier in the week and add their name to the list. Probably this was an attempt to exclude the unruly elements who often disrupted his shows. Initially, he claimed that "the performance is to be to a select company," but a few days later he appended an extra paragraph to the notice running in the *New-York Enquirer*, stating that he was going to "occupy both rooms in the Hall, each large enough to hold six hundred persons."[38] Sales must have been going well, and he wished to reassure fans that the hall could easily accommodate over a thousand patrons.

Yet again this performance was billed as a final one before his departure for England "to fulfill his engagement there." On this occasion, however, Hewlett intended "as a memorial of his gratitude to his audience, to present each gentleman with a correct engraving of himself in the character of Richard the Third with the appropriate costume." This is almost certainly the source of the only known depiction of Hewlett. It is a striking image. In fact, Hewlett is playing not Richard III but Edmund Kean playing Richard III, and, undoubtedly at the black actor's behest, the artist has captured him as he declaims "Off with his head[,] so much for Buckingham. I am myself alone." Part of the art of mimicry was the ability to reduce a subject to an easily recognizable essence, and Hewlett was not the only New Yorker to consider this to be one of Kean's defining stage moments. Seven years previously, in November 1820, after Kean's first New York performance, the theater critic for the *New York Evening Post* had singled out Kean's delivery of precisely these lines as producing an "extraordinary fine effect." Indeed, the "bitter tone of malignant exultation" with which he uttered "so much for Buckingham" could "only be conceived by those who heard, saw and felt it."[39]

It was not merely in his innovative use of the giveaway gimmick that Hewlett brings to mind a modern advertising executive; he also had a copywriter's skill at coming up with pithy slogans. Not only was Hewlett "Shakespeare's proud representative," but he was also the "firm representative of Shakespeare's Hero of Mr. Kean" and even on occasion, and rather more grandiloquently, "Shakespeare's proud representative, of both hemispheres." He also variously billed himself in Philadelphia as the "Philadelphia, New York, and London Coloured Comedian," in New York as the "New York and London Coloured Comedian," and in York, Pennsylvania, perhaps playing to parochial sensibilities determined not to be swayed by what went on in the local metropolises, as the "Coloured Comedian from London."[40] In December 1827, after his notice announcing a performance at the Military Hall had run for one day in the *New-York Enquirer*, Hewlett added the caption "We rise by Merit" to later advertisements, a common enough reference to the developing egalitarian ethos of the new nation, but one that assumed a certain pointedness when an African New Yorker claimed that he too fell under its rubric. The black actor lost few opportunities to advance his name before the paying public. It may even be that the laudatory notice in the *New York American*, signed by "A Friend to Merit," was written by Hewlett himself.[41]

Also important in this regard was Hewlett's unusual relationship with the influential New York editor, Mordecai Noah. In a moment of self-reflection in September 1827, Noah claimed in his new newspaper, the *New-York Enquirer*, that he had "paid more attention to theatricals than most of our contemporaries." This was a fair, if uncharacteristically understated, claim: almost invariably, whichever newspaper Noah happened to be working for contained the most interesting coverage of theatrical activities in New York. The editor, unusually for the time, acknowledged the economic importance of the theater, declaring that acting was a "profession which in one way or other gives subsistence to an immense number of individuals." But for Noah, an inveterate lover of the stage who more often than not finished his day by attending some performance or other, this was only a part of theater's significance: "Of all amusements they [dramatic productions] are the most intellectual, appealing to each variety of taste, and gratifying each order in society." Since three or four thousand patrons attended the theater every night—"people made up of delegations from all ranks and pursuits"—it was "a matter of some importance to a public journalist, that his columns should contain some notice of such institutions."[42]

Yet for all the democratic promise of such claims, it was only with the greatest difficulty that Noah could bring himself to acknowledge the activities of black actors. He ran their advertisements and wrote about them more often than did anyone else, but was incapable of curbing an unpleasant sarcasm whenever he did so. In late March 1826, he reported, "Mr Hewlett, the colored Comedian, called upon us, respectfully, to know, whether, in addition to publishing his play bill, as an advertisement, we would notice his performance at the Spruce-street Theater, this evening." Noah had accepted the advertisement, but "positively refused" the extra request, suggesting that Hewlett should go to the *American* or the *Commercial Advertiser* instead. A few months later, in January 1827, by which time Noah was at the *New-York Enquirer,* he published a brief notice stating that Hewlett had "requested an audience yesterday to take leave on his departure for England in the next packet." The black actor "reminded us," the journalist wrote, "that he makes his valedictory speech and bow to his friends this evening at Dooly's, in a great variety of Entertainments, and requested the usual announcement in the Court Calendar." But in the final months before the ending of slavery on July 4, 1827, Noah could not just leave it at that. He had to add that "Hewlett is patronized by the Manumission Society, who consider him a clever fellow altogether," and that "it is rumored" that the editor of the *Commercial Advertiser*, obviously of a rather more liberal hue than his rival, "has bespoke a box, and there is no doubt that all the cognoscenti and gymnastics will be present."[43]

These conversations tantalize. When Hewlett sat down in Noah's office, how did Noah treat him? Was the white editor as insufferable in person as he was when discussing blacks in print, or did the venom only rise later when he sat at his desk, pen in hand? And what did Hewlett make of these exchanges? Hewlett needed Noah, or someone like him, to make best use of the very limited amount of money he could spend on advertising. Perhaps he endured Noah's condescension as a necessary, albeit unpleasant, aspect of making a living as a black performer in New York, or perhaps, in his guise as the trickster Richard III, the black actor even enjoyed bantering with and manipulating the city's most prominent Jew. Of course we shall never know, but perhaps Hewlett had picked his mark carefully and had the measure of the man in a way that was beyond the powerful editor's comprehension. It could be that, in terms of the psychic damage accruing from their dealings, the black entrepreneur gave as good as he got.

Whatever the final damage to Hewlett's sense of himself may have been, his cultivation of Noah, combined with his skill as a performer, succeeded in making him one of the two best-known blacks in New York in the 1820s and early 1830s. As with the hotelier Cato Alexander, his only rival for this title, Hewlett had achieved name recognition: "Cato's" or "Hewlett" could merely be mentioned in the newspapers, and doubtless in conversation as well, without any need of further explanation. In November 1826, when the writer Mrs. Royall claimed that "New York is generous to a fault, but they do not patronise genius," Noah took it upon himself to respond in the pages of the *New-York Enquirer*. "What! not patronize genius? . . . Is not Mr. Hewlet patronized? Has not the American newspaper a great circulation?" Sarcastically, he then went on to list the anaconda, the large black walnut tree at the Museum, and the Mount Pitt Circus as other well-patronized sites of New York genius. One of the nastier of New York's Bobalition broadsides, dating from 1827 (not coincidentally) and entitled "De Grandest Bobalition," lampooned black preparations for the great event of that year. (These broadsides were scurrilous accounts of black life usually centered on freedom celebrations and rendered in a fake black dialect.) The report of the meeting, supposedly penned by Ourang Outang, the president, included a list of made-up toasts and added "Arter dis las toas dere vas unibersal plaus, an broder Hewlet sing dis song in he bes style." Almost certainly, Hewlett was the only African American to achieve the dubious distinction of being featured, under his own name, in a Bobalition poster. Undoubtedly, however, his name was known in other northeastern cities and quite possibly even further afield. As late as 1838, when the New Orleans Third Municipality gave permission to a "free man of color" to open a theater, the *New Orleans Times-Picayune* suggested that it would be appropriate "to send for Hewlett, the colored tragedian, and open with 'Othello, or the Jealous Nigger.'"[44] To be sure, the occasions on which his name was raised were not meant to be flattering, but in the context of Hewlett's pioneering venture into solo performance, there was no such thing as bad publicity. Had he not achieved "name recognition" among New York's theater-going whites, Hewlett could never have attracted almost one thousand paying patrons to the Military Hall.

Discovering what other African New Yorkers thought of Hewlett's performances is, alas, impossible. Only two faint black voices comment on the black actor. According to the *Spectator*, during the fiasco of Edmund Kean's performance of *Richard III* at the Park Theater in November 1825, the black cheerleader orchestrating the chanting for the beleaguered English star bellowed out, "He debbleish sight better play den Hulet." What was quite surprising about this shouted comment was that it was delivered only days after Hewlett's return to New York following his nine-month absence on the *John & Edward*. The second is a reference of July 1828 in *Freedom's Journal*, the nation's first black newspaper, that is almost Delphic in its opacity: "Editors are pretty saucy beings, and we advise Mr. James H. Hewlett, Comedian &c. &c. &c. to meddle but little with them."[45] Fragmentary and inconclusive though these references are, their tenor probably catches something of Hewlett's relations with at least some other African New Yorkers. The actor was a mulatto, a performer capable of attracting a white audience, and nothing if not prickly: it would not be surprising to find that he had irritated some of his black contemporaries.

Regardless of what other African New Yorkers may have thought about Hewlett, the actor himself was well aware both of his color and of the way blacks were treated in America in general and New York in particular. His open letter to Mathews in May 1824, upbraiding the English actor for ridiculing his skin color and ignoring the "texture of the mind," while also lamenting the "distinctions and classifications" based on complexion that were the rule in America, had made the black performer's views public in quite striking fashion. Even more remarkable was an incident that occurred some twenty months later, which prompted Hewlett to convey his opinions personally to several hundred New Yorkers.

In February 1826, Hewlett gave a benefit performance at a venue in Spruce Street, New York, supposedly one of his last appearances prior to his departure from the city. Reporting for the *New York National Advocate*, Noah, displaying all his customary enthusiasm toward the black actor, wrote that "he gave imitations in tolerable style, of all the popular singers and actors of the age." The audience, however, was rather less tepid, and at the end of the performance demanded that Hewlett take a *"call,"* that is, that he should step out in front of the curtain to acknowledge the applause. The black actor, "in obedience to the public voice," came forward, reluctantly, he claimed, and made a short speech. He told the public that "he was about fulfilling an engagement in London, and therefore would take a respectful leave of New-York," but then, in mid-stride, he slipped into black dialect, adding that as "de Atlantic Ocean would sipparate him from his 'merican bredren, he would soon be in dat country vere dey had no 'stinction of color." The 1820s were precisely the period in which the print convention of black dialect became cemented as a way of marking off newly freed blacks as separate and inferior. That convention was associated with the new forms of discrimination and physical segregation that white New Yorkers introduced in response to black freedom. Not only had Hewlett spoken this dialect back to his audience, but he had also used it to praise England, the enemy of the Revolution and the War of 1812, and the focus of an intense nationalist disdain, as being a place where distinctions of color did not exist. Regardless of the accuracy of the claim, it was meant to throw white New Yorkers' racial prejudices back in their faces.

It was certainly an extraordinary outburst. Although this talented African American actor had put on the mask of "black dialect," the tone of what he said could hardly have been construed as anything but sharply critical. What happened when Hewlett finished speaking is not exactly clear. On February 18, 1826, Noah claimed that the *call* "would have run into a riot had it not been for a vigilant police." But two days later the *Advocate* recanted, stating that it was in error in claiming "that the Police was called upon to prevent a riot" and, furthermore, that "we are assured that the company who attended to witness the entertainments was of a respectable character, and that the strictest order prevailed." The correction then went on, curiously, to note that the Grove Hotel was "kept by Mr. Wauchope, whom we have long known as a worthy and industrious printer."[46] Perhaps the audience did meekly listen to a black man pointing out their shortcomings and then quietly filed out into the night. It seems more likely, however, that Hewlett's speech prompted a vociferous response and not a few threats of violence. After all, Noah, the author of the first report, had been present at James Hewlett's supposed farewell performance and would hardly have got things that far wrong.

In retrospect, the two-year period following James Hewlett's return from sea in November 1825 marked the pinnacle of the black actor's solo career. Not only did Hewlett tour extensively through the towns and cities of the Northeast during this time (and even, on at least one occasion, venture into the South), but he also performed regularly in New York City, establishing himself as the best-known African New Yorker living and working in the metropolis. For all of his pioneering panache, however, there was something unsatisfyingly transitory about the nature of Hewlett's success, and he must have been aware of it. Unfortunately, we have no direct testimony from Hewlett regarding this most interesting period in his professional life, but the fragmentary record of his career that does survive suggests a restless striving to attain a more secure footing in the theatrical world, an effort that would end in failure.

It was no doubt galling to Hewlett that these were also the years in which another African New Yorker actor managed to achieve just such a footing, not in America but in England. Ira Aldridge, almost a generation younger than Hewlett, was born in New York in 1807. His father, Daniel Aldridge, a straw vendor and "strict member of Old Zion," a black church, made sure that the young boy attended the African Free School. He did very well there and won prizes for declamation. Daniel Aldridge wanted his son to enter the church, but, to his father's intense disappointment, the only revelation that young Ira Aldridge experienced occurred not in the House of God but in a theater. Aldridge's interest in "theatrical representations" had been piqued at school, and at some early stage he decided to attend a performance at the Park Theater. It was, as he later recalled, a vivid experience: he had been "bewildered, amazed, dazzled, fascinated, by what to him was splendour beyond all that his mind had imagined."[47] There and then he determined that he would be an actor. For all of its air of self-dramatization, Aldridge's account of his conversion to the theater rings true; something similar had probably occurred to Hewlett a few years earlier, when he first attended a play. What was extraordinary was not so much the impact that the stage had on the two black youths, but that they should have conceived of the idea of taking up acting as a profession. Partly, this may have been the naïvete of youth, but the decision also reflected the new mood of optimism among African New Yorkers as the hated institution of slavery lurched toward its inevitable demise.

Both Hewlett and Aldridge loved the theater passionately, and both possessed a steely determination to succeed as actors in spite of the enormous obstacle to their ambitions that white racism posed. But that was about the end of the similarities between the two men. Aldridge had been well educated at the African Free School; in his memoir he claimed that, after his arrival in England as an eighteen-year-old in 1825, he had attended Glasgow University for a year and a half. Studying under a Professor Sandford, "he obtained several premiums and the medal for Latin composition." Aldridge's biographers Herbert Marshall and Mildred Stock were prepared to accept the fact of his attendance, even though they could uncover no evidence of it from the university itself. Hewlett, probably older by about fifteen years, never had such opportunities, having to rely instead on his wits and verbal dexterity, features honed by his years at sea and on the streets of New York.[48] Martin Delany, the black activist and writer who had met Hewlett in 1836, recollected sixteen years later that he "was not well educated, and consequently, labored under considerable inconvenience in reading, frequently making grammatical blunders." Hewlett certainly impressed Delany as "a great delineator of character" who "possessed great intellectual powers," his success depending "more upon that, than his accuracy in reading," but no one would mistake Hewlett for the much smoother Aldridge.[49] While Aldridge had been shaped by just about the best education whites made available to an African American, Hewlett was more a product of black New York, displaying both the strengths and weaknesses of his origins.

According to the *Memoir and Theatrical Career of Ira Aldridge*, Aldridge was a member of the African Company and made his debut in the role of Rolla in August von Kotzebue's *Pizarro*. No surviving contemporary playbill, newspaper advertisement, or scrap of paper confirms these assertions; the only known link between the actor and the company (and it was only discovered in the last few years) is that Aldridge was beaten up by the brother of one of the white thugs who sacked the theater in August 1822.[50] Aldridge may well have acted with the African Company, indeed he probably did, but it would have been at a time when the company was disintegrating. If Aldridge and his promoters chose to embellish his minor role in the black company just as he embarked on his stage career in London, the reason why is not hard to work out.

Thanks to the enormous success of Charles Mathews's *Trip to America*, the only American stage the English theater-going audience may have known anything about was the one Mathews had depicted in his skit about the black "Roscius" at the "Niggers (or negroes) Theatre." Though other black actors had appeared very occasionally on the English stage, employing Aldridge was a novelty and a risky one at that. Hence the theater tried to capitalize on the American actor's association with Mathews's great hit, no matter how tenuous or fictitious.

Few aspects of Aldridge's early performances in London could have afforded Hewlett much pleasure. The playbills for his debut at the Coburg on October 10, 1825, advertised it as "the first instance in which one of that Complexion has displayed a striking degree of Histrionic Talent, and which has secured him the rapturous Approbation of an enlightened Public on the other side of the Atlantic." To make such a claim was, at best, to dismiss Hewlett's stage performances as second-rate. Moreover, Aldridge began taking over events in Hewlett's career and claiming them for his own. He was being billed as the "The Celebrated Tragedian of Colour from the African Theatre, New York," a description that could only, in fairness, have referred to Hewlett and the rendition of his acting given by Charles Mathews.[51]

After a few weeks, Aldridge dropped all direct references to the African Company in playbills advertising his performances, but years later he was still capitalizing on, indeed encouraging, the English theater-going public's tendency to associate him with

Mathews. The memoir of Aldridge contains an extract of a set speech that the black actor gave at public dinners, in which he claimed that "Mr. Mathews paid a visit to the theatre on one of the evenings of my performance, and this occurrence he has made the vehicle for one of the most amusing anecdotes in his well known 'Trip to America.'" This, of course, was simply not true. But if Aldridge coveted the fame attaching to the character on whom Mathews had based his comic skit, he eschewed all responsibility for the details of that characterization, attributing them to Mathews's art. The black actor pointed out that he had never played Hamlet and that the English comedian had "embellished the whole circumstance with a great many fictitious variations," generously allowing that changes such as these were "pardonable enough in such a work as Mr. Mathews's."[52] The audacity of Aldridge's theft of Hewlett's past is breathtaking. He even incorporated his fictitious version of events into his act, often referring to his role in inspiring one of Mathews's "most whimsical hits," and singing "(in Character) the Celebrated Negro Melody of OPOSSUM UP A GUM TREE."[53] In an 1860 letter to James McCune Smith, then preparing an article about him, Aldridge drew attention to certain published inaccuracies concerning his career, protesting that those guilty of these inaccuracies "confuse me with poor Jim Hewlett."[54] In its most generous interpretation, this claim was disingenuous. Possibly by this time, more than a decade after Hewlett's death, Aldridge even believed his own stories.

What Hewlett made of Aldridge's actions is not known, though he can hardly have been happy about them. News of Aldridge's performances in London in early October 1825 would have begun to filter through to New York in November, the month in which Hewlett was preparing to recommence his solo career. There is, perhaps, one indication of Hewlett's displeasure with Aldridge.

For the first six or seven years of his acting career in England Aldridge used the name "Mr. Keene" rather than his own. (Perhaps Aldridge's eagerness to assume pieces of other people's lives, be it their pasts or their names, reflected the difficulties he had breaking into the theatrical business, but to the modern reader expropriations on the scale of Aldridge's suggest at the least an insecurity, even a confusion regarding his own identity.)[55] Hewlett's return to the stage on November 30, 1825, was, according to the newspapers, supposed to be a one-time event; the *New York Gazette and General Advertiser* reported that he was soon to "return to London to fulfill his engagement at the Coburg," the theater where Aldridge was then performing under the name of Keene. In the *Commercial Advertiser,* Hewlett's show in Greenwich was described "as a sort of parting favor previously to his return to London to supply the place of Kean." If this item referred to Edmund Kean, it is puzzling, because Edmund Kean was then touring America and in fact had finished up in New York on the same day as the reference to him was printed. The reference makes much more sense if Hewlett was talking about Aldridge, or Keene, and that wording—"supply the place of Kean"—contains overtones of a desire on Hewlett's part to assume his rightful place by reclaiming his past from Aldridge/Keene.[56]

As far as we know, the two black actors never met to resolve any differences. Over the next two years Hewlett was constantly on the verge of departing for England, but there is no record of his making the voyage. In January 1826 he was in Philadelphia, performing "prior to his return to London, to fill his engagement at the Cobourg Theatre"; in February he was advertising "his last appearance in Brooklyn, previous to his departure for London"; in late February he made his curtain call speech announcing that "he would soon be in dat country vere dey hab no 'stinction of color," but a month later he was still in New York, claiming that this "grand entertainment" would "be positively the last night of his performance in this city." In late April and then again in late May he made further appearances at the same New York venue. In July 1826 Hewlett advertised his "Farewell Benefit," only, a few months later, to announce another "Farewell Benefit" for September 28, 1826. In late January 1827 a notice in the *New-York Enquirer* stated that Hewlett, "prior to his departure for London, (on the first of February—farewell my native land,) will give his Imitations," but a little more than seven weeks after his promised embarkation in the packet, the black performer was in Alexandria, Virginia. Still, in early December 1827 he was claiming that a show at the New York Military Hall would be "his last performance prior to his departure to England, to fulfil his engagement there."[57]

Hewlett's "threats" of imminent departure may have been merely marketing ploys, but the air of abandonment that marked his "dialect" farewell speech, or even, on another occasion, the visit to Noah to tell him he was about to leave the country, suggest that there was more to it than that. From this distance, Hewlett's indecisiveness seems to be part of a broader pattern. For a second time, someone in London had done him wrong. He had crossed the Atlantic to pursue Mathews in 1824, but without success—a curious failure, since Mathews was performing constantly and could not have been difficult to locate. But later, faced with Aldridge's duplicity, Hewlett did not even make it that far. Perhaps he shied away from personal confrontation with either man. Perhaps, venerating England and English actors as he did, and for all his undoubted ability, he feared that he might fail on the English stage, a defeat that would have been made all the more humiliating because of the younger Aldridge's achievements. What is clear is that Hewlett's failure to achieve any measure of success, or even to try to break onto the English stage, severely restricted his development as an actor. Performing solo undoubtedly had its attractions—it gave Hewlett scope to display the range of his talents as an actor and singer—but could never earn either the cachet or even the thrill that would come from starring in a full-scale dramatic production in a famous and enthusiastically received play. With the exception of Mathews, the stars whom Hewlett imitated performed alongside other actors in plays, and until he could do the same he would always be left wondering just how talented he, a black man, was at these supposedly higher levels of performance. In England, Aldridge had managed to appear on stage alongside white actors with remarkably little fuss being made about his color, but Hewlett could never enjoy the same opportunity in New York. As slavery wound down, racial tension was rising and segregation of the city's blacks was increasing. In this context, the idea of a black actor interacting on stage with white actors, particularly women, was all but unthinkable.

In the scanty record that survives of these years, there are indications that Hewlett felt this deprivation keenly. It is intriguing that he was particularly drawn to the character of the trickster Richard III. His interest in this manipulative character was shared, albeit to a lesser degree and probably for different reasons, by many other New Yorkers; throughout the 1820s, Shakespeare's tragedy was immensely popular in the metropolis and elsewhere in the nation. An irascible theater critic for the *New York American* complained, in 1827, of the numerous "tiresome repetitions of Richard by tragedians and comedians," repetitions that had rendered watching the play "a task; and if the performer is not above mediocrity the task is exceedingly irksome."[58] But the critic was out of step with a public which continued to flock to all manner of productions of the great tragedy. *Richard III* was certainly at the center of Hewlett's career. Almost invariably, Hewlett's solo act included a number of scenes from the play, usually in the form of imitations of Kean, and often a piece from *Richard* concluded the night's entertainment. On several occasions in the years from 1825 to 1827, when Hewlett dropped the mask (which is to say that, instead of imitating a white actor performing a certain role, he performed that role as himself), the character he portrayed was Richard III. In May 1826, for example, he concluded his show at the Grove Hotel in New York by acting the "tent and dying scene in Richard."[59] And, appropriately enough, when Hewlett arranged to have his image engraved, he had himself depicted as Richard. Several newspapers which reported the collapse of the floor at the Greenwich performance noted that the black actor was "vulgarly called 'Dick Hewlett,'" presumably because of his fascination with that dramatic role. The press seems to have found something amusing in this, but their smirks cannot conceal an almost wistful air surrounding Hewlett's behavior, or the reality of white racism denying a talented black individual his fair chance.[60]

The only way for Hewlett to perform his beloved Shakespeare on a New York stage would be in the company of other black actors. From January 1828 to March 1831, there is an almost complete lack of documentation concerning Hewlett's career, but there is some evidence to show that he revived the African Theater in its 1828–29 season. In the inaugural issue of an English publication entitled *The Family Magazine*, which appeared in 1829, an anonymous writer penned several paragraphs on "The Negroes of New York," based on his recent stay there. Having heard "that there was a Negro theatre here in New York," the traveler had "immediately resolved to pay it a visit." When he located it "in a rather retired street," the theater turned out to be "small, but tolerably well fitted up—better, indeed, than in the theatres in many of our provincial towns"; it was also "well lighted" and "the music, for America, was very good." *Julius Caesar* was on the bill that night, and this white observer "sat near the stage" and could not help but notice the black actor playing Brutus; this actor, "after delivering long speeches, asked me twice, in an under-tone, how I liked his acting." Although no names were mentioned in the piece, the actor in question sounds very much like Hewlett. As usual, the writer deployed the usual puns on color in his quest for literary effect, but, for all that, he seems to have been quite taken by the performance: "No sooner had I ceased smiling at the charming Portia, than I was almost thrilled with horror at the dark visages of the conspirators, with their white rolling eyes; and I began positively to shudder at all this Rome in black."

Apparently the patrons of the theater on that night were mostly black; the English traveler alluded to "that disagreeable feeling which comes over me and no doubt over every other White, who finds himself amidst a numerous assemblage of Blacks before he is accustomed to the sight."[61] This supposition raises the vexed and probably unresolvable issue of precisely who made up the audience for these black theatrical performances. Here the evidence is particularly scanty, but, based on what little is available, it seems fair to assume that Hewlett's solo acts drew a different crowd from that which attended performances by a company of black actors. Although whites came too, most of the members of the audience for the African Company's original performances, and for this revival of the company in 1828–29, were African New Yorkers. In contrast, when Hewlett gave his imitations of famous actors, he probably attracted a predominantly white audience, comprised largely of young males who were fast becoming the most important consumers of all kinds of popular entertainment.

Although this was probably not immediately apparent, an audience of this kind spelled trouble for Hewlett. On the one hand, its patronage enabled the black actor to enjoy two years of popularity, but on the other hand, the young white men who frequented his shows were a volatile lot, sometimes dangerously so, combining as they did a curiosity about the spectacle of a black man on stage and occasionally even an appreciation of his talent with an often intense racism. This last point is well illustrated by the recollections, written down decades later, of a white native of Albany, a man who could recall vividly the performances in 1826 of "the African champion, Hewlet" at the Vauxhall Garden in the state capital. Although he acknowledged the high quality of the acting—"this darkey was *some* in Richard and Othello," and "on the stage he tore King Dick to flinders"—his reflections were most notable for their vitriolic nastiness. Not only did he recount with relish some of Hewlett's later troubles in the 1830s, but he also delighted in emphasizing that "of a hot summer's night the audience kept a respectful distance from the foot-lights (penny dips) in consequence of the strong goat-like odor diffused over the garden."[62] This sort of racial slurs and attitudes would prompt before long the savage race riots of 1834, but in the meantime they simmered beneath the surface. Although theater audiences were notoriously boisterous at this time, it seems that Hewlett's shows often brought out the worst in his young white patrons and, almost inevitably, sporadic outbreaks of violence occurred.

Hewlett's audience was also fickle. Perhaps it is only hindsight that makes the point clear, but it does seem that even in these years, the mid-1820s, there was always a sense that Hewlett's popularity could not last. Notwithstanding his virtuosity, his act was still largely a novelty, and inevitably, one feels, young whites would tire of Hewlett's shows and find other ways to satisfy their voyeuristic desire to see blacks performing on stage. The ephemerality of audience taste brings to mind Langston Hughes's elegant epitaph for that brief period a century later when, like moths to a flame, many white New Yorkers were drawn to the goings on uptown: "That spring for me (and I guess for all of us) was the end of the Harlem Renaissance. We were no longer in vogue anyway, we Negroes. Sophisticated New Yorkers turned to Noel Coward."[63] What happened in the late 1820s and 1830s resembled less a turning to Noel Coward than a desire to see Al Jolson, or at least his blackfaced forebears. In 1829, the white entertainer George Washington Dixon, in blackface, sang "Coal Black Rose" at various New York City venues, and the following year T. D. Rice first "jumped Jim Crow." That Hewlett's act would go out of fashion was probably to be expected; that he, a black mimic of famous white actors, would be made redundant by young white men who blacked up their faces and imitated African Americans was the cruelest cut imaginable.

For the period 1828–29 to 1831, virtually nothing is known about Hewlett. Quite possibly he toured. When he performed again in New York in 1831, he advertised himself as the "STAR OF THE WEST." Possibly the black actor tried his luck in Cincinnati and other midwestern cities—all manner of actors were touring those parts of the nation by this time—or possibly this self-description had as much accuracy as his earlier exaggerated billing—a "colored comedian, from London." All that is certain is that when the census taker came around in 1830, Hewlett was living in a household in Varick Street, New York, containing one free black male aged between 36 and 55, one black female in the same category, and another aged between 24 and 36.[64]

For a few months in 1831, however, James Hewlett made another assault on the New York theatrical world. A notice in the *New York Evening Post* on March 4 announced "HEWLETT'S THIRD GRAND CONCERT" (I could find no mention of the two earlier ones) at the New York Museum, at the corner of Broadway and Anthony Street. Curiously, the bill stated that

"Hewlett for this night styles himself Keen. I am myself alone!!!"[65] Read today, these words convey a strange ambiguity. Although originally from *Henry VI*, the quote "I am myself alone" was purloined by Colley Cibber and incorporated into his version of *Richard III* (the standard rendition in the first half of the nineteenth century). The line was associated particularly with Edmund Kean, and Hewlett had had it included in the engraving which depicted him imitating Kean playing Richard III. But in Hewlett's notice the word "Keen" is spelled incorrectly—it is exactly halfway between "Kean," the famous white actor, and "Keene," the name under which the increasingly famous Aldridge was performing. In a context in which Aldridge had stolen some of Hewlett's past, and in which a reference had perhaps been made to the name Aldridge was currently using, the line "I am myself alone" took on another, more pointed, meaning.

Regardless of whether this was the case or not, there were changes in Hewlett's act. Previously, he had called his performance an "entertainment" or a "grand entertainment," but now he used the word "concert," and there does seems to have been much more emphasis on music in his act. Hewlett was now singing twenty or more songs and was accompanied by "a Piano Forte." It appears, then, that after his long absence from the New York stage, Hewlett was casting around, trying to attract back his earlier audience. The following day, a brief advertisement in the *New York American* declared that "WE UNDERSTAND that the Celebrated Tragedian, MR. HEWLETT, takes his FAREWELL BENEFIT at the New-York Museum on MONDAY EVENING." "This man has wonderful abilities," the notice continued, and "we hope to see and hear that his pocket will be strong enough to hold the Cash. He draws tremendous houses."[66] Undoubtedly, Hewlett had attracted thousands of white New Yorkers to see him over the years, but that had been in the 1820s. In retrospect, this advertisement looks less a statement of fact than an attempt to rekindle waning interest in what the black actor had to offer.

Although Hewlett still gave imitations of "several celebrated performers," he now ended the night's entertainment with a rendition of *Sylvester Daggerwood*. In many ways this short comic play, written by George Colman, was ideally suited to Hewlett's talents. Its only scene takes place in the waiting room of a London theater manager's office, where Daggerwood, a provincial actor looking for a job, has whiled away five days, and where Fustian, a playwright with a tragedy to sell, has been waiting three hours. Fustian tries reading his work aloud, but the words continually remind Daggerwood of other speeches in other plays, speeches which he then proceeds to recite, irritating Fustian intensely in the process. After a while, the manager's servant enters and announces that his master has decamped through the back door, whereupon the supplicants depart in disgust, ending the play. Playing Daggerwood, a skilled mimic would recite the speeches in the manner of the famous actors who had performed the roles.

Adapting *Sylvester Daggerwood* might have seemed a clever enough way of trying to eke out a few more full houses from Hewlett's old audience, but it did not work. A few years earlier, in April 1827, the theater critic for the *New York American* had reviewed the performance of an unknown and unnamed tyro actor in the role of Sylvester Daggerwood. For this writer, "the only merit of this character consists in the imitations; of playing there is none." In this case, the young actor had mimicked well-known actors in ways that were "instantly recognized, and drew forth long and loud applause," but "it is not the mere power of imitation that can make the actor." Indeed, wrote the critic, imitation "is a faculty too easily acquired; it requires little study, and once seen, the excitement passes away, and we care not to witness it again."[67] And there was the rub. For this critic, and I am sure for Hewlett too, *Daggerwood* had neither the stature nor the allure of a play by a great playwright such as Shakespeare. Whatever dissatisfaction Hewlett may have felt about the limitations of the roles that circumstances had forced upon him was, however, beside the point; more immediately significant was that even those roles were no longer attracting the crowds.

Hewlett only gave a few performances in early March 1831, but on July 12, the "STAR OF THE WEST" and "Shakespeare's proud representative" reappeared at the New York Museum. Hewlett was to "sing a number of Songs, and give Imitations of several celebrated performers"; in addition, "Mr Hewlitt will take Exhilirating Gas."[68] The promoters did not even manage to spell his name correctly. My guess is that Hewlett's earlier appearances had not drawn as well as expected—expectations doubtless inflated by talk from Hewlett himself—and the proprietors of the New York Museum had insisted that, if he were to reappear in their venue, he would need to demean himself in this manner. Public exhibitions of the effects of laughing gas had been occurring in New York for over a decade. A year earlier, in the same hall in the New York Museum in which Hewlett later performed, a chemist had administered nitrous oxide to members of the public. According to the *New York Evening Post*, the "gas produces great exhilaration, an irresistible propensity to laughter, a rapid flow of vivid ideas, and an unusual fitness for muscular exertion; the taste of this gas is sweet, and its smell peculiar and agreeable; those that have inhaled it once generally wish to inhale it again." As well, a few individuals who had achieved a fame of sorts exhibited themselves after becoming intoxicated on the gas. One such was John Pluck, an ostler at a tavern and "a poor, ignorant, stupid, fellow." In 1825, as part of a protest against an onerous militia system, Philadelphia's Eighty-Fourth Regiment had elected him as their colonel, thus skewering some of the class pretensions associated with the militia officers. Colonel Pluck, all of five feet tall, severely deformed and possibly mentally deficient as well, quickly achieved notoriety throughout the North. In January 1827 he appeared on stage in New York City and had the gas administered to him.[69] This was not a distinguished precedent for Hewlett, and it appears that he used the gas on only the one occasion.

Two months later, in September 1831, still casting around for his audience, Hewlett announced a "FAREWELL BENEFIT." He was no longer associated with the New York Museum and was to appear instead at the Columbian Hall, which had been "newly painted and fitted up for the occasion." The black actor was no longer a solo performer: his "grand concert" would include also the "celebrated Napolitan Minstrels Signors Delcampio, Nulifia and Nortiaco, who will appear with a silver Trumpet which was presented to him by the Emperor Napoleon for his wonderful performance at the coronation." Furthermore, "Mr. H. will have a full band, and Mrs. Hewlet will preside at the piano forte." There is considerable doubt as to whether this program was performed. The advertisement was supposed to run three times in the *Post*, but was printed only once, suggesting that Hewlett had not come up with the money to pay the newspaper.[70]

In the second half of the 1820s James Hewlett had struck a chord with his audience and had prospered, but his attempted comeback in 1831 was a failure. In retrospect, the changes to his act suggest nothing so much as a frenetic, if doomed, search for a way to survive in the changed circumstances of the new decade. Agreeing to perform under the influence of laughing gas was an admission of defeat, something that reduced a talented performer to the level of a curiosity, a taste of what was to come with the rise of P. T. Barnum. One experience of this kind was more than enough for the proud black man. He was going to go down, but he would do so on his own terms, and with a degree of aplomb and a surprising amount of dignity as well. What followed the probably abortive September "farewell benefit" was another period of silence lasting almost three years, and then several appearances in court that charted Hewlett's fall from favor in the city he had tried so valiantly to conquer. It is hardly an edifying story, but then, until very recently, stories of black artists in New York seldom had happy endings.

No matter what he did, Hewlett did it with his own distinctive style. In early June 1834, the *Morning Courier and New-York Enquirer's* police roundsman happened to observe Hewlett making one of his dramatic entrances. "Hewlett, the 'African Roscius,'" the reporter wrote, "strutted into the police office with a most ludicrously consequential air." The actor was there to offer himself as bail for "some sable friend from the Bridewell," and, once he had sworn the requisite oath, "his security was accepted and his friend discharged." In his own inimitable manner, Hewlett began exchanging quips with the policemen idly waiting around the court, "amusing the officers with a touch of his quality," as the reporter put it, when suddenly a Captain Hillman of the ship *America*, who had apparently been trying to track the actor down, strode into the room. The drama of the moment was almost too much for the *Courier's* correspondent: "Had all the ghosts Shakespeare ever imagined presented themselves at once before Hewlett," he wrote somewhat floridly, the black actor "could not have been more horror struck than he was at beholding the captain."[71]

It seems that times had been sufficiently hard to force Hewlett to return to his former occupation. Hillman had needed a steward for the *America* and "Hewlett offered himself to fill the situation."

As always, he had impressed his prospective employer and "by his easy impudence and plausible manner, induced Captain Hillman to engage him." He had started work straight away. Perhaps he never had any intention of sailing, or possibly the mere prospect of working on a ship again brought back unpleasant memories of earlier voyages, but, for whatever reason, two days later he walked off the job. In his statement to the authorities, Hewlett claimed that he "left the ship without his pay" and "knows nothing of the articles he is charged with stealing." According to the captain, however, in only two days Hewlett had "contrived" to steal "several table-cloths, sheets of copper, bottles of wine and porter, the cabin carpet, and a variety of other articles." A dozen bottles of London porter had turned up at a grocery store run by Rogers and Shatzel, and some of the copper sheets were found at Thomas Cosgrove's on Roosevelt Street. Hewlett admitted selling the bottles of porter but claimed that they "were given him by the Captain." As for the copper, he never "even saw any in the ship."[72]

As soon as Hillman had made his charges he departed, leaving Hewlett stranded in the police court. The actor vainly "implored" the magistrates to let him go, "pledging his honour to return to morrow with the necessary bail for his appearance at the sessions." He then turned to one of the magistrates, Alderman Hopson, and asked "do you—can you believe me guilty of the crime with which I am charged [?]" The ensuing exchange was recorded by the industrious *Courier* reporter.

Magistrate Do you want my opinion?
Hewlett Yes, sir, I do.
Magistrate Well, then, I have no doubt of it.
Hewlett Then is Othello's occupation gone. But I know you will take my word for my appearance here tomorrow.
Magistrate There stands the officer with the warrant, ask him.

Hewlett Ah, Mr. Hays, how do you do? You'll let me go till to-morrow, won't you?

Hays Let you go! umph! Let you go to Bridewell.

Hewlett (to the reporters) Gentlemen, don't put me in the newspapers; it will hurt my character.

Hays Come—Start.

Hewlett Well, where's my dungeon; lead me to my straw.

Hays I intend to do so, you scamp.

Hewlett 'Tis not the first time I have slept hard to do the state service.

Hays To be sure it isn't. D'ye remember the silver cup?

Hewlett. No more of that, Hal, an thou lovest me.

   Exeunt Hays and Hewlett.[73]

As that *"exeunt"* suggests, the reporter was well aware that he had witnessed an impromptu dramatic performance. Years of being on stage, acting and mimicking actors, as well as dealing with the inevitable hecklers, must have given Hewlett's act a razor-sharp edge. He was very quick. Here he had remembered, misremembered, or adapted (the precise mix is unknowable; Hewlett's speed almost certainly induced mistakes in the reporter's notes of what happened) lines from *Othello, Henry IV, Part I,* and probably other plays.

A few days later, at his trial for larceny, Hewlett denied the charges, but the result of the proceedings was pretty much a foregone conclusion. There was a certain inevitability too regarding the nature of the actor's performance before the larger audience in the courtroom. According to the *Sun,* Hewlett "acted Shakespeare in the prisoner's box, and marched out with the air of an Othello to the cage."[74] The *New-York Gazette & General Advertiser,* noting that the black actor had "performed Othello to the life," had him giving quotes from *Othello,* to which the Recorder apparently responded with a few lines from the *Merchant of Venice:*

> Thyself shall see the act:
> For as thou urgest justice, be assured
> Thou shalt have justice, more than thou desir'st.

On being sentenced to six months in the penitentiary, "the ebony representative of Shakspeare," as the *General Advertiser* described him, had the final word, slightly changing a couple of lines from the *Merchant of Venice*:

> I am content!
> Sir, I entreat you there with to dinner.

Whereupon Hewlett was marched off to serve his sentence.[75]

This was Hewlett's first conviction, but Hays's passing reference to a silver cup strongly suggests at the very least a prior acquaintance between the two men. It is little more than speculation, but my guess is that sometime after his last known performance in 1831, Hewlett began to get involved with the underworld of New York City. It is unlikely that he would have been associated with anything as crass as breaking and entering or mugging, but his verbal dexterity, his actor's poise, and his mastery of mimicry made Hewlett a natural for the burgeoning occupation of black confidence man.

In part because it was so difficult for urban-dwelling African Americans to scrape together a living, cities such as New York and Philadelphia were alive with a population of black men who lived off their wits and linguistic skills. African American culture had always highly esteemed the man of words, but now the ability to talk well opened up a whole new range of barely legal and illegal possibilities in the rapidly expanding urban centers of the Northeast. Unscrupulous blacks preyed on their unsuspecting fellows: one sold fake lottery tickets to old African American women; another, falsely claiming to be a slave raising money to manumit

himself, solicited contributions from the unwary; another, a New
Yorker, secured a list of African Philadelphians who had migrated
to Haiti, forged letters from the émigrés back to their friends in
which they gave glowing accounts of their new home, and then
charged the "recipients" 37.5 cents for the postage. As the *New
York Evening Post* reported, the poor blacks, anxious for news of
their friends, "seized on them [the letters] with avidity." For the
forger, the scheme was quite "a gainful trade" for some weeks until his scam was uncovered.[76] Moreover, there were always several
blacks willing, for a price, to consult their "dream books" to help
the gullible make the correct choices when they played the fore-
runner of what became the numbers (the game, based on numbers
being drawn in certain lotteries, was illegal). Not only blacks were
gullible. In 1826, the *National Advocate* reported that "in the
neighbourhood of Canal street, a black prophet, who had let his
wool grow for ten years so as to give himself a venerable appearance, has recently opened a shop of fortune telling, and has every
prospect of making a snug little fortune." Respectable whites visited this African New Yorker for a variety of reasons: "Young girls
go to hear of sweethearts and young widows to catch a word of
husbands. Married ladies enter with the hope of listening to the
destiny of their young daughter in baby clothes, or of the boys
who put on their first unmentionables yesterday." As the *Advocate*
concluded, "any occupation may turn the penny if it is shrewdly
followed."[77]

Some of these silver-tongued blacks were operating just within
the law, but others were well and truly outside it. For the most
part, we only hear of members of the latter group when they
slipped up and were caught. On April 23, 1819, Henry Dennis, a
black man who was a servant to a Mr. Ferris Esq., was walking
down Bancker Street when he was approached by another black
man named Tobias Morgan. The smooth-tongued Morgan "entered into conversation" with Dennis and "finally insisted on his

deponent's going with him to take a walk." As Dennis later testified, Morgan "persuaded" him to enter a house in Bancker Street and go into a room "where there were cards on the Table." Another black man named Andrew Thompson came in and joined Morgan in insisting that Dennis play cards with them. At this point Dennis demurred, objecting quite sensibly "to playing cards as he knew nothing about it." Morgan and Thompson then commenced shuffling the deck and playing in front of their mark, betting for drinks on the turn of a card. After a while "they challenged deponent to bet his watch & by the persuasion of Morgan he took out his silver watch to the value of fifteen dollars," and a pair of seals and a key worth five dollars, "& bet with Thompson" on whether "two cards of a particular kind come out together." Not only did Dennis lose the hand, but the fact of his loss had to be explained to him, with Thompson stating that "he had won deponent's watch & accordingly took it up & put it in his Pocket." Their bemused victim watched the pair of black cardsharps play a few more hands, betting on "the turning up of a card or something of the kind." That was about the best description Dennis could manage because, as he kept on claiming, he was "ignorant & know nothing about playing at cards." A short while later, as the pair of conmen were about to leave, the hapless Dennis proposed "to Thompson to play him twelve dollars for the watch as he did not like to lose it." The only thing that prevented Dennis from losing that money as well was that when he returned to his lodgings to collect his savings, Ferris, his somewhat more worldly employer, intervened, advising him to go to the police. Apparently Morgan and Thompson were well known to the local authorities—a notation on their black victim's statement reads: "The above are idle, very bad fellows."[78]

One of the more interesting conmen was Reuben Moore, whom Philadelphia's *Public Ledger* named the "prince of petty swindlers." This black man plied his trade in Philadelphia, New

York, and probably other cities over at least a dozen years. Moore was born free in Philadelphia in 1802, but sometime about 1819 or 1820 he came to New York. According to testimony he gave in 1826, he lived a spartan existence, picking up work "along shore" when he could, eating in cook shops, and paying six shillings a week for his lodging. At the time of his arrest, the only possessions of his found by the police were a few items of clothing and 94 cents. It is, however, doubtful that Moore spent too many hours unloading cargo on the city's wharves, because by this time he had become an accomplished con artist, skilled in the wiles of separating his marks from their money. In the case that had brought him to the attention of the authorities, Moore had "enticed" Peter Harper into an alley in order to hold stakes for a bet, whereupon Moore's accomplice had taken Harper's watch. Moore was convicted and sentenced to a year in prison. In July 1827, only a few months after his release, he was caught again perpetrating much the same sort of scam, colloquially known as "burning."[79] In these schemes, Moore always did the talking, luring the unsuspecting victims into an alley, where one or two black toughs provided the muscle.

In the mid 1830s Reuben Moore turned up again in Philadelphia, where he was arrested at least twice while using a similar stratagem. He would pick out a likely looking white man, often a "raw country lad," and ask him to exchange a five or ten dollar bill for silver, giving as the reason that he wished to enclose a banknote in a letter. Moore would then either seize the note and run off, or, tempting the mark with the prospect of making some easy money, lure him into a nearby alley "to bet on the drawing of cards, and by the aid of an accomplice, soon fleeces him of his money." The second time he was caught, in 1837, he had, according to the *Ledger,* picked the wrong man, a Mr. Marshall from the Northern Liberties, who was "too knowing to be caught by such a trap." Interestingly, when Moore was searched, the police found on him bills on "a broken bank to the amount of $250," as well as "one of those miserable attempts at gaggery, a business card [in] the semblance of a bank note," props suggesting that the plausible black criminal had other swindles in his repertoire. On this occasion, the police had no real evidence against Moore and he was merely sentenced to thirty days for vagrancy.[80]

This was the sort of world in which Hewlett began to move in the 1830s. Doubtless his stint in prison increased his knowledge of the black underworld. Perhaps he was still trying to get back on stage. Years later, Martin Delany claimed that he had seen Hewlett in "a private rehersal, in 1836," but it is unclear exactly what this meant.[81] Certainly no record of any public performances in these years has yet turned up. Indeed, there is silence concerning Hewlett until another court case in 1837, a case which also demonstrated Hewlett's ability to sweet-talk someone into giving him what he wanted, albeit in a rather different fashion.

In March 1837, a destitute white woman by the name of Elizabeth Hewlett was charged with stealing twenty-four dollars' worth of clothing from Olivia McDougal, a black woman. Hewlett had knocked on McDougal's door late one night seeking shelter. Early the next morning she had slipped away with an armload of the black woman's clothing. The ensuing court case revealed some details of Hewlett's history. She was born to a respectable family named Briggs that lived on Staten Island, but in July 1836, when she was twenty-one years of age, she disappeared without trace. McDougal, the black complainant, testified that "a coloured man named Hulett had induced the unfortunate girl to elope with him, and kept her either as his wife or mistress, until she became disgusted with her black Lothario, and abandoned him." The reporter for the *Journal of Commerce* helpfully explained to his readers that "this Hulett is a black fellow whom, it may be remembered, some time back was a candidate for histrionic fame in this and other cities, and not succeeding in that profession, embraced an other which earned him such honors as the Recorder confers in Sessions Court."[82]

By the late 1830s James Hewlett must have been in his mid-forties, possibly even fifty years of age. Briggs was apparently attractive—the *Journal of Commerce*'s reporter described her as "a genteel, interesting looking woman"—and at least two decades younger than Hewlett. The black actor was perfectly well aware of the way white New Yorkers would react to such a union. In his 1824 letter to Mathews, Hewlett had specifically commented on the prejudice against "international marriages," and in the interim that prejudice had only deepened. Indeed, in the vicious riots of 1834, anything that hinted at "amalgamation" had been targeted for violent action by the mobs roaming the city streets. In the event, most of the invective surrounding this 1837 case was heaped on the shoulders of the young woman. The *Journal of Commerce* described the whole affair as "a hideous and lamentable instance of female frailty"; the *Commercial Advertiser* noted that "from her connexion with this vagabond she has reaped sorrow, misery and infamy." As he passed sentence of one month's hard labor, the Recorder thought fit to remark "that nothing but a grossly depraved mind could induce a white woman to cohabit with one of the negro race."[83] Hewlett's career in New York was probably over anyway, a casualty of the vogue for "jumping Jim Crow"—the press in 1837 certainly referred to his acting in the past tense—but the publicity surrounding this incident extinguished any slim chance he had of returning to the stage. Becoming known as a middle-aged black man who had seduced and ruined a respectable young white woman was no way to court popularity with white New Yorkers in the 1830s, 1840s, or indeed at just about any time in the city's history.

Within a few months, Hewlett's life as a conman was revealed to all. In June 1837, a Mrs. Whitlock of Renwick Street made a fatal mistake, taking a dose of arsenic instead of magnesia. As was not uncommon, the inquest was held in the deceased's residence. With his usual confident air, Hewlett walked into the house and behaved as if he were part of proceedings. As the *Morning Herald*'s reporter wrote, "he handed chairs to the gentlemen of the jury and to the coroner, who imagined he belonged to the house." As well, "he poured words of consolation into the ears of the relatives of the deceased, begging them not to cry"; indeed, the recipients of his ministrations "mistook him for the servant of the coroner." He even offered "his assistance in carrying out the coffin." Perhaps Hewlett's performance was too good. One of the residents of the house, a Mr. Vanderzee, unable to take his eyes off the "particularly officious" Hewlett, noticed him slipping a valuable watch into his pocket. The solemn proceedings rapidly deteriorated into farce. Vanderzee "informed Mr. Brown, the coroner, that his nigger had stolen a watch. 'My nigger,' said the coroner in surprise, 'my nigger—he's not my nigger; he belongs to the house!'" After that, things were quickly sorted out. Hewlett was searched, the watch recovered, and "the officious black rascal" taken to the police office.[84]

At his trial a few days later, Hewlett came up with a story about holding the watch for someone else, but no one believed him. Indeed, knowing that he was going to be incarcerated again, he seems to have relished the opportunity to play to the gallery for one final time. According to the *Morning Courier and New-York Enquirer*, "Hewlett defended himself in mock heroic style, to the great delight of the audience, but his eloquence was of no avail, as he was instantly found guilty." The reporter for the *Morning Herald* took down the exchange that occurred at Hewlett's sentencing.

The Recorder Hewlett, the jury have convicted you of a very bad crime. We can send you to Sing Sing or to the Penitentiary, which do you prefer going to?

Hewlett I've no choice. I'll go to whichever your honor pleases.

Recorder Well, we'll adjudge you to the penitentiary for two
years. They'll make a waiter of you, I dare say.

Hewlett I'm much obliged to your honor. I hope if you take a
summer excursion you will allow me to wait upon your honor
at the island. I'll give your honor a capital song if you favor me
with a visit.

Recorder Why—hem—[*in a fit of laughter*] take the black rascal
away!

Unlike some other blacks, who also knew they were going to
prison, Hewlett did not denounce the judge or rail against the
court; personal confrontation was never his style. Instead, in these
unpromising circumstances, he did what he did best—performed
—and probably won at least grudging admiration from all who
saw him. There is, of course, something ineffably depressing
about watching an artist on his way down, particularly when it had
been a shift in audience tastes rather than any decline in the
actor's ability that had rendered his undoubted skills obsolete.
Maybe Hewlett was enough of an optimist not to see things this
way and still envisaged trying his luck again on the New York
stage after his release. If that was the case, he might have taken
heart from the *Morning Herald* reporter's conclusion to his piece
on the actor's appearance in court: "Hewlett possesses uncommon
oratorical talents, and by the drollery of his observations kept the
court and audience in a continual laugh."[85] Not a bad final notice,
but to have seen it, Hewlett would have had to rely on the kindness of a prison guard.

4 | IMITATION

Freedom had changed everything in New York. Slaves had always had a pretty good idea of what being free would be like—and, doubtless, some African New Yorkers could almost taste its sweetness as the last months and days of their negotiated years of "faithful service" dragged by—but most whites were totally unprepared for what would happen once the city's blacks were no longer slaves. In their defense, it was not as though white New Yorkers had before them many examples of slaveowning societies that had successfully ended the institution. Most whites probably unthinkingly assumed that things would go on much as before, or just hoped that blacks would quietly go away. They were completely mistaken. African New Yorkers became a loud and unavoidable presence, assertively enacting on the city's streets and its places of entertainment their own version of what freedom meant. Exponentially more than is the case nowadays, the theater—not only the stage but also the pit, boxes, and gallery—was a place of fantasy where racial tensions and all manner of other social concerns could be played out. Within a few years, in 1849, at the Astor Place Riot, ostensibly caused by a squabble between two actors, more than a score of New Yorkers ended up dead. Theater mattered in early nineteenth-century New York in ways that it no longer does. When James Hewlett and his fellow black actors staged *King Shotaway*, or when Hewlett alone performed *Richard III* in the manner of Edmund Kean, or when George Washington Dixon blacked up and sang "Coal Black Rose," or even when T. D. Rice donned his fantastic costume and his burnt cork and "jumped Jim Crow," the power of their performances derived not only from their own creative genius, but from the way their representations agitated the currents and eddies of racial politics in New York of the 1820s and 1830s.

Now that they were free, African New Yorkers had more scope to experiment with behavior, and whites were palpably aware of their presence in ways they had never been when the city's blacks had been slaves. The result was a cultural mélange in which whites imitated blacks who were already imitating whites (and vice versa). At times it seems that all manner of things, ranging from ways of talking and dressing to making music and dancing, were continually ricocheting between the races. And what made this cultural borrowing all the more piquant—and many on both sides of the racial divide were half aware of this—was that generous helpings of parody were mixed into this process.

Well-read New Yorkers would have been aware that "imitation" had been an important element in stage performance back in Africa. In August 1817, the *American Monthly Magazine and Critical Review* had published, from a book entitled *Voyage to Abyssinia*, an extract to which they had given the heading "Abyssinian Acting." The article gave an account of Totte Máze, "one of the cleverest mimics" the writer had ever seen, who had performed at the African king's court "some finished pieces of acting that evinced very extraordinary native talent." In one of Máze's set pieces, he had given an "imitation" of "the behaviour of a chief in battle, who had not been remarkable for his courage," at first being pompous and overbearing, but, as the enemy approached, more cautious, and finally being reduced to cringing on his knees begging for mercy. In another sketch Máze "imitated the over-strained politeness" of a "courtier, paying a first visit to a superior." Not only did these performances elicit admiration and much applause from the Abyssinians, but they also impressed the writer, who noted that "in all these representations, the tones of his [Máze's] voice were so perfectly adapted to the different characters and his action so thoroughly appropriate that it gave me very unexpected gratification."[1]

A dozen years later, in May 1829, the *Democratic Press* selected and printed a "particularly curious and interesting" extract from Hugh Clapperton's recently published *Second Journey into the Interior of Africa*. The lengthy (for a newspaper) selection described a performance put on before a king and a large audience drawn from the surrounding area. The actors were "dressed in large sacks, covering every part of the body: the head most fantastically decorated with strips of rags, damask silk, and cotton, of as many glaring colours as it was possible." The first act consisted of dancing and tumbling; the second was an elaborate acting out of "catching the boa constrictor"; the third, and most pertinent here, was a representation of the "white devil." The actor playing this part was left in the center of the performance space. As his sack gradually dropped down, it revealed a "white head" and a body exhibiting "the appearance of a human figure cast in white wax, of the middle size, miserably thin, and starved with cold." The "whitefaced" figure "frequently went through the motion of taking snuff, and rubbing its hands; when it walked, it was with the most awkward gait, treading as the most tender footed white man would do in walking bare footed, for the first time over new frozen ground." But if the locals were delighted by the performance, "enjoy[ing] the sight, as the perfection of the actor's art," Clapperton had been less taken by it, even though the spectators "often appealed to us, as to the excellence of the performance, and entreated that I would look and be attentive to what was going on." The English traveler merely "pretended to be fully as much pleased with this caricature of a white man as they could be," even though, he grudgingly added, "certainly the actor burlesqued the part to admiration."[2]

But New York natives who remained ignorant of Africa did not have to look this far afield to find such a mixture of imitation and parody, of exaggerated behavior and burlesque. On July 11, 1834, during one of the worst race riots in the city's history, the editor of *The Transcript* published an article under the inflammatory headline of "ATTEMPTED PRACTICAL 'AMALGAMATION.'" The piece blamed the "self-sufficient conceits" that had been "thrust into the heads of our black population, by the fanatic zealots" promoting "immediate abolition and amalgamation." A few days earlier a "colored gentleman" had climbed up "the stoop of a respectable boarding-house in Nassau street," paused while "restoring the economy of his rustling silk cravat," grasped the doorknob "with scrupulous exactness . . . between the thumb and forefinger of his dainty right hand, and gently rapped it once and again, making of course, twice." "It was," the writer continued smugly, "a genteel rap, intended as such, and carried, in its very sound, an unmistaken indication of superiority." After the black man had ascertained from the landlady that there was indeed an unoccupied room, the following exchange ensued:

"May I be permitted to see it?"
"The gentleman who wishes board is at liberty to inspect it."
"Madam, I am that gentleman."

Needless to say, the "modish African" was "very emphatically and unexpectedly given to understand that he could not be accommodated." According to *The Transcript*, the black man did not take his refusal well: "his indignant spirit straightway waxed warm, his astonished eyes, gleaming lightning, dilated to the very utmost stretch of their 'orbicular extent,' and he 'grinned horribly a ghastly smile.'" As he wandered off, "he was heard to mutter something about 'equal rights,'" and to recite, "by way of self-consolation," a couplet from Thomas Gray's famous elegy:

> Full many a flower is born to blush unseen,
> And waste its sweetness on the desert air.[3]

The ending of slavery had resulted in a revolution in black behavior, and the tone of this article—its supercilious malevolence and the way the author, by archly putting lines from the famous poet in the black man's mouth, highlighted what he obviously thought was the absurdity of this turn of events—only served to emphasize an underlying white uneasiness at this new situation.

It was not just that blacks were imitating whites; worse, some blacks were clearly aspiring to behave in a fashion similar to that of the white upper class. John Jackson, a 26-year-old "dandy black man," had been the "confidential servant" of one Thaddeus Phelps, Esq., "a gentleman residing in Greenwich-st." for most of 1832. During that time, as he confessed in court, he was "in the practice of stealing money from the house whenever he could lay his hands on it, to the amount of twenty dollars at a time." That was bad enough, but compounding the crime were the young black man's lavish purchases with the purloined money. When the authorities examined his "exceedingly fashionable apartments" in Church Street, they found "wine and other luxuries upon his sideboard," as well as "a dozen superior mahogany chairs, a large mirror, a splendid work table, a cake tray, richly plated candlesticks, silver spoons, mantel ornaments &c. &c." Indeed, according to the *Courier and Enquirer*, the contents of the premises "left not a doubt that the servant's establishment was intended to imitate if not to exceed the costliness of the master's."[4] To many whites the city seemed to be overflowing with blacks who were equally audacious.

Yet this sort of behavior had been going on for some time, ever since significant numbers of African New Yorkers started to secure and define their freedom. A dozen years previously, in late 1821, a case of "criminal conversation" provided one of the minor scandals of the day. Although this instance lacked the "pin money—splendid equippage—elopements—duels and doctors commons," which, according to the *National Advocate*, were the "regular gradations" of "an established case of English crim con," the fact that all the principals were black gave the event enough notoriety for one printer to advertise that he was going to bring out a full account of the trial in pamphlet form within a few days of its conclusion. John Furguson, "a decent young man of color," had brought suit against Thomas Thompson, "an old and experienced beau," for seducing his wife, a much younger and "very handsome" mulatto. Attracted by the idea of "moving in rather higher and more splendid circles," the wife had abandoned "her husband, child and home, and fled with the defendant." According to the *Republican Sentinel*, Furguson's wife's expectations were met by Thompson, who "was possessed of property to a considerable amount!" Since her elopement, Furguson's wife had "had the pleasure of making a tour to the 'Springs,'" that is, the fashionable resort of Saratoga Springs, where Hewlett had performed at least once, and her "Beau Nash" could be seen driving her around New York in "a polished gig 'tandem,' with a retinue that would do honor to a Queen." After lengthy consideration of the evidence, the jury found for the plaintiff and awarded him $250 and costs. This case prompted Mordecai Noah to editorialize in the *Advocate* that blacks were making "a dash at the higher walks in life" and even attempting "to imitate their more fashionable neighbours." Deploring these developments, the influential editor linked them, in his own inimitable fashion, to the folly of allowing any blacks the "elective franchise."[5]

The most revealing site of this sort of social-climbing behavior was the black ball. In 1836, the police roundsman for the *Herald* opined that "Every body may not know that the sons and daughters of Africa have their private balls, soirées, and parties and more than that," but by this date few living in the metropolis could have been unaware that such events were regular occurrences. Although occasional mentions of black balls survive in the historical record from earlier in the century, it was in the 1820s and 1830s that these affairs attained a size and frequency that made them a striking and notorious facet of city life.[6] Several times a year in New York and Philadelphia, during the winter "season," up to three or four hundred blacks, reportedly as many as six hundred on at least one occasion, would dress up in their best outfits, make their way often by carriage to the hall hired for the night, and dance waltzes and cotillions until the early hours of the morning.

These balls intrigued and fascinated whites. In part, they opened a window into what the *Advocate* labeled "High Life Among the Colored Folks," providing racy glimpses of an urban milieu that confirmed all the prevailing stereotypes of black people. While Adam Hodgson, a traveler, was enjoying dinner at a New York house in 1824, his host inadvertently opened a letter addressed to one of his servants; it contained an invitation to "a ball and supper." Few locals would have demurred from Hodgson's observation that "The negroes seem always ready for a frolic, as it is called."[7] Assertions of black frivolity particularly irritated some black reform-minded activists, including most notably one of the editors of *Freedom's Journal*, the nation's first African American newspaper. In 1828 he editorialized that he had "been much tried during the past winter, upon hearing the daily accounts of balls, cotillion parties, &c. in which many of our respectable colored friends have seen proper to indulge in this our city of New-York." A few moments spent assessing the costs of these events, the editor continued, should convince "many who are now great admirers of Balls, &c. . . . that all this waste of time, and health, and money, is highly impolitic, and might easily be dispensed with." The saturnine editor recommended that his fellow blacks should instead "devote their leisure hours to the more important subject of self-cultivation."[8]

Smaller affairs tended to pass unnoticed, but the larger ones often received newspaper coverage. In late February 1828, the *Pennsylvania Gazette* opened its account of a black fancy dress ball by calling it a "joke of no ordinary magnitude"—almost as if blacks behaving like whites was self-evidently ridiculous. The editor of *Freedom's Journal* disputed the *Gazette*'s piece, attempting to discount both the details of the story and the larger implications about black life, but he was wasting his ink.[9] Highly sensitive to what whites might think and, in this case, entering the lists on grounds determined by white newspapers, he missed completely the positive aspect of the exciting cultural convulsion that accompanied slavery's demise, and also failed to appreciate the combative edge that ordinary blacks were imparting into the free black culture they were creating in northern urban centers.

As a matter of course, newspapers reported disturbances associated with some of these balls, with the assumption that blacks who attended balls were behaving with ludicrous effrontery. In August 1833, after dancing and drinking most of the night away at one such event, a number of blacks slowly and noisily ambled up Broadway at between two and three o'clock in the morning. The watch found this behavior irritating enough to warrant incarcerating several of the party for the rest of the night, and the *Courier and Enquirer* thought it worthy of a few lines of print.[10] Newspapers eagerly seized upon incidents that provided the opportunity to peer at "black life," particularly if the material was lively and could be written up humorously. After a ball held in February 1835, Granville Bryant charged Henry Bennet, a "modest looking little yellow man," with assault and battery. The *Sun*'s reporter spent some time describing the complainant; Bryant was "a tall dandy looking gentleman, of quadroon blood," wearing "a nice embroidered shirt bosom," "divers fine clothes over his precious body," and "with hair frizzled up, and a dainty pair of gloves on his hands." At the ball, he had "danced and coquetted, smirked and smiled," but had ended up quarreling with a young black woman, over whom he had thrown a cup of coffee and whom he called a "a d—d black——." Bennet and several other blacks had ejected Bryant from the ball, and it was for that that he was suing them. When Bryant had finished what the *Sun* described as his "mincing story," the magistrate threw everyone out of his court. Not even bothering to temper its language, the *Transcript* simply reported that Bryant had called the woman "a black bitch."[11]

For all the sarcasm and supposed humor in the newspaper coverage of blacks balls, press stories revealed an underlying brittleness in the white reaction to them: there was something unnerving about the aggressive way black New Yorkers and Philadelphians were refusing to fade quietly into the background and asserting their right to do whatever whites did. Partly it was African Americans' flamboyant clothing, partly their use of the accoutrements of elite white life, such as carriages, but overall it was the clamorous way in which blacks were occupying the public space which whites had unthinkingly assumed was theirs alone that disconcerted them. At an event organized to raise money for Greek

Freedom, the *New-York Enquirer* pointedly noted that, at the start of the evening, there had been a queue of horses and carriages in Orange Street waiting for their black passengers to alight; at another ball two years earlier, the bustle in Mulberry Street had been controlled, according to the *New-York National Advocate*, by black managers "ordering the white drivers to turn 'de horses head to Pump street.'" "It is worthy of remark," commented the *Pennsylvania Gazette*, following another of these affairs in 1828, "that many of the coaches . . . were attended by white coachmen and *white footmen*," a fact that made the newspaper wonder "how long it will be before servants and masters change places."[12] There can be little doubt that these were exactly the kinds of impressions that the blacks in question were trying to plant in white minds.

Every now and then, when white authorities interfered in a heavy-handed manner, a black spokesman would make it explicit that a new order was being established and that blacks were no longer prepared to behave as slaves. The morning after the Police Magistrate and a dozen members of the watch had closed down a ball in Mulberry Street in March 1825, about forty blacks appeared in court. "With a bold front and confident brow," the manager of the establishment in which the event took place stepped forward and "made a speech." Even the supposedly comic black dialect in which the address was rendered could not conceal the black man's anger: he demanded to know "for what dey disturb peaceable black people cause dey had a party—dey hab rights —dey pay dare money and dey behave as well as the vite gentleman vat go to de City Hotel—and dey hand de vine and cake about on a vaiter like dem vite folks at de Washington Hall and de Greek Ball." Three years later, in the early hours of the morning and after another of these functions, two mulatto women, interrupted by the watch while quarreling in the street, were hauled off to the Police Office. The magistrate, whom the *New-York En-*

quirer described as "benevolence himself," proceeded to lecture them on the "consequences of dissipation," pointing out, among other things, that "the follies of the upper classes are too often imitated instead of their virtues." Cutting to the quick of the issue, one of the women retorted sharply: "If the big white folks dance why should not people of color?"[13]

In the case of these black balls, the sources are even more than usually skewed by derogatory white attitudes. The newspaper stories lack shade or nuance; they are almost invariably written from a perspective external to the events themselves, concentrating not on the actual ball but on blacks' behavior in the street on their way to or home from it. And, of course, all stories are permeated with an overbearing "humor." Even the racist stories, however, hint that black balls signified rather differently to African American participants; that they were in fact firmly enmeshed in the filaments of the city's black life. In late 1823, it was announced that a ball to aid the beleaguered Greeks (engaged in a war of independence from the Turks) was to be held at the Mercer Street Theater, where Hewlett and his fellow black actors had given most of their performances. The event was to take place on January 1, 1824, "the anniversary of the Abolition Society," as the organizers noted. Clearly they hoped that their call to freedom-loving black citizens would "be felt with peculiar force on that day, which cannot fail most powerfully to recall to the descendants of Africans, the blessings of freedom." Some three years later, another ball to aid the Greeks' struggle for independence was held in a hall festooned with banners from the Manumission Society.[14]

A story published in the newly established *Philadelphia Monthly Magazine* described a fancy dress affair held in Philadelphia in February 1828 and presented a view from the inside of one of these balls. As with all such pieces, it meant to lampoon the black revelers, but in this case its four-page length provides enough detail to open up other possible readings. According to the writer, the African Philadelphians who attended, "excited by a laudable spirit of emulation," were copying, however comically and ineptly, functions staged by whites. Here he followed the usual cues taken by other newspaper writers, dismissing such events as risible clones of the practices of white society, but in this case some of the particulars the writer described undermined the general impression he attempted to convey. He reported, for instance, that a large map of Africa had been rendered in charcoal on the dance floor and that opposite the band there shone an imposing transparency, designed by a black, which depicted, among other things, the Abolition Society breaking the shackles of slaves, and a vessel about to sail for Liberia. There were also, during the evening, positive references to Haiti, the black republic established after a successful revolution against the French colonial administration. Organizers of the ball had resolved "by acclamation" to invite to it any Haitian army or navy officers who happened to be in town, and one such notable who did attend became the star of the evening; his "easy manners and fascinating address gave all the ladies and gentlemen present a favorable opinion of the state of society in that island." Most importantly, however, the orchestra had been put together by Frank Johnson. Johnson, easily the most famous African American composer and bandleader in the antebellum years, had performed with Hewlett and was noted for his talent at syncretizing European forms and the rhythms of the African American dancing cellars, creating a culturally distinctive sound.[15]

African American balls were multifaceted and complex events that can be interpreted in several ways. A considerable element of "copying" or "imitating" white American practices was in effect, as blacks took from what they found around them in order to restructure their lives now that they were free. But the process of building a social structure was more intricate than that. Even if the origins of the black balls lay in white American culture, that was just a starting point: northern blacks infused these events with their own cultural imperatives, creating something that was new. Participating in events that had cultural significance for themselves, they also, at least in part, parodied the behavior of whites. In its turn, the way in which African New Yorkers and African Philadelphians transformed the ball would have its own reverberations in white practices: the most obvious example is the distinctive "distortion" that Frank Johnson, and probably other lesser known black musicians, gave to waltzes and cotillions at the white balls, where their playing was in much demand.

At one and the same time, then, these black balls were part imitation, part parody, and part showy performance of a northern urban African American culture. They must also have been something else—something that historians in their bookish dourness often omit from their renditions of human behavior—namely fun. Dressing up to the nines, and beyond; hiring a coach and a white driver to take oneself downtown; making a grand entrance; mingling and gossiping with friends and acquaintances; eating supper and drinking—these were enjoyable things for people to do. Then, of course, there was the music and the dancing—first the clipped precision of cotillions and the sweeping grace of waltzes, but as the evening wore on, some of the formal clothing was shucked off or at least loosened, and the alcohol had taken its toll, there was the dimming of the lights, a slowing down of the music, and dancing of a rather different sort. This, as those who had started their lives as slaves must have particularly appreciated, was the way freedom was meant to be.

For many whites, the obvious joyfulness of much of this display, the sense that blacks seemed to be having more fun than were their former owners, was unsettling. But if black behavior was in some measure repellent, it was also curiously alluring. The furtive glimpses of these balls and other sites of entertainment that northern whites perceived as they walked the streets of their city, or events they read about in the newspapers, suggested an unrestrained and sexualized black milieu that allowed whites to project vicariously their own guilty fantasies onto black bodies. This fascination with black balls and other aspects of black life provided material from which Clay and others created their ubiquitous caricatures of African Americans, and also background for the skits and short pieces by blackface stars of the 1830s that were the wildly popular precursors to the minstrel show. In September 1833, for example, the best known of these artists, T. D. Rice, was performing at New York's Bowery Theater in *Life in Philadelphia*. This play was a farce, the theater's publicist claimed, "written with great spirit" in order to display the "Ethiopoian Mobility of Philadelphia in all their glory—supper, champagne, bustle and balls." Rice portrayed a "North Carolina negro undergoing his initiation into the mysteries of high life under the tutilage of Bonaparte a Philadelphia Swell," a ploy that allowed the actors full reign to cavort through situations that were "strikingly ludicrous," and that elicited from the audiences "the merriest bursts of laughter."[16]

In some form or other, blacks had been imitating whites for centuries, but now that African New Yorkers were no longer slaves, that form of behavior was simply more apparent to all manner of whites. But what was even more novel about these years in New York, and elsewhere in the North, was the unprecedented number of whites who took to imitating, parodying, and burlesquing blacks. This too was a result of freedom. It was as though the now-free blacks were more visible than they had ever been as slaves, and their activities were attracting the eye of "witty" whites. Yet the humor had an edge. "Black dialect" and the various "humorous" stories that were told about blacks were designed to separate blacks from whites, to ensure that although all were now free, the two groups could not be confused.

In early January 1813, when *Poulson's American Daily Advertiser*, a Philadelphia newspaper, reprinted from the *Boston Weekly Messenger* a supposedly comic piece in "black dialect" entitled a "Dialogue Between Sambo & Cuffy," the editor thought it necessary to append a brief notice. "It must be recollected," he warned his readers, "that the people of colour in Boston talk in a dialect peculiar to themselves, of which here is an excellent specimen."[17] Perhaps there were some minor peculiarities of African Bostonian English that marked its speakers off from African Philadelphian or African New Yorker English, although this would hardly have caused problems of comprehension. More to the point, there was as yet no accepted way of rendering black speech on the printed page. It is easy enough to find examples of "black dialect" in the newspapers or almanacs of the New York or Philadelphia or Boston of the 1790s, but such material was a mere trickle; by the 1810s and 1820s it turned into a torrent.[18] With increased volume came standardization and the development of an orthography of "black dialect." The conventions of this white version of black speech—the inclusion of numerous malapropisms and the use of phonetic spellings, for example—were being worked out in the northern cities in the early decades of the nineteenth century, at the same time that large numbers of free blacks were becoming a highly visible presence. "Black dialect" comprised a curious mixture: one ingredient was an occasional closely observed representation of the way in which some blacks did actually speak; the other ingredient was a complete invention of black speech forms. Overall, this amalgam of fact and fantasy purported to show, often in the most demeaning and unpleasant fashion possible, that blacks were comically inept imitators of their supposed betters, and that even if now free, they remained clearly differentiated from whites. Refined and above all amplified by the minstrel show, this manufactured black dialect, with all its pernicious legacy of racial denigration, has lasted down to our own time.

Back in 1813, the editor of *Poulson's Advertiser* felt compelled to include his warning about "black dialect," but that would have been one of the last occasions on which such a warning would have been thought necessary, for this was the period in which the whites invented what was known as "Bobalition." Starting in 1808, African Bostonians celebrated the abolition of the slave trade by staging, on July 14, a parade through town which ended up at the African church, where they listened to a sermon delivered by some dignitary or other. From the outset this celebration won enthusiastic support and for almost a quarter of a century it was one of the highlights of the year for black Bostonians. Not surprisingly, its very success prompted a surly, ill-tempered, and occasionally violent response from many white Bostonians. An account of the 1820 march printed in the *New England Galaxy* gives a good indication of these attitudes. For the *Galaxy's* writer, the event was an unwanted display by "a mob of negroes, whose parade and pageantry are as useless, unmeaning, and ridiculous, as their persons and the atmosphere which surrounds them in these hot days are offensive and disgusting." "Quietness and order can hardly be expected," he continued, "when five or six hundred negroes, with a band of music, pikes, swords, epaulettes, sashes, cocked hats, and standards, are marching through the principal streets." The "scene" was one of "farce and mummery," a "ridiculous piece of buffoonery."[19]

In the early 1810s, some whites created a series of broadsides on the occasion of the parade, labeling the event "Bobalition." These posters were plastered all over the city in advance of the procession. Language and imitation were at the core of Bobalition. The very term was a verbal play on the supposed inability of blacks clearly and properly to enunciate the word "abolition": just like a young child, they had inserted an extra syllable, mangling the word and demonstrating once more that they were incapable of emulating their white betters. "Bobalition" was a particularly wounding invention, ridiculing as it did that which most African Northerners held dearest—their recently attained freedom. Filled with a maladroit and malapropic black dialect, these lengthy and elaborate broadsides proved to be at least as popular with whites as were the actual processions with African Bostonians. For the period to 1830, some twenty or so of these posters are known to have survived. Newspapers joined the campaign of denigration, publishing so-called comic toasts in black dialect given at the celebratory dinners. Gradually, Bobalition conjured up the comic black and was no longer necessarily associated only with the July parade. Thus a pamphlet consisting of a several-page-long poem and entitled *The Pick Nack* proclaimed on the cover that it had been "delivered before the Bobalition Society and published at their request," and was "respectfully dedicated to Misse Phillisse Malissa Wangum." The Bobalition broadsides and all the attendant material constituted perhaps the earliest extensive and regular seam of black caricature in America.[20]

Bobalition may have started in Boston, but it tapped into a mood prevalent elsewhere in the North and was easily translated to other locales. As early as February 1819, on a boat somewhere near the Bay of Biscay, William Faux, an English traveler en route to America, was regaled with an account of ludicrous toasts supposedly given at the latest Boston free black celebration of "as they term it the *Boblition* of the slave trade." "I give this anecdote, as I heard it from an American," the bemused Englishman noted, before sharply concluding that "contempt of the poor blacks, or niggers, as they are there called, seems the national sin." A few years later, though, the term was being used in London itself to satirize the passage of the bill abolishing slavery in the West Indies. By the 1820s Bobalition had become a catch-all term that embodied a churlish and spiteful response to the new status of free blacks, a term that was instantly recognizable in Boston, Philadelphia, New York, and even in London.[21]

Editors often filled their own newspapers with material taken from other publications, and some of the Boston material made its way to New York City. In July 1822, for example, the *New York Evening Post* reprinted from the *Boston Daily Advertiser* a series of nine toasts in black dialect, supposedly given at the recent celebration of the "anniversary of the Abolition of Slavery." A few local white wits saw in slavery's demise in 1827, and the inauguration of an annual black celebratory parade, an opportunity to try their hand at establishing Bobalition in New York. They produced at least one broadside—De Grandest Bobalition—(it conferred on Hewlett the dubious honor of being mentioned by name) and plastered it up around the city. In addition, the *New-York Spy* ran a Bobalition story. Two years later, in the aftermath of the march celebrating the end of slavery, someone offered a piece for publication to the *New York American*; the editor, however, refused to print the article, announcing in his paper that "*Bobalition* is too broad for our taste."[22] Bobalition, then, was certainly known in New York, although it never attained there anything like the prominence it had in Boston.

If, in Boston, the disturbing spectacle of assertive blacks parading through the main streets had provoked Bobalition, and thus the institutionalization of "black dialect" as the way in which "print" and later "stage" blacks were expected to speak, in New York the white response to black stage performance fulfilled much the same function. As William Brown, James Hewlett, and other black actors staged their own version of freedom at the African

Grove and other venues, white New Yorkers took away an entirely different lesson from these performances. Although unwittingly —holding those black actors responsible for the fevered inventions of their white contemporaries would hardly be fair—the actors were not only present at but central to one of the moments that made the minstrel show possible. In Boston, those responsible for Bobalition were, and would remain, anonymous; in New York, the writer who was central to the development of "black dialect" and minstrelsy was well known.

Right from the first story about the African Grove, Mordecai Noah was intrigued by what he viewed as the mimicked details of black life, particularly in their language. As he wrote in the *National Advocate* in early August 1821, "in their address; salutations; familiar phrases; and compliments; their imitative faculties are best exhibited." He then illustrated his point by transcribing snatches of conversation overheard after the band in the garden had finished playing (and, interestingly, the first speaker here and the holder of the same disparaging opinion of the music as Noah's was almost certainly Hewlett):

You like [the] music, Miss? Can't say I like it much. I once could play Paddy Cary, on the Piano; our young ladies learnt me. Did you eber hear Phillips sing, "Is dare a heart dat neber lov'd,"? I sing xactly like him; Harry tell us some news. De Greeks are gone to war wid de Turks. Oh! dat's bery clever; and our gentlemen said at dinner yesterday, dat de Greeks had taken Constantinople, and all de wives of de Dey of Algiers. O shocking! Vell, Miss, ven is de happy day; ven vill you enter de matrimony state? Dat's my business: Gentlemen mus'nt meddle with dese delicate tings. Beg pardon, Miss. O! no offense.

As he went on, Noah was unable to resist pointing out the political implications of what he portrayed as the upper-class pretensions of newly freed blacks: "Harry, who did you vote for at de election? De fedrilists to be sure; I never wotes for de mob. Our gentlemen brought home tickets, and after dinner, ve all vent and woted."[23] Possibly the inclusion of the many "v's" here, certainly jarring to modern ears, was part of an attempt to capture the Dutch inflection in African New Yorker English. At any rate, readers of the *Advocate* over the ensuing weeks and months witnessed a rapid development in the way in which black speech was represented: in later stories about the black actors and in numerous pieces about other aspects of black life—all of them grist for the newspaper's mill—Noah exhibited a much surer hand, deftly employing a black dialect still instantly recognizable as such today.

For Noah, the activities of Hewlett and the other black actors were emblematic of the larger problems posed by the behavior of African New Yorkers, and much of the bite in a couple of imaginative skits he published in his paper derived from the way he creatively fused these concerns. The first—written in late June 1823, when Brown was trying desperately to hold his theater company together with a benefit performance of *The Drama of King Shotaway*—was in the form of a playbill, similar both to the ones the black actors were papering all over New York and to the Bobalition broadsides then being run off in Boston in anticipation of that year's celebration. It began: "On ———day evening, (and on every evening until further notice) will be presented at the Skunk Point, corner of Orange and Cross streets, *a nuisance* in 3 acts interspersed with a variety of abuse &c. &c." The cast included, among others, Drunkencuff, Profane Tom, and Noisy Sam, played respectively by Mr. Ethiop, Mr. Mandingo, and Mr. Creole. The first act would be "a masquerade of Ethiopeans" and "a Dance, together with the method of Blockading Side Walks in Sea Ports." In the second, "Messrs. Cuff, Tom and Sam" would display "intoxication, profanity, riot &c. &c. in which Mrs. Diana will prove herself champion," and in the third, the players would "amuse the audience with many new and absurd gestures." The entire spectacle would finish at one in the morning to the "general annoyance of the peace and security of the good citizens in the vicinity." A brief note was appended: "No person admitted, who voted in favor of the Missouri bill, or who are in favor of the slave states."[24]

Noah must have been quite taken with this piece because a few weeks later he published a sequel. Under the heading "Cross and Orange streets"—at the intersection of these streets lay Five Points, rapidly developing a worldwide reputation as the epitome of urban squalor—he noted that this neighborhood was "celebrated for riots, dram drinking, and an assemblage of blacks, who herd in large squads." Noah then urged that those "who are for liberating the slaves of the south had better pay a visit to these haunts of freemen." What followed was what the editor described as "a mild *jeu d'espirit*," a much longer imaginative piece that refined and followed through on many of the ideas raised earlier. The first part read:

GRAND CONCERT OF DE BOB-LINK SOCIETY
"De times hab changed,"
But we hab not.

In consequence of *great couragement* bin had had at skunk point for *dram-tick* beformance, de managers will gib grand consert ebery evening dis week.

De public is spectfully formed dat a new gumpany of *Africans* habe kommenced *noying* de *pop-lace* at de above place. De *ladies* and *gemmen* of dis *korps* are ferior to *none* in point of *low*

language, and de *vulgar talons* of some of latter are *first rate*.
De entertainments dat will be brot up consist chiefly in grate
woe-call powers.

Leader of de music	Nig Crow-well
Overture to Back-us.	Sam Screetch-owl

Song　　Why should we de *watchman* fear,
　　　　　　Since when deir call'd dey neber hear,
　　　　　　　　　Tom Whip-poor-will.

Duet　　Say, will you *treat*? or shall I go?
　　　　　　Dear dimple chops, it *must* be so.
　　　　　　　　Bet Sawbill and Jack Pigeonwing

Song　　If de *marsh-all* should come, how de *neighbours*
　　　　　would laugh,
　　　　　　But, as we'rre only *so many*, he only catch *half*.
　　　　　　　　Prince Nighthawk

Song　　When we done *make tread mill* crack,
　　　　　　Light as *feders* we come back,
　　　　　　Ready wid more *saucy slack*.
　　　　　　　　　Dick Jackdaw

Song　　Street Spector sleeps *late* in de morn,
　　　　　　Maybe *sick*, he eat too much *corn*,
　　　　　　Get de *fever* as sure as he born.
　　　　　　　　　Antony Duck-eye

Duet　　Peacock *mark*, he rader dark,
　　　　　　Yet *strut* as big as *white man*,
　　　　　　And *sulkey Jay*, bote night and day
　　　　　　Will make much *noise* as *he* can.
　　　　　　　　Caesar Snipe and Dinah Duck
　　　companied on sheep skin fiddle by Dick Webfoot.

The piece goes on at some length in much the same vein, climaxing with a riot on the street. In a final note, the author stated that the authorities were invited "to *witness* our new *immorally scenes*, trusting dey will not *any-mad-vert too closely* pon de *new actors*."[25]

This "Grand Concert" piece was demeaning and derogatory; it used black dialect to lampoon African New Yorkers and played on all the stereotypes of free blacks that newspaper editors, Noah in particular, were doing their best to establish. And yet, as was usually the case with Noah, there is something more here. Note that he drops the obvious nomenclature of "Profane Tom" and the like from the earlier piece in favor of naming the many singers to ground the bird motif permeating the "Grand Concert." Not only did this strategy cleverly give the piece a thematic unity, but it also relied on knowledge of the details of black life. Birds were of great importance in African American culture, particularly in dance and music. All manner of slave dances—the buzzard lope and pigeon wing for example—gained their names from the movements of birds. Herein, of course, lay part of the potency of "Jump Jim Crow." One of Frank Johnson's most popular tunes was the "Bird Waltz," which imitated the "chirping of the canary bird so distinctly and so natural that the keenest perception cannot discover the difference."

Most revealing of all, though, was Noah's use of the word "Bob-Link" in the title. This, of course, sounds very much like "Bobalition," conjuring up all manner of derogatory associations. But the bobolink was actually a bird (*Dolichonyx oryzivorus*). As W. T. Lhamon, Jr. has noted, the bobolink "is a field bird, a new world passerine, rarely vagrant in Europe, whose male's brown underparts and face change to black while it breeds in spring." The bird was well known to African New Yorkers—Bob Rowley, one of the most honored and highly skilled dancers on the shingle at Catharine Slip, performed under the name of "Bobolink Bob"—and to white New Yorkers as well.[26] A few years after

Noah wrote his "Concert," Lydia Maria Child wrote eloquently and wonderingly of the bird. In the middle of one of her *Letters from New York*, she digressed to describe a mockingbird imitating the bobolink.

> The short, quick, "bob-a-link," "bob-a-link," he could master very well; but when it came to the prolonged trill of gushing melody, at the close of the strain—the imitator stopped in the midst. Again the bob-o'-link poured forth his soul in song; the mocking-bird hopped nearer, and listened most intently. Again he tried; but it was all in vain. The bob-o'-link, as if conscious that none could imitate his God-given tune, sent forth a clearer, stronger, richer, strain than ever. The mocking-bird evidently felt that his reputation was at stake. He warbled all kinds of notes in quick succession. You would have thought the house was surrounded by robins, sparrows, whippoorwills, black-birds, and linnets. Having shown off his accomplishments, he again tried his powers on the all-together inimitable trill. The effort he made was prodigious; but it was mere talent trying to copy genius. He couldn't do it. He stopped, gasping, in the midst of prolonged melody, and flew away abruptly, in evident vexation.[27]

It was almost as though by referring to the "bobolink" Noah allowed that there was an irreducible genius to black life that could not be reproduced. For all of the critic's pyrotechnics and the mockingbird's display, entertaining enough in their own right, neither was going to capture the sound of the bobolink.

If Noah, on occasion, may have conceded the inimitability of African American culture, he still took every opportunity to make derisory comments about black life. At times, it was almost as though Noah could not help himself. Down in Philadelphia in late December 1828, he dropped in on the Mayor's Court, listened to a few minutes of testimony, and quickly penned a sketch entitled "A Scene in Coloured Society," which the local *Democratic Press* published a few days later. Henry Washington had begun his testimony by noting that "I saw this lady, now my wife, some time 'go and got much entached to her—spend my time with her and get in love." Another black named Durham, a rival for this woman's affections, continued to pester her even after she married Washington, frequently turning up on the newlyweds' doorstep. Finally, Washington warned Durham off, sparking a "good many hard words," which, in turn, upset his wife, who "took hold of me and got me qualified." In the course of the ensuing brawl Durham sank his teeth into Washington's thumb and Washington reciprocated by biting Durham's nose. A bystander testified that he thought that Washington "would have eat the very face off of him." The case, as such, was completely inconsequential, yet another minor domestic drama to be sorted out on Monday morning by the petty courts. To Noah, however, it cast a light into the goings on of blacks, in a way that revealed their sexual foibles and also highlighted their fumblings with the English language, always to be contrasted with Noah's own neatly turned bon mots. The piece concluded with the observation that neither party had "appeared much injured, although it is probable they will each of them carry the marks of the other's teeth to his grave."[28]

The way Mordecai Noah and other newspaper editors chose to portray African New Yorkers percolated through into a number of other cultural genres. It was almost certainly Noah's publicity splash that made the famed English actor Charles Mathews aware of the very existence of the black performers in the first place. And what Mathews saw in these actors' performances (and here, of course, we must judge by the way he later chose to represent the spectacle) was shaped by the newspaper-formed popular perception of vainglorious free blacks misconstruing what they would imitate. It is almost inconceivable that Mathews, with his interest in both the theater and in searching out material for *A Trip to America*, failed to read the *National Advocate* when he was in New York. To be sure, Mathews was probably even more interested than Noah in the use of language, but, in a very real sense, the most famous scene of Mathews's long and illustrious career brought the words and ideas of Mordecai Noah to the transatlantic stage. It was this that caused the theater historian Samuel Hay to label Noah, and not the usual suspect, T. D. Rice, as "the father of Negro minstrelsy."[29]

Similarly, the way blacks were portrayed in numerous popular prints by Edward Clay and other caricaturists drew its inspiration from the press. The clearest example of this influence is found in one of the lithographs in Clay's *Life in New York* series. The image was set in the police office, which, by 1829 (the lithograph's date), had become the venue where much of the domestic strife and irritable dissension (the usual accompaniments of life in the crowded metropolis) among New York blacks was sorted out. In the picture two black men are vying for the attention of a black woman who lived in an oyster cellar—"Miss Arminton did give me the witching glance, which told me as plain as eye could speak that [I] was the more welcome visiter"—and the action centers on the handkerchief displayed prominently on the podium. The idea for the caricature came from an actual case that was reported in the *Morning Courier and New-York Enquirer:* Clay's rendering of the dialogue is virtually identical with that in the newspaper's account.[30] The depiction in this and numerous other contemporary images is, of course, derogatory, but the reason why such caricatures worked for their white viewers was the very familiarity of the scenes. Clay's lithograph depicted scenes which they read about in the newspapers or claimed to see on the city streets every day.

And, most importantly, when they gave their renditions of black life, the early blackface performers were also inspired by what they had actually seen. T. D. Rice, easily the most gifted and influential of the minstrel performers, was quite explicit about this process. When, in late 1833, the editor of the *New York Mirror* attacked Rice's performance of the song "Jim Crow" and of the opera *Oh! Hush!* at the Bowery Theater, Rice responded with a lengthy letter to the editor of the *Morning Courier and New-York Enquirer*. In this clever and cutting demolition of his critic, only a small part of which is relevant here, Rice claimed that he had "merely sought to give a sketch of the lowest classes, something in the same style with Tom and Jerry." Indeed, Rice had been told that *Tom and Jerry* was "itself imitated from a style of humble life drama, exceedingly popular even among the audiences more fastidious in their tastes, of other countries." "I am sorry that the niggar affectation of white manners [and here again we have a white imitating blacks who were already imitating whites] should be so annoying to the *Mirror*," he continued, "but there was a precedent for this sort of 'high life below stairs' in the farce of that name." Rice was referring here to an English commonplace, but, as he would have been well aware, "high life below stairs" or some variant of the term was commonly used in the United States also, to characterize pretentious and *arriviste* aspects of urban black behavior.[31]

With all this "imitation" going on, it was probably inevitable that blacks would be mistaken for whites and vice versa. In 1820s and 1830s New York people had a fascination with "passing," whether intentional or not, and a number of stories revealing much about race relations were freely circulating. In early February 1835, the *Morning Courier and New-York Enquirer* informed its readers of recent goings on in Albany. When it became known that a Justice of the Peace had "lately married an Irish girl to a full blooded negro," a "mob" gathered and "took the matter in hand,

and blackened his [the Justice of the Peace's] face." The "outraged justice" had defended his action in the local papers, claiming that he was told the woman was a mulatto and that he would not have married the "interesting couple" had he realized that the woman was white. "We presume so," the *Courier*'s writer opined, "but couldn't he tell a fair skinned daughter of Erin, from a mulatto, when he saw her?"[32] But for all the outrage of the Albany mob, or the self-righteous certainty of the *Courier*, an increasing number of whites were having just as much difficulty as had the Albany justice in working out who was who. Now that most African Americans living in the North were no longer slaves and were dressing and disporting themselves on the city sidewalks in newly assertive ways, all manner of whites had moments of confusion when dealing with their black neighbors.

For many whites a well-dressed black was an at least slightly comic figure, but such observations also carried an underlying sense of disquiet, a fretful complaint at the blurring of the former, relatively clear-cut racial boundaries. William Blane, an English gentleman who visited Philadelphia in the early 1820s, recollected that "frequently," on being "desirous of ascertaining whether the beauty of some finely dressed female was equal to her attire," he had "perceived under a huge Leghorn bonnet and lace cap, the black face and great white eyes of a negress." Quite often he "could hardly help laughing, so ludicrous was this contrast." A decade later, the traveler S. A. Ferrall was walking down Broadway in New York when he "was struck with the figure of a fashionably dressed woman, who was sauntering before me." Having overtaken her, Ferrall turned around, only to be shocked. "O angels and ministers of ugliness!" Ferrall later wrote, "I beheld a face, as black as soot—a mouth that reached from ear to ear—a nose, like nothing human—and lips a full inch in diameter!" Both of these travelers derided blacks for copying white behavior—

Blaine wrote of African Americans being "so eager to imitate the fashions of whites"—but, unnerved by the apparent success of these particular African Americans in managing to look like whites, the two white men had marked themselves off by lampooning the blacks' facial features.[33] To be sure, demeaning caricatures of Africans and African Americans had a long history, but as the viciousness of Ferrall's description suggests, such negative portrayals of black people took on a new importance at a time when other barriers were crumbling.

It was not merely travelers or strangers who experienced the embarrassment of mistaking someone's racial identity, and when such incidents occurred, they commonly made their way into the newspapers. In June 1834, the *Sun* recounted how a local white dandy's attention was attracted by "a tall and elegant female figure before him" while he too strolled down Broadway. From behind, he was taken by her "majestic mien," sent into "rhapsodies" by her "neat little ancles," and "enchanted with her taste in dress," but, as she "stopped to cheapen an article of ornament at a store," he passed her, "turned around, looked her full in the face, and behold she was black!!!" Another young white man out on a "spree" came across a black girl on the Bowery. He went up to her and said "Good evening—O, I beg your pardon—I thought you was white!" She quickly responded that she "thought he was a good for nothing booby," whereupon the aggrieved man tore off the young woman's bonnet and ripped it into pieces.[34]

Whites were also mistaken for blacks. Often this was the result of the white, for whatever reason, wearing blackface. Very early one morning in June 1829 "a well dressed young man was seen reeling in Broadway." From "a little distance," the obviously inebriated man "was taken for a negro," but on closer examination it turned out that "his shining black complexion was only the effect of a beautiful coat of oil-paint, which some *friend* had laid on."

Occasionally, though, the confusion occurred without artificial assistance. Five years later a "highly respectable gentleman" from the South checked into one of the Broadway hotels. As a result of "long exposure to the sun," the man was rather dark-skinned; indeed, according to the *Sun*, "at first sight" he would "be mistaken for one a little touched with the 'niggur blood.'" As soon as the landlord laid eyes on him, the agitated man ran upstairs to find his wife, exclaiming to her, "Wife, wife, did you know there was a real niggur down stairs?" She doubted that this could be so, but her husband was adamant: "Curse me if it aint a true bill." He went on to add that "I've no doubt the rascal will want to marry one of our daughters before he goes away!" "O Lord!" the startled wife exclaimed. Eventually, the landlord confronted the guest: "I beg your pardon, sir—but—but—." "Ah, yes I understand you," the guest replied, and gave him his card on which was the name "Colonel———, of Charleston, one of the most respectable citizens of South Carolina." The piece ended by noting that "the joke was too good to lose" and that "the Colonel laughed heartily" as he regaled the gentlemen in the sitting room with the story that evening.[35]

As a number of historians have pointed out, this was the period in which "whiteness" was being invented, primarily by various ethnic groups that sought to distinguish themselves from blacks, but in the 1820s and 1830s that process was nowhere near complete.[36] In 1826, one white New Yorker, angry at what he perceived as blacks trampling all over "us poor white people," signed his letter to the *New-York Enquirer, "An Unfortunate White Man."* But this was just an early manifestation of consciousness of "whiteness," regardless of how clear things may have seemed to this aggrieved white. Indeed, from today's perspective, what seems remarkable about these years in which Hewlett trod the boards in New York was the fluidity of racial categories. The key here is the language used in everyday speech. Finding examples of this language is obviously difficult, although there are a couple in the records of court cases (one of the few places where the language of ordinary people is occasionally transcribed without calculated distortion). In late 1817, George Angus was convicted of the assault and battery of Michael Quinn. At one point in the events that led up to the assault, a very angry Angus ended up outside Quinn's locked door, shouting abuse that could be heard by everyone in the neighborhood. According to the court papers, the words he used were: "If I could get the door open I would murder you, and when I get it open I will murder you, I want to be hanged for you, I am shure god would not be angry with me for shivering an Irish man." Just for good measure, Angus added, at the top of his voice, that "they merchants that brings the Irish negroes to this country, their ships ought to go to the bottom and be damd."[37]

A second example of the fluidity of racial categories occurred a bit over a decade later in the summer of 1828. As was the case on most Sundays, New York's African Church had been pelted with stones during service, an offense that was not only dangerous in itself but also forced the worshippers to keep the doors shut. This, in summer, often caused members to faint from the heat. On this occasion, one Peter Corcoran was detained and charged. Corcoran was not present in court at his trial, but James Harris, a member of the church, swore that he had seen Corcoran throwing stones. At this point the Judge intervened and asked the witness a question: "Is Corcoran a white man?" The black man simply replied "He passes for a white man."[38] Of course, for all of Harris's efforts to highlight the slipperiness of Corcoran's racial status, that uncertainty would soon be resolved. Ironically, throwing stones at black churches and physically harassing black people on the city streets became valued badges of whiteness for young Irish men.

Perhaps the most important site where tensions over racial categories were played out was the theater. It was a liminal space that excited the passions and held an element of danger. An incident from 1834 illustrates the point. One evening in May, the officer attached to the Park Theater for the purpose of maintaining order "was attempting to remove a black girl from the gallery because she made a noise." At this point Edward Jackson, a black sailor on leave from the brig *United States*, came to the girl's assistance, and the pair of them "completely stripped the officer of his pantaloons, and tore them in pieces." According to the *Sun*, the officer was left "in not a very modest situation among the gentlemen and ladies of the gallery."[39] But, of course, the *Sun* reporter was being sarcastic; for him the onlookers to this spectacle were neither gentlemen nor ladies. The gallery was for prostitutes, poor whites, and above all African New Yorkers. It was a place where, periodically, authority ran the risk of being debagged.

For some New Yorkers at least, the theater was also the site of their deepest fantasies. In April 1833, the *Morning Courier and New-York Enquirer* published an extraordinary story about a "young lady not quite out of her teens, who from some unknown motive had long indulged a curiosity to view the Park Theater from the gallery." She had come up with plan after plan in order "to gratify this inclination to view the audience and stage, from the topmost point of access"—and clearly this "inclination" had little to do with the excellence of the view of the stage to be thus afforded. On the last Friday in March 1833, she was finally ready to put her latest ploy into action. The young lady donned "an old bonnet and some cast off clothing of a servant in the kitchen." This, however, left her face bare. Since a veil would have been "rather out of keeping with the place and character she was about to assume, recourse was had to a coat of oil and lampblack." Garbed thus in a black woman's ragged old clothing, a pair of black gloves, and with her face "besmeared," the young lady "hied for the Theater." At this point, the sexual frisson of it all bubbled over into the *Courier and Enquirer*'s story, as the writer described the young woman ascending "the almost endless stair case to the gallery, with some little dread, it is true, but still a dread almost overcome by the pleasing hope of so shortly having her curiosity gratified by realizing a scene which she had long anticipated, and as ardently desired." She purchased a ticket with no trouble, sat down off by herself and gazed "with satisfaction upon the scenes which presented itself beneath her." But as the benches filled up, she came into closer proximity with other denizens of the gallery, and "the eyes of some of her sooty companions detected the cheat." Although the writer thought this was "a catastrophe which she had not anticipated," I would suggest that the fear of being unmasked had never been far from the young woman's mind and was the source of a good part of the thrill. The young lady was "shoved and jostled about," and some of "the real simon pures"—an extraordinary way to describe blacks—"insisted [that] she was a witch and others the old boy [that is, the devil]." Indeed, a few "were so indignant at the imposition, and the insult presumed from the vile attempt to assume their color" that more extreme action seemed likely, until the attending police officers rescued her and took her to the watch house. By this time, the lampblack and oil, "regularly laid on" several hours ago, had streaked: her "repeated wiping of tears" had leached the "jet black" from around her eyes and some of the watch "affected to believe she was something more than earthly." When she regained her composure, the young lady "confidentially" informed the person in charge who she was, and he "withdrew her from the gaze of the watchmen, and kindly conducted her to her residence."[40]

It was a story that struck deep societal chords and revealed miscegenant longings that pervaded New York in the 1820s and 1830s. This was the difficult environment—of attraction and repulsion, sex and violence, love and theft—in which the newly freed African New Yorkers had to make their way. And there, for some ten years, James Hewlett had managed to defy the odds and fashion a career on the stage. What seems remarkable now is how few people seem to have considered it particularly noteworthy that it was a black man who was delineating the ways of white actors on stage. In these early years of black freedom, with the pattern of race relations not yet fully worked out and alternative possibilities still in play, a black man could mimic whites and young white men could black up and perform their fantasized version of African American life. But this uneasy balance would not last long. Within a few weeks of the young lady's memorable evening at the Park Theater, across town at the Bowery Theater, T. D. Rice began his phenomenal run of performances of Jim Crow. The lithograph of the "*fifty seventh* night of Mr. T. D. RICE" in "his original and celebrated extravaganza of JIM CROW," an evening on which the theater "was thronged to an excess unprecedented in the records of theatrical attraction," captures something of the sensation he caused.[41] Rice's genius lay in the way he distilled these societal longings into Jim Crow, satisfying vicariously the desires of young white upper-class ladies and boisterous white male clerks through his blackface representations of African American life. For Hewlett the writing had already been on the wall in 1831, with the failure of his return to acting, and as far as is known, he never appeared on a New York stage after Rice's dazzlingly successful theatrical triumph.

EPILOGUE

The maw of the New York prison system did not consume James Hewlett; there was a twist or two left in his remarkable story. If he served out his two-year sentence, he must have been released in mid-1839, by which time he would have been in his fifties. There can have been little prospect of work for him in the city in which he had spent most of his life. Not only was he a jailbird, with two stints in prison behind him, but he was widely known as the black man who had debauched a respectable woman decades younger than himself, an unforgivable sin for most white New Yorkers. Who, after the success of T. D. Rice and his blackfaced epigones, would still want to see this black actor perform his delineations of white stars? Against odds like these, a dignified Hewlett opted for a quiet departure from New York and exile.

Although not the first well-known African American to choose to leave America—the boxer Tom Molineaux, and Hewlett's *bête noire*, Ira Aldridge, had long since set out from New York to try their luck in England—James Hewlett was among the pioneers, in this as in so much else. The trickle of expatriates in the nineteenth century would become a steady stream in the twentieth; it would include such black luminaries as Josephine Baker, W. E. B. Du Bois, Richard Wright, James Baldwin, and Sidney Bechet.[1] White Americans had always been willing to welcome a black on the end of a broom or a shovel, but those aiming at anything more ambitious were likely to arouse their displeasure. For many blacks trying to forge careers as writers, painters, musicians, and actors, the stifling atmosphere of America was too much. Exile offered the chance of an environment untrammeled by their own country's particularly corrosive and debilitating brand of racism. In Hewlett's case, it gave the actor an opportunity to try his luck in a place where some episodes in his past were unlikely to be known and where blackface acts had yet to take hold.

Possibly Hewlett just took a passage on the first boat leaving New York on which he could get a position as a steward, but, with the benefit of hindsight, we can see a certain logic in his decision to disembark at Port of Spain in Trinidad. It was an area with which he was familiar. Fifteen years before, on the ill-fated voyage of the *John & Edward*, that vessel had docked at La Guaira ("Laguira" in the newspaper), Venezuela, barely forty miles away. Possibly the *John & Edward* called in at Port of Spain as well, or if it remained in La Guaira for a few days loading and unloading cargo, the usually adventurous black traveler may have journeyed there himself, just as he would later visit Toulon while the boat was docked in Marseilles. More importantly, though, developments in Trinidad before Hewlett's journey must have given a familiar resonance to Port of Spain, making it seem, in some ways, not unlike New York of the 1820s, the city of Hewlett's heyday.

Port of Spain is the largest city on the small island of Trinidad, which lies only about ten miles off the Venezuelan coast. Slavery arrived in Trinidad very late. A few West Africans had been imported to work on cacao plantations in 1702, but, until a flurry of plantation development toward the end of the century, the island had remained a backwater. By 1783, there were barely three hundred slaves on Trinidad, but by 1797 an influx of French planters had pushed that figure to almost 10,000. In 1797, the British attacked Port of Spain and not only replaced the Spanish as rulers of the island, but very quickly began nibbling away at the civil and political rights of Trinidad's substantial free black population. Many black Trinidadians, property owners and professionals, resented this treatment; in 1823, a delegation traveled to England and lobbied, successfully, to have their rights restored. On August 1, 1834, slavery was legally abolished in Trinidad, as it was throughout the British West Indies. Supposedly, abolition was to be followed by six years of apprenticeship, but this system quickly collapsed. By the time Hewlett arrived in 1839, Trinidad was awash with native Carib, Spanish, French, English, and African influences and a polyglot population of Africans, Europeans, and creoles. The African New Yorker actor had alighted in a society coping with newly freed ex-slaves, in this case a majority of the island's inhabitants.[2] It was a situation carrying strong echoes from Hewlett's past.

In early December 1839, a small notice in the *Port of Spain Gazette* announced that "Mr. Hewlett, from the Royal Cobourg Theatre, London, will have the honor of opening the 'Royal Victoria Theatre,' in Camaridge Street." It seems that the black actor's "imitations, recitations, and songs. &c. &c. &c." were successful: he gave more performances, and the price of tickets went up, admission to the pit rising from three quarters to one dollar. As well, in a move reminiscent of a strategy Hewlett had employed at the Military Hall in New York in 1827, tickets were no longer on sale at the door but had to be purchased in advance from the offices of the two newspapers. The program for these Port of Spain shows was also familiar: Hewlett performed selections from his favorite play, *Richard III*, probably in the manner of various actors, and assumed the character of Rolla in a series of extracts from *The Death of Rolla*. He also made some adaptations to the local circumstances. With a nod to French planters, Hewlett gave imitations of the opera singer Senora Garcia of the "Theatre Royal, at Paris." Finally, too, Hewlett also managed at last to perform the role of Othello, if only for a few minutes. Judging from the terse description in the program, this must have been an extraordinary moment. Boldly mixing genres, in ways that had delighted his African New Yorker audience and nonplussed Euro-Americans, Hewlett as Othello sang "The Banner of the Battle" and "The Marseilles Hymn, and the Parisienne," the latter in English.[3] What a spectacle: a black man, an African New Yorker, performing extracts from *Othello;* incorporating in his performance an English rendition of "The Marseilles Hymn"; on a stage in Port of Spain; before an audience of British colonial officials, French planters, and newly freed blacks. Indeed, this is a fine example of the cross-cultural possibilities attendant on slavery's slow demise in the Atlantic World.

In late December 1839, the *Port of Spain Gazette* noted that "the 'Proud Representative of Shakespeare's Heroes,' we are glad to hear, is going rapidly a-head." The editor had "heard" (doubtless after a visit from Hewlett) that the black actor was "now engaged in preparing for the Stage, a short piece, *his own composition*, descriptive of life in Port of Spain, a sort of Tom and Jerry affair, light and lively, full of entertainment and fun." The piece went on to praise Hewlett: "he is a most deserving man, and a true as well as a 'proud representative' of the Poet's Heroes," and "positively superior to Kean in some of his personations," although many thought "very justly perhaps, that he 'does' Macready better." Hyperbolically, the editor continued: "He is great in all he undertakes, nor is his greatness limited to the stage." He is "an Author as well as a Player," and "his commonest efforts read like blank verse." A brief note, supposedly penned by Hewlett to the Governor, concluded the short article: "Mr. Hewellit Returnes thancks for his kindness and in Closes 4 tickts as Every Prepreations has been maid For his Esecellncy." "It is not often that a document like *that*, glistens in our pages," the editor noted superciliously. "He deserves all the success that he has obtained, and has a fair chance of Immortality."[4] It was, as sports commentators the world over are fond of quoting, *déjà vu* all over again. As "Hewlett's" supposed letter to the Governor reveals, no recognized conventions had thus far been invented in Trinidad for rendering black speech onto the printed page. It would be Hewlett's own adaptation of *Tom and Jerry* that would give Trinidadians of all hues and origins their first stage representation of their own society—one can only wonder whether he intended to include a slave auction. Judging by this piece in the *Gazette*, Hewlett even appears to have found a Port of Spain version of Mordecai Noah, a newspaper editor who publicized, and even grudgingly praised him, while assaying more than enough backhanders to make sure that the stereotypes of blacks were undisturbed.

At any rate, this story is the last known contemporaneous reference to James Hewlett. If he made other stage appearances in the Caribbean, no trace of his passage through the islands has yet been unearthed. Some blacks who went into exile never returned to the United States—Charles B. Hicks died in Surabaya; Baker, Bechet, and Wright in France—but it is likely that Hewlett did go back to the city in which he had first trod the boards. The black activist Martin Delany stated in 1852 that the actor had "died in New York a few years ago."[5] There is even a chance that Hewlett may have taken a few last bows on a New York stage. Writing of 1842 or 1843, an English traveler, a Mrs. Felton, noted that "the blacks, who are never behind in rivalling their superiors, contrive to keep open one, and sometimes two theatres." She herself had not witnessed a performance, but another guest at the boarding house in which she was lodging had regaled everyone at breakfast "with an account of his last night's entertainment at the black theatre, where a sable 'Richard' was the point of attraction." The speaker went on to note that "in order to please his audience, the crooked-backed monarch politely accommodated his language to the meridian of the place: whenever the word 'York' occurred, he invariably altered the text, and called it 'New York!'"[6] For all the vagueness and second-hand nature of Felton's description, it certainly sounds as though the actor in question could have been Hewlett, reprising perhaps for the last time his favorite role. No one has yet managed to uncover any other traces of this theatrical venture, but if it did occur, and if the actor referred to was Hewlett, he seems to have been as unlucky as ever in his timing. Early 1843 saw the arrival of a new theatrical sensation—the Virginia Minstrels, the first fully fledged minstrel show.

I have lived with James Hewlett, off and on, for much of the last decade, and, at least in my mind's eye, the telling of the spare facts of his demise is fleshed out by images of the Bud Powell-like character, played with such dignity and power by Dexter Gordon in Bertrand Tavernier's 'Round Midnight, returning from Paris to die in New York City. My inability to see Hewlett properly into his grave does not matter much in the larger scheme of things, but it still nags, hindering closure to my book. Perhaps that is why I would start the film of Hewlett's life with an aging Mordecai Noah in the mid-1840s (he died in 1851 at the age of 65), reading in the newspaper a one- or two-sentence announcement of Hewlett's death, a notice that probably did exist, but that I have failed to find. Noah would say something like "The nigger is dead," yet for all the ugliness of the words, his voice would convey a wistful affection.

Hewlett's absence from most histories of New York, of theater, or even of African Americans is still surprising. He was well known at the time, publicly living out much of his adult life on stage, in the courts, and in newspapers, all this providing more than enough material to fashion a story of his trajectory through the New York of the 1820s and 1830s. How, then, should he be remembered? What collage of images should flash up on my imagined screen as the credits run? Certainly, it should include a scene from one of those early performances of Brown's company that so thrilled its black supporters, perhaps Hewlett as Richard III stagily asking a white traveler in the audience for his opinion of one of his show-stopping speeches; or perhaps, Hewlett, again as solo performer, imitating Kean, tearing "King Dick to flinders," or using his fine voice to give a rendition of Otello in song, as played by the Garcias. But those images should also include a depiction of Hewlett on stage, under the influence of laughing gas, of his surreptitious slipping of the watch into his pocket at the inquest, of his court appearances and imprisonment, the assemblage ending with Hewlett on stage in Port of Spain, incorporating an English rendition of the "Marseillaise" into his acting out of the role of Othello. Yet the actor has an at once larger and more symbolic burden to bear. If the successes of the black theater company and of Hewlett in the 1820s were part of the cultural convulsion that so electrified black New York as the hated institution of slavery wound down, a sign of alternative possibilities for relations between the races, then the closing down of the company and the later decline of Hewlett also signaled the eclipse of those possibilities as nervous whites, recoiling from the realities of black freedom, preferred disenfranchisement, segregation, riot, and minstrelsy. Not until the Harlem Renaissance of a century later would a similar level of attention be paid to African New Yorker actors, indeed to African New Yorker life. In the end, then, and for all the promise of his early years on stage in New York, and the dignity of his decline, Hewlett's failure is depressingly familiar. But then this is a story of black New York, and tales of dreams deferred do not have happy endings.

NOTES

INTRODUCTION

1. Ralph Ellison, "The Little Man at Chehaw Station: The American Artist and His Audience," in John F. Callahan, ed., *The Collected Essays of Ralph Ellison* (New York: Modern Library, 1995), pp. 515–19.

2. As is well known, in the 1990s the great playwright August Wilson denounced colorblind casting. See Henry Louis Gates, Jr., "The Chitlin Circuit," in Harry J. Elam, Jr., and David Krasner eds, *African American Performance and Theater History: A Critical Reader* (New York: Oxford University Press, 2001), pp. 132–48. *New York Times*, June 3, 1999.

3. James Weldon Johnson, *Black Manhattan* (New York: Atheneum, 1968 [orig. 1930]), p. 80.

4. Everyone working in New York theater history is indebted to George Odell's remarkable multivolume compilation of sources. His third volume includes many of the *National Advocate* references to the black company. See George C. D. Odell, *Annals of the New York Stage.* Vol. 3, *1821–1834* (New York: Columbia University Press, 1928), pp. 34–37, 70–71, 224, 228, 293, 536, and 594. As well, the account, based on Writers' Project material but not published until much later, in Roi Ottley and William Weatherby, *The Negro in New York: An Informal Social History, 1626–1940* (New York: Praeger, 1969), pp. 72–73, seems to be the basis for the common mistake of dating the theater's end at 1829. Basing their research mostly on the material in Odell, several writers concerned with black theater have given brief versions of this early theatrical endeavor. See Herbert Marshall and Mildred Stock, *Ira Aldridge: The Negro Tragedian* (Washington D.C.: Howard University Press, 1993 [orig. pub. 1958]), pp. 28–47; Errol Hill, *Shakespeare in Sable: A*

History of Black Shakespearean Actors (Amherst: University of Massachusetts Press, 1984), pp. 11–16; Samuel A. Hay, *African American Theatre* (New York: Cambridge University Press, 1994), pp. 5–14, 16–17, 136–38. See also William Over, "New York's African Theatre: The Vicissitudes of the Black Actor," *Afro-Americans in New York Life and History*, 3 (1979): 7–14; Jonathan Dewberry, "The African Grove Theatre and Company," *Black American Literature Forum*, 16 (1982): 128–31. Even as outstanding an example of what is possible in theater history, *The Cambridge History of American Theatre*, a volume of almost 500 pages of text, deals with the black actors in a few dozen words. See Don B. Wilmeth and Christopher Bigsby, eds., *The Cambridge History of American Theatre*. Vol 1, *Beginnings to 1870* (New York: Cambridge University Press, 1998). For brief mentions of the black actors in recent African American histories see, for example, Graham Russell Hodges, *Root & Branch: African Americans in New York & East Jersey, 1613–1863* (Chapel Hill: University of North Carolina Press, 1999), pp. 197–98; James Oliver Horton and Lois E. Horton, *In Hope of Liberty: Culture, Community and Protest Among Northern Free Blacks, 1700–1860* (New York: Oxford University Press, 1997), pp.160–61 and 164. And in recent New York histories, see Paul A. Gilje, *The Road to Mobocracy: Popular Disorder in New York City, 1763–1834* (Chapel Hill: University of North Carolina Press, 1987), pp. 156–57; Anthony Gronowicz, *Race & Class Politics in New York City before the Civil War* (Boston: Northeastern University Press, 1998), pp. 89–91; Edwin G. Burrows and Mike Wallace, *Gotham: A History of New York City to 1898* (New York: Oxford University Press, 1999), pp. 487–88. More recently, three very well researched studies have been completed. See Marvin Edward McAllister, "White People Do Not Know How to Behave at Entertainments Designed for Ladies and Gentleman of Colour: A History of New York's African Grove/African Theatre" (Ph.D. diss., Northwestern University, 1997) and George A. Thompson Jr., *A Documentary History of the African Theatre* (Evanston, Ill.: Northwestern University Press, 1998). George Thompson has been an indefatigable researcher and has managed to dig up and publish all manner of material that was hitherto completely unknown. Without Thompson's research, I would still have published this book, but, particularly in the post-1835 material, it would have looked rather different. And as this book was being sent off to the publisher another well-researched article was published: Michael Warner with Natasha Hurley, Luis Iglesias, Sonia Di Loreto, Jeffrey Scraba, and Sandra Young, "A Soliloquy Lately Spoken at the African Theatre: Race and the Public Sphere in New York City, 1821," *American Literature*, 73 (2001): 1–46. Lastly, several years ago

Carlyle Brown wrote a play about the African Company. See Carlyle Brown, *The African Company Presents Richard III* (New York: Dramatists Play Service Inc., 1994).

1. THE END OF SLAVERY

1. *The Sun*, August 26, 1834.

2. *New York American*, Oct. 1, 1827.

3. *New-York Herald*, March 29, 1815. On voting restrictions, see Alexander Keyssar, *The Right to Vote: The Contested History of Democracy in America* (New York: Basic Books, 2000), pp. 54–60.

4. *New York American*, Feb. 25, 1826. For how important it was for runaway slaves trying to "pass as free" to tell a story well, see David Waldstreicher, "Reading the Runaways: Self-Fashioning, Print Culture, and Confidence in Slavery in the Eighteenth Century Mid-Atlantic," *William and Mary Quarterly*, 56 (1999): 243–72. More generally, see Ann Fabian, *The Unvarnished Truth: Personal Narratives in Nineteenth Century America* (Berkeley: University of California Press, 2000).

5. Statement of Edward Latham, *The People v. Edward Latham*, filed March 6, 1816, District Attorney Indictment Papers, Municipal Archives of the City of New York.

6. Ira Rosenwaike, *Population History of New York City* (Syracuse: Syracuse University Press, 1972), p. 16.

7. Quoted in Edwin G. Burrows and Mike Wallace, *Gotham: A History of New York City to 1898* (New York: Oxford University Press, 1999), p. 450.

8. Rosenwaike, *Population History*, p. 16.

9. Shane White, *Somewhat More Independent: The End of Slavery in New York City, 1770–1810* (Athens: University of Georgia Press, 1991), pp. 3–55.

10. Harry B. Yoshpe, "Record of Slave Manumissions in New York During the Colonial and Early National Periods," *Journal of Negro History*, 26 (1941): 81, 80, 96, 97.

11. Report of the Standing Committee of the New York Manumission Society, March 18, 1814; April 19, 1814; in the Papers of the New York Manumission Society, New York Historical Society.

12. Report of the Standing Committee of NYMS, Dec. 19, 1809; Oct. 2, 1815; Feb. 3, 1812.

13. Statements of Aaron Black, Jane Ford, Daniel S. Tyler, & Power of Attorney, *The People v. Aaron Black*, filed Jan. 5, 1826, DAIP.

14. *The People v. Amos Broad* filed Feb. 25, 1809, DAIP; *The Trial of Amos Broad and His Wife, On Three Several Indictments for Assaulting and Beating Betty, a Slave, and Her Little Female Child Sarah, Aged Three Years* (New York: Henry C. Southwick, 1809), quote on p. 11.

15. Report of the Standing Committe of the NYMS, April 11, 1809.

16. Statement of Joseph Corlies, *The People v. Lavau,* filed Nov. 12, 1814, DAIP; statement of Phoebe Dodge, *The People v. John Plume,* filed Nov. 11, 1815, DAIP; statement of Charles McLean, *The People v. Jacob Brown,* filed Sept. 5, 1817, DAIP.

17. Statement of Isaac Heddy, *The People v. Josiah Muir,* filed July 9, 1813, DAIP; statement of Eleanora Traghata, *The People v. Eleanora Pienard,* filed May 3, 1815, DAIP.

18. Statement of John Towt, & loose bit of paper, *The People v. John Towt,* filed June 14, 1813, DAIP.

19. Statement of Phoebe Stewart, *The People v. Anthony, slave of Phoebe Stewart,* filed Nov. 7, 1805, DAIP; statement of Reveste Chaux, *The People v. Jane (a Black),* filed May 7, 1807, DAIP.

20. *The People v. Betsey Paulding,* filed Feb. 4, 1817, DAIP; *The People v. Robert Warnock,* filed June 4, 1817, DAIP; *The People v. Betsey Paulding,* filed Oct. 14, 1818, DAIP; *The People v. Betsey Paulding,* filed Nov. 10, 1818; Minutes of the Standing Committee of the NYMS, Feb. 6, 1818.

21. John Stanford, *An Authentic Statement of the Case and Conduct of Rose Butler, Who Was Tried, Convicted, and Executed for the Crime of Arson* (New York: Broderick and Ritter, 1819); *New York Evening Post,* June 11, 1819.

22. Statement of Jemima, *The People v. Jemima a slave of William Wright,* filed June 21, 1810, DAIP; statement of Charlotte, *The People v. Charlotte a black girl,* filed June 7, 1811, DAIP; statement of Rose, *The People v. Rose a black girl,* filed Dec. 4, 1811, DAIP. For an example that probably did not reach the authorities, see Elizabeth Bleeker's notation in her diary that her "black Girl" had tried to burn her father's house down by setting a fire in the garret. "Diary of Elizabeth Bleeker 1799–1806," Dec. 19, 1805, New York Public Library.

23. Statement of Euphemia Clark, *The People v. Margaret (a black) and Diana (a black),* filed Dec. 8, 1806, DAIP; statement of Eleanor Rankin, *The People v. Eleanor Rankin,* filed Dec. 8, 1806, DAIP; letter from H. G. Livingston and statement of Lucy, *The People v. Lucy (a slave of H. G. Livingston),* filed June 11, 1808, DAIP. See also a note in the papers of *The People v. Margaret Rodgers,* filed Oct. 7, 1809, DAIP, that "this wench is probably as Dangerous a person as any in New York having as is is strongly suspected stolen $500 from her master and poisoned her mis-

tress who died not long since." In this case she was convicted of grand larceny.

24. Statement of Sophie Tardy, *The People v. Bet (a slave of John G. Tardy)*, filed Oct. 6, 1814, DAIP.

25. Statements of Mary Underhill and John C. Gillen, *The People v. Joseph Pulford*, filed Dec. 9, 1819, DAIP. On kidnapping more generally, see Carol Wilson, *Freedom at Risk: The Kidnapping of Free Blacks in America, 1780–1865* (Lexington: University Press of Kentucky, 1994).

26. *New York American*, Nov. 27, 1829.

27. Story from *Daily Advertiser* repeated in *New York American*, July 24, 1829.

28. *New York American*, Nov. 26, 1829; August 14, 1829; *The Sun*, June 20, 1834; Moses Roper, *A Narrative of the Adventures and Escape of Moses Roper From American Slavery* (Philadelphia, 1838), in Yuval Taylor, ed., *I Was Born a Slave: An Anthology of Classic Slave Narratives*, 2 vols. (Chicago: Lawrence Hill Books, 1999), vol. 1, p. 515; *New York Spectator*, July 14, 1821.

29. Statement of J. M. Gervais, *The People v. Marcelle, Sam, Benjamin Bandey and 20 Others*, filed Oct. 9, 1801, DAIP; Paul A. Gilje, *The Road to Mobocracy: Popular Disorder in New York City, 1763–1834* (Chapel Hill: University of North Carolina Press, 1987), pp. 147–49.

30. Statement of John McManus, *The People v. John Byas*, filed July 15, 1819, DAIP; *The People v. William Sockum et al.*, filed Oct. 9, 1826, DAIP; *National Advocate*, Sept. 20, 1826; *New-York Enquirer*, Sept. 20, 1826; *New York American*, Sept. 20, 1826; *New York Evening Post*, Sept. 21, 1826; *New York Spectator*, Sept. 22, 1826. See also Gilje, *Mobocracy*, pp. 150–53.

31. *Morning Courier and New-York Enquirer*, July 13, 1833; *New York Journal of Commerce* reprinted in *Public Ledger*, Dec. 28, 1836.

32. Rosenwaike, *Population History of New York City*, pp. 18, 36.

33. White, *Somewhat More Independent*, pp. 31–32; 143–45; 155; 190–91.

34. *New York Gazette and General Advertiser*, Jan. 3, 1803; White, *Somewhat More Independent*, pp. 154–56.

35. Statement of Tom Johnson, *The People v. Tom Johnson*, filed Oct. 3, 1819, DAIP; *National Advocate*, July 14, 1826; *Morning Courier and New-York Enquirer*, March 15, 1833.

36. James W. C. Pennington, *The Fugitive Blacksmith* (London, 1849) in Taylor, ed. *I Was Born a Slave*, vol. 2, p. 138.

37. *The Sun*, Nov. 21, 1833.

38. Francis J. Grund, *Aristocracy in America*, 2 vols. (London: Richard Bentley, 1839), vol. 1, pp. 281–82; *New York Spectator*, Dec. 18, 1829.

39. On Downing, see John H. Hewitt, "Mr. Downing and His Oyster-house: The Life and Good Works of an African-American Entrepreneur," *New York History*, 74 (1993): 229–52. On Toussaint, see *Memoir of Pierre Toussaint, Born a Slave in St. Domingo* (Boston: Crosby, Nichols, 1854) and Arthur and Elizabeth Odell Sheehan, *Pierre Toussaint: A Citizen of Old New York* (New York: P. J. Kenedy & Sons, 1955). On Cato Alexander, see James Grant Wilson, ed., *The Memorial History of the City of New-York*, 4 vols. (New York, 1892–93), vol. 3, p. 137; Tyrone Power, *Impressions of America; During the Years 1833, 1834, and 1835*, 2 vols. (Philadelphia: Carey, Lea and Blanchard, 1836), vol. 1, p. 45. See, for example, a story in the *National Advocate*, Jan. 29, 1824, describing a "dashing young blade" driving extremely fast and dangerously—the "horses were soon headed for Cato's, where all cares and misfortunes are quietly forgotten."

40. "Diary of a Journey Through the United States, 1821–24," 3 vols. Vol. 1, pp. 155–56, New York Historical Society; statement of Peter Joseph, *The People v. Peter Lewis et al.*, filed Oct. 2, 1821, DAIP.

41. On the larger process, see Elizabeth Blackmar, *Manhattan for Rent, 1785–1850* (Ithaca: Cornell University Press, 1989).

42. *The American*, Sept. 19, 1820; *New York American*, August 15, 1823; letter to the foreman of the Grand Jury, *The People v. John L. Martin*, filed April 14, 1827, DAIP; statement of Doctor Knapp, *The People v. Barclay Fanning*, filed May 14, 1830, DAIP.

43. *Morning Courier and New-York Enquirer*, July 27, 1833; Feb. 1, 1833. For a recent account of Five Points, albeit one that does not take sufficient account of the role of African Americans in the 1820s and 1830s, see Tyler Anbinder, *Five Points: The 19th-Century New York City Neighborhood That Invented Tap Dance, Stole Elections, and Became the World's Most Notorious Slum* (New York: Free Press, 2001).

44. *New York American*, August 3, 1825.

45. Coroner's Report for John Richards, a Black Man, January 20, 1804, Historical Documents Collection, Queens College, City University of New York; *New York American*, July 8, 1829.

46. *The Sun*, Dec. 31, 1834.

47. Statement of Maria Louisa Souque, *The People v. Nancy (a Black)*, filed Dec. 4, 1807, DAIP; *Trial of Amos Broad and His Wife*, p. 31; statement of Amos Broad, *The People v. Betty (a Black)*, filed Oct. 15, 1810, DAIP.

48. Statement of James Arden, *The People v. James Arden*, filed April 11, 1811, DAIP.

49. *Letters from John Pintard to His Daughter Eliza Noel Pintard Davidson*, 4 vols. (New York: Printed for New York Historical Society, 1940), vol. 1, pp. 137, 145, 205.

50. *Morning Courier and New-York Enquirer*, Nov. 24, 1832.

51. *New-York Enquirer*, August 10, 1827.

52. *Morning Courier and New-York Enquirer*, August 3, 1833; *New-York Spectator*, Jan. 25, 1822; *Morning Courier and New-York Enquirer*, Jan. 26, 1833.

53. *The Sun*, March 5, 1834; *New-York Enquirer*, Dec. 9, 1828.

54. *New-York Enquirer*, Sept. 22, 1826.

55. Report of the Standing Committee of the New York Manumission Society, Sept. 24, 1816; Oct. 2, 1816; Feb. 9, 1818; Feb. 11, 1818; Feb. 17, 1818, Papers of the New York Manumission Society, New York Historical Society.

56. Statements of James Boardman, *The People v. John Chadwick & Anthony Robertson*, filed Oct. 17, 1818, DAIP.

57. *New-York National Advocate*, April 22, 1826.

58. *New-York Spectator*, May 21, 1822; *Daily Advertiser*, Jan. 20, 1826; *New York American*, Oct. 31, 1826.

59. *The American*, Oct. 2, 1820; *Commercial Advertiser*, April 17, 1832; *New York American*, July 23, 1830.

60. Bayard Still, "New York City in 1824: A Newly Discovered Description," *New-York Historical Society Quarterly*, 46 (1962): 137–70, quotation from p. 149.

61. *New York Evening Post*, June 7, 1828. For a similar story, see also *New York Evening Post*, July 10, 1830.

62. Thomas F. De Voe, *The Market Book: A History of the Public Markets of the City of New York* (New York, 1970 [orig. pub. 1862]), pp. 344–45.

63. *The Sun*, Sept. 12, 1834.

64. Statement of Leonard Baum, *The People v. Edward Ball & Henry Dunlap*, filed Nov. 17, 1825, DAIP.

65. Petition to the Corporation of the City of New York, August 12, 1817, reprinted in Paul A. Gilje and Howard B. Rock, eds., *Keepers of the Revolution: New Yorkers at Work in the Early Republic* (Ithaca: Cornell University Press, 1992), pp. 218–21; statement of Jas. Gardner, *The People v. William Sammons*, filed August 13, 1819, DAIP; statement of William Allen, *The People v. Henry Butler & Julian Butler*, filed August 19, 1819, DAIP; statement of William Gee, *The People v. Thomas Covert*, filed Sept. 9, 1819, DAIP; *New York Evening Post*, August 24, 1820.

66. Petition of the subscribers, *People v. William Slam*, filed August 16, 1826, DAIP; *New York American*, Feb. 18, 1826.

67. Statement of Garrit Heyer Jr., *The People v. Leonard Emmons*, filed May 8, 1812, DAIP; *Morning Courier and New-York Enquirer*, Dec. 11, 1834.

68. *The American*, August 24, 1820; *Morning Courier and New-York Enquirer*, Feb. 25, 1830.

69. See Shane White and Graham White, *Stylin': African American Expressive Culture from Its Beginnings to the Zoot Suit* (Ithaca: Cornell University Press, 1998).

70. *National Advocate*, August 3, 1821; *New-York Columbian*, August 23, 1820.

71. *National Advocate*, June 5, 1826.

72. Henry Bradshaw Fearon, *Sketches of America: A Journey of Five Thousand Miles through the Eastern and Western States of America* (London: Longman, Hurst, Rees, Orme, and Brown, 1818), p. 9; James Stuart, *Three Years in North America*, 2 vols. (Edinburgh: Robert Cadell, 1833), vol. 1, p. 29; Stephen Davis, *Notes of a Tour in America in 1832 & 1833* (Edinburgh: Waugh & Innes, 1833), p. 75; Carl David Arfwedson, *The United States and Canada in 1832, 1833, and 1834*, 2 vols. (London: Richard Bentley, 1834), vol. 1, pp. 27–29; E. T. Coke, *A Subaltern's Furlough: Descriptive of Scenes in Various Parts of the United States* (New York: Harper, 1833), p. 139.

73. *New York American*, Dec. 6, 1821; *Morning Courier and New-York Enquirer*, Nov. 28, 1829.

74. William Dunlap, *A Trip to Niagara; or, Travellers in America. A Farce in Three Acts* (New York: E. B. Clayton, 1830), pp. 12–13; White and White, *Stylin'*, pp. 116–18.

75. *National Advocate*, May 18, 1815; *New York Spectator*, August 5, 1825.

76. Statement of Isaiah Kip, *The People v. Hannah Elliot et al.*, filed May 8, 1812, DAIP; statement of Henry Olmstead, *The People v. William Isaacs and Joseph Owens*, filed Jan. 7, 1819, DAIP; statement of Francis Laforest, *The People v. Hannah Prior*, filed March 11, 1820, DAIP.

77. *National Advocate*, June 22, 1822.

78. *National Advocate*, July 9, 1822; June 21, 1823; *New York Evening Post*, Sept. 22, 1826.

79. Blackmar, *Manhattan for Rent*, p. 114.

80. *The American*, June 20, 1821.

81. *National Advocate*, June 21, 1823.

82. Piece from *Montreal Gazette* reprinted in *New York Evening Post*, July 22, 1829; Fearon, *Sketches of America*, pp. 58–60; J. S. Buckingham, *The Slave States of America*, 2 vols. (New York: Negro Universities Press, 1968 [orig. pub. 1842]), vol. 2, p. 112.

83. For white disruption of services at the African Union Church, see statement of Jas Harris, *The People v. Peter Cochran*, filed June 6, 1828, DAIP, or the African Church in the 12th Ward, see statement of Henry Graves, *The People v. Timothy Duffy et al.*, filed July 14, 1829, DAIP. For a fascinating account from a white involved in harassing black churches in Philadelphia, see William Otter, *History of My Own Times*, ed. Richard B. Stott (Ithaca: Cornell University Press, 1995 [orig. pub. 1835]).

84. *Commercial Advertiser*, Jan. 4, 1828.

85. *A Memorial Discourse by Reverend Henry Highland Garnet. With an Introduction by James McCune Smith, M.D.* (Philadelphia: Joseph M. Wilson, 1865), pp. 20–21; Report of the Standing Committee of NYMS, Nov. 14, 1809; Jan. 9, 1810.

86. *New-York Enquirer*, April 14, 1827.

87. *New-York Enquirer*, June 13, 1827; *Freedom's Journal*, June 29, 1827; *Freedom's Journal*, July 18, 1828. See also Shane White, "'It Was a Proud Day': African Americans, Festivals, and Parades in the North, 1741–1834," *Journal of American History*, 81 (1994): 13–51.

88. *New-York Enquirer*, March 28, 1927.

89. *New York American*, July 6, 1827.

90. *New York American*, July 6, 1827.

91. Statement of Henry White, *The People v. Jack Robinson & Murray*, filed August 12, 1825, DAIP. On disruption by coachmen and carters, see James Boardman, *America and the Americans* (London: Longman, Rees, Orme, Brown, Green, and Longman, 1833), pp. 309–11.

92. *Memorial Discourse by Reverend Henry Highland Garnet*, pp. 24–26.

93. See Shane White, "The Death of James Johnson," *American Quarterly*, 51 (1999): 753–95.

2. STAGING FREEDOM

1. *National Advocate*, Sept. 21, 1821.

2. Lawrence W. Levine, "William Shakespeare and the American People: A Study in Cultural Transformation," in Levine, *The Unpredictable Past: Explorations in American Cultural History* (New York: Oxford University Press, 1993), pp. 139–71; David Grimsted, *Melodrama Un-*

veiled: American Theater & Culture (Berkeley: University of California Press, 1987), p. 119; Gary Taylor, *Reinventing Shakespeare: A Cultural History from the Restoration to the Present* (London: Vintage, 1991), p. 200.

3. See Levine, "'Some Go Up and Some Go Down': The Meaning of the Slave Trickster," in Levine, *The Unpredictable Past*, pp. 59–77, and Lawrence W. Levine, *Black Culture and Black Consciousness: Afro-American Folk Thought from Slavery to Freedom* (New York: Oxford University Press, 1977).

4. *National Advocate*, Sept. 19, 1822.

5. *National Advocate*, Dec. 28, 1818.

6. *New York Evening Post*, June 2, 1827; *National Advocate*, Dec. 18, 1824. See also Graham Hodges, "'Desirable Companions and Lovers': Irish and African Americans in the Sixth Ward, 1830–1870," in Ronald H. Bayor and Timothy J. Meagher, eds., *The New York Irish* (Baltimore: Johns Hopkins University Press, 1996), pp. 107–24; Leslie M. Harris, "From Abolitionist Amalgamators to 'Rulers of the Five Points': The Discourse of Interracial Sex and Reform in Antebellum New York City," in Martha Hodes, ed., *Sex, Love, Race: Crossing Boundaries in North American History* (New York: New York University Press, 1999), pp. 191–212.

7. *National Advocate*, April 12, 1820.

8. *The Sun*, Oct. 23, 1834.

9. Quoted in Levine, "William Shakespeare and the American People," p. 142.

10. [James McCune Smith], "Ira Aldridge," *Anglo-African Magazine*, 2 (1860): 27–28.

11. *Morning Courier and New-York Enquirer*, July 2, 1833.

12. *National Advocate*, August 3, 1821; [Smith], "Ira Aldridge," p. 28.

13. *National Advocate*, August 3, 1821. On Noah, see Jonathan D. Sarna, *Jacksonian Jew: The Two Worlds of Mordecai Noah* (New York: Holmes and Meier, 1981); Michael Schuldiner and Daniel J. Kleinfeld, *The Selected Writings of Mordecai Noah* (Westport: Greenwood Press, 1999); and for an interesting comic strip version of Noah, Ben Katchor, *The Jew of New York* (New York: Pantheon Books, 1998).

14. *National Advocate*, Sept. 21, 1821. Most of the documents I have used to piece together my story of the black actors have been reprinted in full in George A. Thompson Jr., *A Documentary History of the African Theatre* (Evanston, Ill.: Northwestern University Press, 1998). The book is indispensable for anyone interested in the history of these black actors.

15. W. Jeffrey Bolster, *Black Jacks: African American Seamen in the Age of Sail* (Cambridge, Mass.: Harvard University Press, 1997), pp. 102–30,

quotations on p. 121. For the motley possibilities of the Atlantic world, see Peter Linebaugh and Marcus Rediker, *The Many-Headed Hydra: Sailors, Slaves, Commoners, and the Hidden History of the Revolutionary Atlantic* (Boston: Beacon Press, 2000).

16. *National Advocate*, Sept. 25, 1821.

17. *New York American*, Nov. 10, 1821.

18. *City-Hall Recorder*, Nov. 1821; *Commercial Advertiser*, Nov. 22, 1821; *New York American*, Nov. 21, 1821; *National Advocate*, Nov. 19, 1821.

19. *People v. Charles Taft*, filed Nov. 6, 1821, District Attorney's Indictment Papers, Municipal Archives of the City of New York.

20. Edwin G. Burrows and Mike Wallace, *Gotham: A History of New York City to 1898* (New York: Oxford University Press, 1999), p. 416.

21. Statement of Thomas Drumgold, *People v. Charles Taft*.

22. [Smith], "Ira Aldridge," pp. 27–28; story from the *Brooklyn Star* reprinted in *National Advocate*, Dec. 30, 1825.

23. *The People v. James Hewlett*, filed Oct. 14, 1813, DAIP; *National Advocate*, Sept. 23, 1815.

24. [Thomas Hamilton], *Men and Manners in America* (Edinburgh: William Blackwood, 1834), pp. 96–97.

25. *New York Spectator*, Nov. 18, 1825; *New York American*, Nov. 15, 1825.

26. Statements of Richard Brown, Harry Foster, and Bow Jackson, *The People v. Harry Foster et al*, filed Dec. 5, 1823, DAIP.

27. *National Advocate*, Oct. 27, 1821. The handbill is mentioned, with no further reference as to where it was located, in Roi Ottley and William Weatherby, eds., *The Negro in New York: An Informal Social History, 1626–1940* (New York: Praeger, 1967), p. 73.

28. *National Advocate*, Jan. 9, 1822.

29. For the presentation to Noah, see *New York American*, Jan. 3, 1822. *National Advocate*, Jan. 9, 1822.

30. *Republican Sentinel* story reprinted in *New York Evening Post*, Jan. 10, 1822.

31. *New York Spectator*, Jan. 18, 1822. The *Spectator* was in fact a compendium of items from the *Commercial Advertiser*. This piece appeared in the *Advertiser* a day or two earlier, but due to the accident of availability, I read the *Spectator*, not the *Advertiser*, for most of 1822.

32. According to Sarna: see his *Jacksonian Jew*, p. 7.

33. *New York Spectator*, January 18, 1822.

34. Marvin Edward McAllister, "'White People Do Not Know How

to Behave at Entertainments Designed for Ladies and Gentlemen of Col-our': A History of New York's African Grove/African Theater" (Ph.D. diss., Northwestern University, 1997), pp. 181–86. On *Metamora*, see Jill Lepore, *The Name of War: King Philip's War and the Origins of American Identity* (New York: Alfred A. Knopf, 1998), pp. 191–226.

35. *Republican Sentinel*, reprinted in *New York Evening Post*, Jan. 10, 1822.

36. *National Advocate*, July 22, 1822.

37. *New York Spectator*, August 13, 1822. Twaites evinced some knowl-edge of the stage. It is possible, indeed likely, he was the same "Twaits" mentioned in a review of a performance of *The African* in the *New York Evening Post*, Oct. 10, 1810. He was described there as an "acting man-ager," who, ironically, in his performance "cannot (animated as he is) give life to slaves."

38. *Sports of New York. By Simon Snipe. Containing an Evening at the Af-rican Theatre. Also a Trip to the Races! With Two Appropriate Songs* (New York: n.p., 1823), pp. 3–16. The only known copy of this small pamphlet is at the New York Historical Society.

39. [Smith], "Ira Aldridge," pp. 27–28.

40. Statements of William Mulineaux (sic) and Warwick Stouton, *The People v. William Molineaux*, filed March 17, DAIP; Stuart M. Blumin, ed., *New York by Gas-Light and Other Urban Sketches by George G. Foster* (Berkeley: University of California Press, 1990), p. 145. See also Shane White, "The Death of James Johnson," *American Quarterly*, 51 (1999): 753–95, and for a particularly insightful discussion of this issue of the commercialization of African American leisure in contemporary Amer-ica, Robin D. G. Kelley, "Playing for Keeps: Pleasure and Profit on the Postindustrial Playground," in Wahneema Lubiano, ed., *The House That Race Built: Black Americans, U.S. Terrain* (New York: Pantheon Books, 1997), pp. 195–231.

41. Tyrone Power, *Impressions of America; During the Years 1833, 1834, and 1835*, 2 vols. (Philadelphia: Carey, Lea and Blanchard, 1836), vol. 1, p. 45; *The People v. Cato Alexander*, filed May 11, 1819, DAIP; statement of Cato Alexander, *The People v. John Ryan*, filed July 5, 1826, DAIP.

42. Statements of Eliza Alexander, William A. Tyson, Cato Alexander, Thomas Blake, and Charles Blake, *The People v. George Luke et al.*, filed March 16, 1831, DAIP.

43. *Allen Royce and others v. Robert Mitchell et al.*, August 11, 1822, New York City Police Court Records, Cases Dismissed, Municipal Archives of the City of New York; statement of William Brown, *The People v. George Bellmont*, filed Sept. 10, 1822, DAIP.

44. *National Advocate*, April 15, 1822.

45. *New York Evening Post*, August 13, 1822.

46. *Commercial Advertiser* reprinted in *New York Spectator*, August 20, 1822.

47. *The People v. James Belmont*, filed August 12, 1822, DAIP; *James Hewlett v. Abraham Cox*, Dec. 3, 1822, Police Court, Cases Dismissed.

48. *National Advocate*, July 23, 1822.

49. *Memoir and Theatrical Career of Ira Aldridge, The African Roscius* (London: Onwhyn, [1849]). McAllister claims that, although in the third person, this memoir was written by Aldridge. I agree that this appears highly likely; if he did not write it, he was at the very least involved. McAllister, "'White People Do Not Know How to Behave," p. 238.

50. *Memoir and Theatrical Career of Ira Aldridge*, pp. 10–11.

51. Peter Neilson, *Recollections of a Six Years' Residence in the United States of America* (Glasgow: David Robertson, 1830), p. 20.

52. Grimsted, *Melodrama Unveiled*, pp. 94–96, quote from Kemble on p. 95.

53. *New York Spectator*, August 13, 1822; *Sports of New York*, pp. 3–16.

54. Neilson, *Recollections of Six Years' Residence*, p. 20.

55. *Memoir and Theatrical Career of Ira Aldridge*, p. 11.

56. Neilson, *Recollections of Six Years' Residence*, p. 20; *Family Magazine* reprinted in *Nottingham and Newark Mercury*, May 22, 1830, in Thompson, *A Documentary History of the African Theatre*, p. 186.

57. Basil Hall, *Travels in North America*, 3 vols. (Graz, Austria: Akademische Druck—u. Verlagsanstalt, 1965 [orig. pub. 1829]), vol. 1, p. 6; James Stuart, *Three Years in North America*, 2 vols. (Edinburgh: Robert Cadell, 1833), vol. 2, p. 555.

58. John Palmer, *Journal of Travels in the United States of North America and in Lower Canada, Performed in the Year 1817* (London: Sherwood, Neely, and Jones, 1818), pp. 285–86.

59. *Commercial Advertiser*, reprinted in *New York Spectator*, Feb. 19, 1822.

60. "Diary of a Journey Through the United States, 1821–24," 3 vols., vol. 3, August 28, 1823, New York Historical Society.

61. *New-York Enquirer*, May 13, 1828; *The Sun*, Dec. 17, 1833.

62. *The Transcript*, July 23, 1834.

63. See, for example, *Freedom's Journal*, Sept. 12, 1828, reporting on a camp meeting at Flushing in late August: "Capt. Peck states that he carried 3,700 persons of colour from New-York, for the encampment, and besides there were a great number of carriages, waggons and horsemen." See also "A Methodist"'s letter to the *Commercial Advertiser*, Sept. 10,

1832, complaining of the proposed camp meeting at Sing Sing while the fever remained unabated. As he noted, "It is a well known fact, that almost all the domestics, who are members of the Methodist Church '*will go*' to camp meeting, let the consequences be what they may; often times putting the families in which they live to great inconvenience. At this period, many families have just returned to the city, whence they had been driven by the pestilence, and their situation is such that they cannot with propriety permit their domestics to go off to attend such meetings." Stuart, *Three Years in North America*, vol. 2, p. 555.

64. *New-York American*, May 24, 1828.

65. Mrs. Felton, *American Life: A Narrative of Two Years' City and Country Residence in the United States* (Boulton Percy, England: Printed for the Authoress, 1843), pp. 56–57.

66. *National Advocate*, Sept. 21, 1821.

67. Ibid.; *Commercial Advertiser* reprinted in *New York Spectator*, Jan. 18, 1822.

68. Joe Cowell, *Thirty Years Passed Among the Players in England and America*, 2 vols. (New York: Harper & Brothers, 1844), vol. 2, pp. 63–64.

69. *Commercial Advertiser*, reprinted in *New York Spectator*, August 13, 1822.

70. *National Advocate*, Sept. 21, 1821; *Sketches of Mr. Mathews's Celebrated Trip to America* (London: J. Limbird, [1824?]), pp. 10–11.

71. Quoted in Shane White and Graham White, *Stylin': African American Expressive Culture from Its Beginnings to the Zoot Suit* (Ithaca: Cornell University Press, 1998), p. 82.

72. *Family Magazine*, reprinted in *Nottingham and Newark Mercury*, May 22, 1830, in Thompson, *A Documentary History*, p. 186; *National Advocate*, Sept. 21, 1821; *Commercial Advertiser*, reprinted in *New York Spectator*, August 13, 1822.

73. *Sports of New York*, pp. 3–16.

74. *Memoir and Theatrical Career of Ira Aldridge*, p. 11.

75. *National Advocate*, Oct. 12, 1822.

76. *National Advocate*, Jan. 20, 1823.

77. *New York American*, March 3, 1823.

78. *National Advocate*, Sept. 26, 1826; A. Greene, *A Glance at New York: Embracing The City Government* (New York: A. Greene, 1837), pp. 67–68.

79. *New York American*, Dec. 6, 1821.

80. *National Advocate*, July 9, 1822; *James Hewlett v. Abraham Cox*, Dec. 3, 1822, Police Court, Cases Dismissed, Municipal Archives of the City of New York. See Cox's advertisement in the *New York American*, Jan. 2, 1822. George Thompson first uncovered this similarity. See Thompson, *A Documentary History*, p. 126.

81. Broadside reprinted in Thompson, *A Documentary History*, pp. 126–27.

82. Broadside reprinted in Laurence Hutton, *Curiosities of the American Stage* (New York: Harper & Brothers, 1891), p. 97; Peter George Buckley, "To the Opera House: Culture and Society in New York City, 1820–1860" (Ph.D. diss., State University of New York at Stonybrook, 1984), pp. 355–357. (This excellent work has been enormously helpful in writing this book. It should have been published a long time ago.)

83. *New York Evening Post*, March 3, 1823; Jan. 13, 1824.

84. *New York American*, Feb. 2, 1827.

85. William B. Wood, *Personal Recollections of the Stage* (Philadelphia: Henry Carey Baird, 1855), pp. 295–97.

86. George C. D. Odell, *Annals of the New York Stage. Vol. 3, 1821–1834* (New York: Columbia University Press, 1928), pp. 70–71. Odell quotes from a broadside which seems to be no longer extant. Thompson was unable to find it. See *A Documentary History*, p. 136.

87. *National Advocate*, July 4, 1823.

88. *National Advocate*, May 26, 1823 and Thompson, *A Documentary History*, p. 130.

89. Quoted in Edward Ball, *Slaves in the Family* (New York: Ballantine Books, 1999), p. 307; and also in Jeffrey Robert Young, *Domesticating Slavery: The Master Class in Georgia and South Carolina, 1670–1837* (Chapel Hill: University of North Carolina Press, 1999), p. 187. (There are minor differences in the transcription of the quotes.)

90. Poster reprinted in Thompson, *A Documentary History*, p. 140.

91. *Providence Gazette*, Dec. 3, 1823.

92. Broadside reprinted in Thompson, *A Documentary History*, p. 144.

3. SHAKESPEARE'S PROUD REPRESENTATIVE

1. Richard L. Klepac, *Mr Mathews At Home* (London: The Society for Theatre Research, 1979), pp. 17–19, 23.

2. Mrs. Mathews, *A Continuation of the Memoirs of Charles Mathews, Comedian*, 2 vols. (Philadelphia: Lea & Blanchard, 1839), vol. 1, pp. 239–40.

3. *Sketches of Mr. Mathews's Celebrated Trip to America* (London: J. Limbird, [1824?]), pp. 9–10.

4. Mrs. Mathews, *A Continuation of the Memoirs*, vol. 1, pp. 275–76.

5. *New York American*, April 28, 1824.

6. *National Advocate*, May 8, 1824.

7. Ibid.

8. Broadside reprinted in George A. Thompson Jr., *A Documentary History of the African Theatre* (Evanston, Ill.: Northwestern University Press, 1998), pp. 126–27.

9. *National Advocate*, Oct. 9, 1824.

10. Mrs. Mathews, *A Continuation of the Memoirs*, vol. 1, p. 292.

11. *New York Evening Post*, Nov. 19, 1825.

12. *New York Gazette and General Advertiser*, Dec. 2, 1825; *New York Daily Advertiser*, Dec. 2, 1825; *New York Spectator*, Dec. 6, 1825.

13. *Baltimore Patriot*, Sept. 24, 1822, quoted in Klepac, *Mr Mathews*, p. 18.

14. *New York Evening Post*, Nov. 17, 1825. On Kean, see also Peter Buckley, "To the Opera House: Culture and Society in New York City, 1820–1860" (Ph.D. diss., State University of New York at Stony Brook, 1984), pp. 168–76.

15. See, for example, *New York Gazette and General Advertiser*, Dec. 2, 1825.

16. *Brooklyn Star*, Dec. 15, 1825; *Brooklyn Star* reprinted in the *National Advocate*, Dec. 30, 1825. *Poulson's American Daily Advertiser*, Jan. 9, 1826; Jan. 10, 1826; and Jan. 12, 1826, reprinted in Thompson, *A Documentary History*, pp. 167–69.

17. Eileen Southern, *The Music of Black Americans: A History*, 3rd ed. (New York: W. W. Norton, 1997), pp. 107–11.

18. *Poulson's American Daily Advertiser*, Jan. 14, 1826; Jan. 18, 1826, in Thompson, *A Documentary History*, pp. 170–71.

19. *Brooklyn Star*, Feb. 2, 1826; *New-York National Advocate*, Feb. 18, 1826; March 30, 1826; April 10, 1826; May 20, 1826; *New-York Enquirer*, July 21, 1826; Sept. 27, 1826.

20. *New-York National Advocate*, April 10, 1826.

21. *National Advocate*, Nov. 3, 1826.

22. *New-York Enquirer*, Jan. 27 1827; Nov. 29, 1827.

23. *York Gazette*, May 8 and 29, 1827; *York Recorder*, May 8, 1827; all in Thompson, *A Documentary History*, pp. 183–84.

24. *Alexandria Gazette*, March 24, 1827; March 30, 1827. I am indebted to Dale Cockrell for these references. I should add that they caught me completely by surprise, as I had not expected to find Hewlett performing in the South, and indeed had not looked in newspapers there. I should add that pursuing this sort of material in newspapers is pretty much like looking for a needle in a haystack. Subsequent brief forays into obvious southern newspapers in months when I did not know where Hewlett was, turned up nothing more—but this means little.

25. *The Sports of New York, by Simon Snipe* (n.p., 1824) in Thompson, *A Documentary History*, pp. 150–51.

26. *Brooklyn Star* reprinted in the *National Advocate*, Dec. 30, 1825.

27. *New York American*, April 27, 1826.

28. *National Advocate*, Nov. 3, 1826.

29. On the star system, see Bruce McConachie, "American Theatre in Context, from the Beginnings to 1870," in Don B. Wilmeth and Christopher Bigsby, eds., *The Cambridge History of American Theatre*. Vol. 1, *Beginnings to 1870* (Cambridge, 1998), pp. 147–56. See also the other essays in this excellent volume.

30. John Dizikes, *Opera in America: A Cultural History* (New Haven: Yale University Press, 1993), pp. 3–12; *New York Evening Post*, Nov. 30, 1825. See also Karen Ahlquist, *Democracy at the Opera: Music, Theater, and Culture in New York City, 1815–60* (Urbana: University of Illinois Press, 1997).

31. *Poulson's American Daily Advertiser*, Jan. 9, 1826; *New-York National Advocate*, March 30, 1826; April 10, 1826.

32. *Poulson's American Daily Advertiser*, Jan. 14, 1826, in Thompson, *A Documentary History*, p. 170; *Brooklyn Star*, Feb. 2, 1826.

33. *Poulson's American Daily Advertiser*, Jan. 14, 1826, in Thompson, *A Documentary History*, p. 170; *New-York National Advocate*, May 20, 1826.

34. *New York American*, April 27, 1826; *Brooklyn Star* reprinted in the *National Advocate*, Dec. 30, 1825.

35. *Poulson's American Daily Advertiser*, Jan. 9, 1826, in Thompson, *A Documentary History*, p. 167; *York Gazette*, May 8, 1827, in Thompson, *A Documentary History*, p. 183; *New York Daily Advertiser*, Dec. 2, 1825.

36. Richard Waterhouse, *From Minstrel Show to Vaudeville: The Australian Popular Stage, 1788–1914* (Kensington, NSW: University of New South Wales Press, 1990), pp. 47–97.

37. [James McCune Smith], "Ira Aldridge," *Anglo-African Magazine*, 2 (1860): 27–28.

38. *New-York Enquirer*, Dec. 4, 1827; Dec. 7, 1827.

39. *New-York Enquirer*, Dec. 7, 1827.

40. *Poulson's American Daily Advertiser*, Jan. 9, 1826, in Thompson, *A Documentary History*, p. 167; *Brooklyn Star*, Dec. 15, 1825; *York Star*, May 8, 1827, in Thompson, *A Documentary History*, p. 183.

41. *New-York Enquirer*, Dec. 7, 1827. The repeated use of the word "merit" is certainly interesting.

42. *New-York Enquirer*, Sept. 15, 1827. A decade later, Asa Greene made a weaker claim of theater's importance, although his numbers were

larger than Noah's: "There are supposed to be, on an average, about 5,000 persons nightly attending the different theatres in New York. Of these, nearly, or quite, one half are strangers. Hence the theatres are best filled during the spring and autumn, when there are most country merchants, and other persons from abroad, in the city." A. Greene, *A Glance at New York: Embracing the City Government* (New York: A. Greene, 1837), p. 38.

43. *New-York National Advocate*, March 30, 1826; *New-York Enquirer*, Jan. 27, 1827.

44. *New-York Enquirer*, Nov. 29, 1826; "De Grandest Bobalition," New York Historical Society; *New Orleans Times-Picayune*, no date, 1838, in Thompson, *A Documentary History*, p. 209.

45. *New York Spectator*, Nov. 18, 1825; *Freedom's Journal*, July 18, 1828.

46. *New-York National Advocate*, Feb. 18, 1826; Feb. 20, 1826.

47. *Memoir and Theatrical Career of Ira Aldridge, the African Roscius* (London: Onwhyn, 1849), p. 10. On Aldridge, see also Herbert Marshall and Mildred Stock, *Ira Aldridge: The Negro Tragedian* (Washington, D.C.: Howard University Press, 1993 [orig. pub. 1958]) and Bernth Lindfors, "'Nothing Extenuate, nor Set Down Aught in Malice': New Biographical Information on Ira Aldridge," *African American Review*, 28 (1994): 457–72.

48. *Memoir and Theatrical Career of Ira Aldridge*, p. 12; Marshall and Stock, *Ira Aldridge*, pp. 48–49.

49. Martin Delany, *The Condition, Elevation, Emigration, and Destiny of the Colored People of the United States* (Philadelphia, 1852), in Thompson, *A Documentary History*, p. 213.

50. *Memoir and Theatrical Career of Ira Aldridge*, pp. 10–11. He was probably the brother of the Bellmont involved in sacking Brown's theater. See *The People v. James Belmont*, filed August 12, 1822, District Attorney Indictment Papers, Municipal Archives of the City of New York.

51. Marshall and Stock, *Ira Aldridge*, pp. 40, 43, 53–55.

52. *Memoir and Theatrical Career of Ira Aldridge*, p. 11.

53. Marshall and Stock, *Ira Aldridge*, pp. 82–83.

54. Ibid., p. 39.

55. According to the *Memoir and Theatrical Career of Ira Aldridge*, pp. 8–9, a document Aldridge at least was heavily involved in and probably wrote, he came from a princely line and spent the first eight years of his life in Senegal. There is now no doubt that he was born in New York.

56. *New York Gazette and General Advertiser*, Dec. 2, 1825; *Commercial Advertiser*, Dec. 2, 1825.

57. *Poulson's American Daily Advertiser*, Jan. 9, 1826; *Long Island Star*,

Feb. 2, 1826, in Thompson, *A Documentary History*, p. 172; *New-York National Advocate*, Feb. 18, 1826; March 30, 1826; *New York American*, April 27, 1826; *New-York National Advocate*, May 20, 1826; *New-York Enquirer*, July 21, 1826; Sept. 27, 1826; Jan. 27, 1827; *Alexandria Gazette*, March 24, 1827; *New-York Enquirer*, Dec. 4, 1827.

58. *New York American*, Sept. 6, 1827.

59. *New-York National Advocate*, May 20, 1826.

60. *Commercial Advertiser*, Dec. 2, 1825; *New York Daily Advertiser*, Dec. 2, 1825.

61. *Family Magazine* reprinted in *Nottingham and Newark Mercury*, May 22, 1830, in Thompson, *A Documentary History*, pp. 186–87.

62. George Stone, "Reminiscences of Albany Theatricals," in Joel Munsell, *Collections on the History of Albany from Its Discovery to the Present Time* (Albany: J. Munsell, 1867), vol. 2, p. 46. I am indebted to Paul E. Johnson for this reference.

63. Quoted in David Levering Lewis, *When Harlem Was in Vogue* (New York: Alfred A. Knopf, 1981), p. 261.

64. Census entry reprinted in Thompson, *A Documentary History*, p. 189.

65. *New York Evening Post*, March 4, 1831.

66. *New York American*, March 5, 1831.

67. *New York American*, April 6, 1827.

68. *New York Evening Post*, July 12, 1831.

69. See *New-York Columbian*, Feb. 3, 1821, for a story about a Dr. Preston taking gas. *New York Evening Post*, June 2, 1830. For Pluck taking gas, see *New York American*, Jan. 20, 1827. On Pluck, see Susan G. Davis, *Parades and Power: Street Theatre in Nineteenth-Century Philadelphia* (Philadelphia: Temple University Press, 1986), pp. 78–96. On laughing gas, see Ellen Hickey Grayson, "Social Order and Psychological Disorder: Laughing Gas Demonstrations, 1800–1850," in Rosemarie Garland Thomson, ed., *Freakery: Cultural Spectacles of the Extraordinary Body* (New York: New York University Press, 1996), pp. 108–20. On later developments associated particularly with P. T. Barnum, see James W. Cook, *The Arts of Deception: Playing with Fraud in the Age of Barnum* (Cambridge, Mass.: Harvard University Press, 2001).

70. *New York Evening Post*, September 12, 1831.

71. *Morning Courier and New-York Enquirer*, June 17, 1834.

72. Ibid.; statement of James Hewlett, *The People v. James Hewlett*, filed June 20, 1834, District Attorney Indictment Papers, Municipal Archives of the City of New York.

73. *Morning Courier and New-York Enquirer*, June 17, 1834.

74. *The Sun*, June 21, 1834. See also *The Sun*, June 17, 1834.

75. *New-York Gazette & General Advertiser*, June 23, 1834.

76. *New York Evening Post*, March 12, 1830; *Public Ledger*, Dec. 31, 1836; *New York Evening Post*, May 25, 1825.

77. *National Advocate*, March 3, 1826.

78. Statement of Henry Dennis, *The People v. Andrew Thompson & Tobias Morgan*, filed May 6, 1819, DAIP.

79. *Public Ledger*, Feb. 16, 1837; statement of Reuben Moore, *People v. Reuben Moore and Thomas Williams als Peter Williams* filed April 14, 1826; *People v. Anthony Woodward et al.*, filed July 6, 1827, DAIP. On "burning," see *New York Daily Express*, August 11, 1838; *New York Evening Star*, August 11, 1838.

80. *Public Ledger*, Dec. 10, 1836; *Public Ledger*, Feb. 16, 1837.

81. Martin Delany, *The Condition, Elevation, Emigration, and Destiny of the Colored People*, in Thompson, *A Documentary History*, p. 213.

82. *Journal of Commerce* reprinted in *New York Evening Post*, March 15, 1837, in Thompson, *A Documentary History*, pp. 202–203.

83. *Journal of Commerce* reprinted in *New York Evening Post*, March 29, 1837, in Thompson, *A Documentary History*, p. 204; *The Herald*, March 29, 1837, in Thompson, *A Documentary History*, p. 204.

84. *Morning Herald*, June 12, 1837 in Thompson, *A Documentary History*, p. 205.

85. *Morning Courier and New-York Enquirer*, June 20, 1837, in Thompson, *A Documentary History*, p. 207; *Morning Herald*, June 20, 1837, in Thompson, *A Documentary History*, pp. 206–207.

4. IMITATION

1. *American Monthly Magazine and Critical Review*, 1 (1817): 322–23.

2. *Democratic Press*, May 6, 1829.

3. *The Transcript*, July 11, 1834.

4. *Morning Courier and New-York Enquirer*, Jan. 26, 1833.

5. *National Advocate*, Sept. 26, 1821; *Republican Sentinel* story reprinted in *New York Evening Post*, Sept. 29, 1821.

6. *The Herald*, July 26, 1836. For earlier mentions of balls, see, for example, statement of Ann Maria Legree, *The People v. Ann Maria Legree*, filed August 2, 1808, District Attorney Indictment Papers, Municipal Archives of the City of New York, where a black servant took her mistress's dress "to wear to a Ball and after the Ball was over she went . . . to look at

herself in a glass"; statement of Nancy, *The People v. Nancy a Black Girl a Slave of J. Johnson*, filed December?, 1809, DAIP, where a slave took a pair of shoes, "put them on and went to a Ball in Little Water Street."

7. Adam Hodgson, *Letters from North America, Written During a Tour in the United States and Canada*, 2 vols. (London, 1824), vol. 2, p. 115. I am grateful to George A. Thompson, Jr. for this reference.

8. *Freedom's Journal*, March 14, 1828.

9. Ibid. The *Pennsylvania Gazette* piece was reprinted in its entirety in *Freedom's Journal*.

10. *Morning Courier and New-York Enquirer*, August 2, 1833.

11. *The Sun*, Feb. 18, 1835; *The Transcript*, Feb. 18, 1835.

12. *New-York Enquirer*, March 13, 1827; *New York National Advocate*, March 18, 1825; *Pennsylvania Gazette* reprinted in *Freedom's Journal*, March 14, 1828.

13. *National Advocate*, March 18, 1825; *New-York Enquirer*, Dec. 9, 1828.

14. *New York Evening Post*, Dec. 31, 1823; *New-York Enquirer*, March 13, 1827.

15. "The African Fancy Ball," *Philadelphia Monthly Magazine*, 2 (1828): 53–57.

16. *Morning Courier and New-York Enquirer*, Sept. 2, 1833.

17. *Poulson's American Daily Advertiser*, Jan. 2, 1813.

18. For the 1790s, see Shane White, *Somewhat More Independent: The End of Slavery in New York City, 1770–1810* (Athens: University of Georgia Press, 1991), pp. 66–75.

19. *New England Galaxy*, July 14, 1820. For the Boston parades, see also Shane White, "'It Was a Proud Day': African Americans, Festivals, and Parades in the North, 1741–1834," *Journal of American History*, 81 (1994): 13–51.

20. *The Pick Nack, or Adventures of the Heroes of the Salt River Bulletin* (n.d., n.p.). The only copy of this pamphlet I have seen is held by the American Antiquarian Society. On Bobalition, see David Waldstreicher, *In the Midst of Perpetual Fetes: The Making of American Nationalism, 1776–1820* (Chapel Hill: University of North Carolina Press, 1997), pp. 336–42; Joanne Pope Melish, *Disowning Slavery: Gradual Emancipation and "Race" in New England, 1780–1860* (Ithaca: Cornell University Press, 1998), pp. 171–83; White, "It Was a Proud Day."

21. W. Faux, *Memorable Days in America: Being a Journal of a Tour to the United States* (London: W. Simpkin and R. Marshall, 1823), p. 9; Shane White and Graham White, *Stylin': African American Expressive Culture*

from Its Beginnings to the Zoot Suit (Ithaca: Cornell University Press, 1998), pp. 111–13.

22. *New York Evening Post*, July 19, 1822; "De Grandest Bobalition," New York Historical Society; *New York American*, July 8, 1829.

23. *National Advocate*, August 3, 1821.

24. *National Advocate*, July 1, 1823.

25. *National Advocate*, August 27, 1823. Virtually the same piece was reprinted a few years later, *Hawk and Buzzard*, Sept. 15, 1832. This fugitive newspaper is held by the American Antiquarian Society. I am indebted to W. T. Lhamon, Jr. for this reference.

26. W. T. Lhamon, Jr., *Raising Cain: Blackface Performance from Jim Crow to Hip Hop* (Cambridge, Mass.: Harvard University Press, 1998), p. 4.

27. Lydia Maria Child, *Letters From New York*, ed. Bruce Mills (Athens: University of Georgia Press, 1998), p. 120.

28. *Democratic Press*, Jan. 7, 1829.

29. Samuel Hay, *African American Theatre: An Historical and Critical Analysis* (Cambridge: Cambridge University Press, 1994), p. 13.

30. *Morning Courier and New-York Enquirer*, Sept. 30, 1829.

31. *Morning Courier and New-York Enquirer*, Oct. 12, 1833. For use of "High Life Below Stairs" as a caption, see, for example, *National Advocate*, March 2, 1825.

32. *Morning Courier and New-York Enquirer*, Feb. 2, 1835.

33. [William Blane], *An Excursion Through the United States and Canada During the Years 1822–23. By An English Gentleman* (London: Baldwin, Craddock and Joy, 1824), p. 25; S. A. Ferrall, Esq., *A Ramble of Six Thousand Miles Through the United States* (London, 1832), p. 10.

34. *The Sun*, June 4, 1834; Feb. 4, 1834.

35. *Journal of Commerce* reprinted in *Democratic Press*, June 22, 1829; *The Sun*, June 23, 1834.

36. See David R. Roediger, *The Wages of Whiteness: Race and the Making of the American Working Class* (London: Verso, 1991); Noel Ignatiev, *How the Irish Became White* (New York: Routledge, 1995); Matthew Frye Jacobson, *Whiteness of a Different Color: European Immigrants and the Alchemy of Race* (Cambridge, Mass.: Harvard University Press, 1998). See also Laura Browder, *Slippery Characters: Ethnic Impersonators and American Identities* (Chapel Hill: University of North Carolina Press, 2000).

37. *The People v. George Angus*, filed April 10, 1818, DAIP.

38. *New York American*, July 16, 1828.

39. *The Sun*, May 14, 1834.

40. *Morning Courier and New-York Enquirer*, April 3, 1833.

41. On Rice and the minstrel show, see Eric Lott, *Love and Theft: Blackface Minstrelsy and the American Working Class* (New York: Oxford University Press, 1993); Dale Cockrell, *Demons of Disorder: Early Blackface Minstrelsy and Their World* (Cambridge: Cambridge University Press, 1997); Lhamon, *Raising Cain;* William J. Mahar, *Behind the Burnt Cork Mask: Early Blackface Minstrelsy and Antebellum American Popular Culture* (Urbana: University of Illinois Press, 1999).

EPILOGUE

1. On exile, see, for example, Tyler Stovall, *Paris Noir: African Americans in the City of Light* (Boston: Houghton Mifflin, 1996).

2. Lisa Clayton Robinson, "Trinidad and Tobago," in Kwame Anthony Appiah and Henry Louis Gates, Jr., eds., *Africana: The Encyclopedia of the African and African American Experience* (New York: Basic Books, 1999), pp. 1881–85.

3. *The Port of Spain Gazette*, Dec. 13, 1839; Dec. 17, 1839; *The Trinidad Standard*, Dec. 17, 1839; all in George A. Thompson Jr., *A Documentary History of the African Theatre* (Evanston, Ill.: Northwestern University Press, 1998), pp. 222–24.

4. *The Port of Spain Gazette*, Dec. 24, 1839, in Thompson, *A Documentary History*, pp. 224–25.

5. Martin Delany, *The Condition, Elevation, Emigration, and Destiny of the Colored People of the United States* (Philadelphia, 1852) in Thompson, *A Documentary History*, p. 213.

6. Mrs. Felton, *American Life: A Narrative of Two Years' City and Country Residence in the United States* (Bolton Percy, Eng.: for the authoress, 1843), pp. 37–38. I am indebted to Dell Upton for this reference.

ACKNOWLEDGMENTS

I enjoy very much writing about New York while living in Sydney, but that ten-thousand-mile distance between the two cities (26 hours of flying from when the wheels leave the ground in Sydney) does create the odd logistical problem. Money helps to overcome such obstacles, and, over the last few years, the Australian Research Council has funded me in an extremely generous fashion. Indeed, without the ARC Large Grant for *Stories of Freedom in Black New York*, which paid for my travel, computers, research assistance, and time free from teaching, I shudder to think how much longer this book would have taken and how different it would have ended up looking.

This book was conceived, mostly researched, and entirely written in Australia, and my debts in this country are numerous. I have been either a student or a member of staff in the History Department at the University of Sydney since I was seventeen years of age (and that was a long time ago); indeed, for my sins, I am currently chair of the department. It has been, on the whole, a wonderful place to be educated and to work, and I owe much to past and present members of the department for their support. In particular, I would like to thank Stephen Garton, Stephen Robertson, and Glenda Sluga for reading this manuscript and for putting up with me as a friend. One of the perks of working at an institution such as the University of Sydney is that I get to hire research assistants who are much smarter than I am: in this case, Clare Corbould and Ben Urwand were terrific. Elsewhere in the University, Moira Gatens has tried to keep me sane, and elsewhere in Australia, Richard Bosworth, Greg Dening, Nick Gebhardt, David Goodman, Rhys Isaac, Donna Merwick, John Salmond, and Ian Tyrrell have all substantially contributed to the intellectual environment in which I work.

It is now more than a quarter of a century since I first met Richard Waterhouse. He taught me as an undergraduate and graduate student and has been a colleague for decades. Over the years he has offered me astute advice and guidance on the writing of history and much else besides—I am grateful for his friendship. I have known Graham White for the same length of time. During the last couple of decades we have both taught together and written together, and working with Graham has been one of the main pleasures of my academic career. (I should add here that, contrary to the assumption of various reviewers of our last book, we are not related.) Not only is Graham White the most gifted editor I have ever seen, but he is also extremely knowledgeable about African American culture. He is the person I have in mind as I write; indeed, I cannot imagine letting anyone else read my prose unless he has first covered it with his almost indecipherable pencil scribblings. The dedication to this work is merely public acknowledgment of the very large debt I owe to my friends Graham White and Richard Waterhouse.

In America, I must begin with the libraries and repositories in which I completed my research. The Municipal Archives of the

City of New York hold a fascinating range of material, most of it barely looked at by scholars. Ken Cobb and his staff have done everything possible to facilitate my research and I am very grateful for their help. I also thank the staff at the New York Historical Society, New York Public Library, the newspaper section in the Library of Congress, and the Library Company (especially the incomparable Phil Lapsansky), for all their help over the years.

I have had a great time writing this book and, more than was the case with any of my previous work, felt that I was part of a shared enterprise of uncovering African New York's past. E-mail has had an enormous impact in lessening the isolation of those who write about America from outside its borders. I am also extremely fortunate in my colleagues and friends. For passing on material or suggestions from their own work or reading a few pages of my manuscript or talking to me about my project, I am grateful to Peter Agree, Jeff Bolster, Dale Cockrell, Leslie Harris, Graham Hodges, Dick Hutson, Paul Johnson, George A. Thompson, Jr., and Dell Upton. I would particularly like to thank Ira Berlin, Alex Bontemps, Deborah Kaplan, Robin Kelley, Larry Levine, Rip Lhamon, Leon Litwack, Roy Rosenzweig, David Waldstreicher, and Mike Wallace, for their shrewd and sharp readings of early versions of this book. At Harvard University Press, I would like to thank Anita Safran, David Lobenstine, and especially Joyce Seltzer for their help in converting my manuscript into this book.

My largest obligations are to my long-suffering family. I am fairly difficult to live with when I am writing a book—but, as they have pointed out, I always seem to be writing a book. Meeting Lexie Macdonald is the best thing that has happened in my life; her love and support are what has made this book, and much else besides, possible. Macdonald White came into this world at about the same time I began the actual writing of *Stories* and undoubtedly slowed down its completion, but there are far too many books and I am not entirely sure that any of them are read by anyone anyway. Mac (who derives an inordinate amount of pleasure whenever we drive past one of "my restaurants") is the joy of our lives. And last, I have to mention Scout Macdonald, who wants to see his name in print again.

INDEX